The Besterman World Bibliographies

The Besterman World Bibliographies

Law

& International Law

A BIBLIOGRAPHY OF BIBLIOGRAPHIES

By Theodore Besterman

TOTOWA, N. J.
Rowman and Littlefield

1971

Published by
Rowman and Littlefield
A Division of
Littlefield, Adams & Co.
81 Adams Drive
Totowa, N. J. 07512

★

★

Typography by George Hornby
and Theodore Besterman

ISBN 0-87471-051-0

Contents

Preface

I have explained in the Introduction to the successive editions of *A World bibliography of bibliographies* why I decided to arrange it alphabetically by specific subjects. Since that decision was taken, and after prolonged experience of the book in use, I have had no reason to regret it, nor among the many letters I have received from librarians has there been a single one complaining of the alphabetical form of the *World bibliography*.

The *World bibliography of bibliographies* covers all subjects and all languages, and is intended to serve reference and research purposes of the most specific and specialised kind. Yet contained in it are broad and detailed surveys which, if relevant entries throughout the volumes are added to them, can serve also the widest reference inquiries, and be useful to those who seek primary signposts to information in varied fields of inquiry.

Therefore I can only thank Rowman and Littlefield for having gathered together all the titles in some of the major fields found throughout the 6664 columns of the fourth edition (1965-1966) of *A World bibliography of bibliographies*.

These fields are:

1. Bibliography
2. Printing
3. Periodical Publications
4. Academic Writings
5. Art and Architecture
6. Music and Drama
7. Education
8. Agriculture
9. Medicine
10. Law
11. English and American Literature
12. Technology
13. Physical Sciences
14. Biological Sciences
15. Family History
16. Commerce, Manufactures, Labour
17. History
18. Geography

Of course these categories by no means exhaust the 117,000 separately collated volumes set out in the *World bibliography*, and the above titles will be added to if librarians wish for it.

Th. B.

Notes on the Arrangement

An Alternative to critical annotation

Consider what it is we look for in a normal bibliography of a special subject. Reflection will show, I think, that we look, above all, for completeness, just as we do in a bibliography of bibliographies. We desire completeness even more than accuracy (painfully uncongenial though it is for me to make such a statement); for in most cases a bibliography is intended to give us particulars of publications to which we wish to refer; thus we can always judge for ourselves (waiving gross errors) whether the bibliographer has correctly described these publications. On the other hand, anything that is omitted is lost until rediscovered.

The question is, therefore, whether it is possible to give some indication of the degree of completeness of a bibliography without indulging in the annotation which is impossible in a work of the present scope and scale. It seemed to me that this could be achieved, to a considerable extent, by recording the approximate number of entries set out in it. This method is, of course, a rough-and-ready one, but experience shows that it is remarkably effective: and I hope that its novelty will not tell against it.

The recording of the number of works set out in a bibliography has another advantage in the case of serial publications: it displays in statistical form the development of the subject from year to year—often in a highly significant manner.

This procedure, then, is that which I have adopted, the number of items in each bibliography being shown in square brackets at the end of the entry. This, I may add, is by no means an easy or mechanical task, as can be judged from the fact that this process, on the average, just about doubles the time taken in entering each bibliography.

Supplementary information in footnotes

I have said that this method of indicating the number of entries is intended to replace critical treatment; but it is not possible to exclude annotation altogether, for a certain minimum of added information is indispensable. Consequently many of my entries will be seen to have footnotes, in which the following types of information are recorded: a few words of explanation where the title is inaccurate, misleading, obscure, or insufficiently informative; a statement to that effect where a work is in progress, where intermediate volumes in a series have not been published, or where no more have been published; an attempt to clarify complicated series; a note that a book was privately printed or in a limited number of copies, where this does not exceed 500, or in some abnormal manner, as on one side of the leaf, on coloured paper, or in a reproduction of handwriting, or with erratic pagination; when I have come across copies containing manuscript or other added matter, I have recorded the fact; substantial corrections and additions to bibliographies are sometimes published in periodicals, and I have noted a good many of these—but without aiming at anything even remotely approaching completeness, the attainment of which would be impossible. Various minor types of information are also occasionally to be found in the footnotes.

Owing to the great increase in the number of bibliographies reproduced directly from typewritten copy, such publications are designated by an asterisk at the end of the entry; this device saves a good deal of space.

Place of publication

The place of publication is not shown when it is London in the case of an english book and

Paris in the case of a french one. In the case of a series or sequence of entries, however, the absence of a place of publication means that it is the same as the place last shown in the series. The same applies to the names of editors and compilers. The place of publication is given as it appears on the titlepage, but prepositions are omitted even if violence is done to grammatical construction.

The Order of entries

Under each heading the order of the entries is chronological by date of publication; in the case of works in successive volumes or editions the chronological order applies to the first volume or edition. In suitable long headings an additional chronological order by period covered has been created; see, for instance, France: History, or Drama: Great Britain.

Method of collating

An effort has been made, so far as space allows, to give detailed and accurate information of the kind more usually found in small bibliographies. For instance, I have paid special attention to the collation of bibliographies in several (or even numerous) parts or volumes. It is, in fact, difficult to understand why it is usually considered necessary to give collations of works in a single volume, where difficulties seldom occur (from the point of view of systematic bibliography), but not of a work in several volumes, where confusion much more frequently arises. An occasional gap in the collations of such publications will be noticed. This is because, naturally enough, I have not been able in every case to see perfect sets; and I have thought it better to leave a very small number of such blanks rather than to hold up the bibliography indefinitely.

Serial publications

Where successive issues of a serial publication are set out, the year or period shown is usually that covered by the relevant issue; in such cases no date of publication is given unless publication was abnormal or erratic in relation to the period covered.

Bibliographies in more than one edition

Where a bibliography has gone into more than one edition I have tried (though I have not always been able) to record at least the first and latest editions. Intermediate editions have also been recorded wherever it seemed useful to do so, that is, for bibliographies first published before 1800, and for those of special interest or importance; but in general intermediate editions, though examined, have not been recorded.

Notes

Transcription of titles

Titles have been set out in the shortest possible form consistent with intelligibility and an adequate indication of the scope of the bibliography; omissions have of course been indicated. The author's name, generally speaking, is given as it appears on the titlepage, amplified and interpreted within square brackets where necessary.

Anonymous bibliographies

Far too large a proportion of bibliographical work is published anonymously. This is due, in part, to the all too common practice of library committees and similar bodies of suppressing altogether or of hiding in prefaces the names of those who have compiled bibliographies and catalogues for them. I have spent a good deal of time in excavating such and other evidences of authorship, and the result may be seen in the large number of titles preceded by names enclosed within square brackets.

Th. B.

Law, laws.

1. *Bibliographies*

E[UGÈNE] DRAMARD, Bibliographie de la bibliographie générale du droit français et étranger. 1893. pp.[iii].120. [775.]

2. *Periodicals*

[GEORGES] FLEURY and [MAURICE] GODEFROY, Catalogue des périodiques français et étrangers de la bibliothèque de l'université d'Aix-Marseille. Section du droit et des lettres à Aix. Faculté des sciences de Marseille: Annales (vol.xvi, supp.2): 1907. pp.3–61. [1000.]

PÉRIODIQUES. Université de Bordeaux: Bibliothèque: Section de droit: Bordeaux 1917. pp.19. [350.]

A SELECTED list of latin american periodicals containing laws and legal information. Pan american union: Columbus memorial library: Bibliographic series (no.28): Washington 1942. ff.[ii].27. [225.]*

SURVEY of libraries' holdings of legal periodicals. University of London: Institute of advanced legal studies: 1949. pp.[iii].41. [550.]*

— [another edition]. A survey of legal periodicals held in british libraries. University of London: Institute of advanced legal studies: Publication (no.1): 1949. pp.vii.52. [750.]

— Second edition. 1957. pp.ix.82. [1200.]

VERZEICHNIS deutscher juristischer periodika. Max Planck-institut für ausländisches und internationales privatrecht: Tübingen 1952 &c.

in progress.

AUNE AUTTI and KAUKO SIPPONEN, Yhteisluettelo Suomen tieteellisissä kirjastoissa olevista ulkomaisista lainopillisista aikakaus- ja sarjajulkaisuista. Helsinki 1956. pp.215. [1063.]

C[ARLOS] E. MASCAREÑAS, Catálogo de publicaciones periódicas y revistas jurídicas francesas.

Consejo superior de investigaciones científicas: Instituto de derecho comparado: Colección: Bibliografías (no.5): Barcelona 1958. pp.50. [150.]

KÄTE HOEDT, Rechts- und wissenschaftliche zeitschriften der universität Bonn. Bonner beiträge zur bibliotheks- und bücherkunde (vol.7): Bonn 1961. pp.215. [1189.]

MYRNA [S.] FELICIANO, Checklist of legal periodicals available in the law library. University of the Philippines: Library: Research guide (no.4): Quezon City 1963. ff.[ii].22. [200.]*

3. *History and early printed books*

CHARLES BUTLER, Horæ juridicæ subsecivæ: a connected series of notes, respecting . . . the principal codes, and original documents, of the grecian, roman, feudal and canon law. 1804. pp.xvi.631. [50.]

— — The second edition. 1807. pp.iii–xvi.238 [50.]

[EUGÈNE FRANÇOIS JOSEPH] TAILLIAR, Notice de manuscrits concernant la législation du moyen-âge. [Douai 1846]. pp.viii.5–135. [31.]

issued as an appendix to H. R. Duthillœul, Catalogue . . . des manuscrits de la Bibliothèque de Douai.

FRANK H. NOBLE, Catalogue of the Hammond historical law collection, in the Law library of the State university of Iowa. Iowa City 1895. pp.[iv]. 52. [600.]

G. GAVET, Sources de l'histoire des institutions et du droit français. Manuel de bibliographie historique. 1899. pp.iii–xi.783. [2000.]
not limited to french law.

V. E. HRABAR [VLADIMIR EMMANUILOVICH GRABAR], De legatorum jure tractatuum catalogus completus ab anno MDCXXV usque ad annum MDCC. Dorpati Livonorum 1918. pp.xvi.311. [200.]

[ELIZABETH NORTON], The Transylvania library. A list of rare and curious old works on medicine, law, and the humanities printed before 1700. Transylvania college: Bulletin (vol.xi, no.3): Lexington, Ky. 1919. pp.51. [law: 27.]

RAFAEL DE UREÑA Y SMENJAUD, Los incunables jurídicos de España. Madrid 1929. pp.55. [100.]

A LIST of selected books from the tercentennial exhibition of the Harvard law school library. Cambridge (Mass.) 1936. pp.[ii].18. [164.]

KAROL KORANYI, Bibliografia historycznoprawna za lata 1926–1936. I. Wydawnictwo

Towarzystwa naukowego we Lwowie (1st ser., vol.xii): Lwowie 1938. pp.xv.499. [8054.]
no more published.

R[ENÉ] SUAUDEAU, Introduction aux études d'histoire du droit. 1944. pp.56. [110.]

CARLOS A. LUQUE COLOMBRES, Libros de derecho en bibliotecas particulares cordobesas, 1573–1810. Universidad nacional de Córdoba: Instituto de estudios americanistas: Cuaderno de historia (vol.ix): Córdoba, Argentina 1945. pp.xvii.80. [200.]

[ROBERT FEENSTRA and J. W. BOSCH], Livres anciens de droit d'origine étrangère imprimés aux Pays-Bas. Essai de bibliographie et catalogue de l'exposition . . . de Breda. Université d'Amsterdam: Bibliothèque: Amsterdam 1953. pp.viii.72. [500.]

KAROL KORANYI ant JADWIGA KORANYIOWA, Bibliografia historyczno-prawna za lata 1937–1947. Towarzystwo naukowe w Toruniu: Roczniki (vol.lv): Torún.
i. 1953. pp.xi.247. [4424.]
ii. 1959. pp.477. [7305.]
in progress.

N[IKOLAI] P[ETROVICH] DMITREVSKY, Указатель специальной литературы по всеобщей истории государства и права. Москва 1957. pp.108. [1500.]

EXPOSITION "Droit et jurisprudence", Bibliothèque de l'abbaye de St. Winoc. Manuscrits, incunables, imprimés XVIe et XVIIe siècles. Journées internationales de la Société d'histoire du droit des pays flamands, picards et wallons: [Bergues 1960]. ff.5. [50.]

ÉLÉMENTS de bibliographie sur l'histoire des institutions et des faits sociaux, 987–1875.

[1926–1956]. Par Gabriel Lepointe et André Vandenbossche. 1958. pp.[v].v.232. [3324.]

[*continued as:*]

Bibliographie en langue française d'histoire du droit 987–1875.

1957–1959. Par G. Lepointe, Marguerite Boulet-Sautel et A. Vandenbossche. [1961]. pp.xiii.195. [1408.]

1960. 1962. pp.[xii].219. [1636.]

in progress.

4. *Manuscripts*

GOTTLIEB HUFELAND, Vorläufige nachricht von den juristischen schätzen der Wirzburger universitätsbibliothek, besonders dem rechtsbuch Alarichs. Bamberg &c. 1805. pp.98. [150.]

HEINRICH AMANN, Præstantiorum aliquot codicum mss. qui Friburgi servantur ad iurisprudentiam spectantium notitia. Friburgi Brisgaviæ 1836–1837. pp.[vi].20.31+viii.72. [25.]

EMIL JULIUS HUGO STEFFENHAGEN, Catalogus codicum manuscriptorum Bibliothecae regiae et universitatis regimontanae. Fasciculus I. Codices ad iurisprudentiam pertinentes. Regimonti 1861. pp.x.94. [500.]

[KARL] TH[EODOR] PYL, Die Rubenow-bibliothek. Die handschriften und urkunden der von Heinrich Rubenow 1456 gestifteten juristen- und artisten-bibliothek zu Greifswald. 1865. pp.[iii].iv.196. [law: 750.]

[ALFRED VON WRETSCHKO], Die rechtshandschriften der universitätsbibliothek. Innsbruck 1904. pp.41. [200.]

R[UDOLF] HELSSIG, Die juristischen handschriften. Katalog der handschriften der Universitätsbibliothek zu Leipzig (part VI, vol.iii): Leipzig 1905. pp.xliii.372. [1500.]

G[OTTFRIED] KENTENICH, Die juristischen handschriften der Stadtbibliothek. Stadtbibliothek: Beschreibendes verzeichnis der handschriften (vol.ix): Trier 1919. pp.xviii.104. [300.]

A SELECTION of legal manuscripts and printed books for the visit of the state bar of California. Henry E. Huntington library: San Marino [1934]. pp.26. [63.]

S[VEN] STELLING-MICHAUD, Catalogue des manuscrits juridiques (droit canon et droit romain) de la fin du XIIe au XIVe siècle conservés en Suisse. Travaux d'humanisme et renaissance: (vol.xi): Genève 1954. pp.130. [187.]

MARCEL GOURON and GENEVIÈVE MALAVIALLE, Exposition de manuscrits juridiques à l'occasion de [*sic*] 1er Congrès international d'histoire du droit écrit. Archives départementales de l'Hérault: [Montpellier] 1957. ff.6. [29.]*

5. *General*

GIOVANNI NEVIZZANO, Inuentarium librorū in vtroq; iure hactenus impressorū. Lugduni 1522. pp.[38]. [1000.]

—— [another edition]. Index librorum omnium qui in vtroq; iure hinc inde eduntur. Venetiis 1525. pp.[34]. [1000.]

IVRISCONSVLTORVM vitæ, vetervm qvidem, per Bernardinum Rutilium. . . . Recentiorvm vero, ad nostra usq; tempora, per Ioannem Fichardum francofurtensem. Ad hæc indices duo locupletissimi omnium scriptorum in iure tam pontificio quàm ciuili . . . per Io. Neuizanum, Lud. Gomessium, & Io. Fichardum collecti. [Edited by Nicolaus Gerbelius]. Basileæ [1537]. pp.7.[xvii].263. [xlix]. [1500.]

[MARCO BENAVIDIO MANTOVA], Epitoma virorum illvstrium qui vel scripserunt vel jurisprudentiam docuerunt in scholis. . . . Authore Mantua. Patavii 1553. ff.72. [232.]

a copy in the Bibliothèque nationale contains ms. notes.

GIOVANNI BATTISTA ZILETTI, Index librorvm omnivm nomina complectens, in vtroq; ivre tam pontificio qvam caesareo, ad hanc diem editorum. Venetiis 1559. ff.[ii].48. [1500.]

— — [another edition]. Indices dvo, avctorvm et tractatvvm vniversi ivris, . . . in vnvm congestorum. 1584. pp.[161]. [2000.]

JOHANN FICHARD, Vitae recentiorum jureconsultorum . . . quibus accessit etiam opusculum . . . Mantuae Patavini Virorum illustrium. Patavii 1565. pp.xi.ff.65. [325.]

JOAN. WOLFGANGUS FREYMONIUS, Symphonia juris utriusque chronologica. Francofurti 1574. pp.xvi.918. [22,500.]

JOHANN WOLFGANG FREYMON, *ed.* Elenchvs omnivm avctorvm sive scriptorvm, qvi in ivre tam civili qvam canonico . . . claruerunt. . . . Initio qvidem a . . . Ioanne Neuizano, Ludouico Gomesio, Ioanne Fichardo, & Ioanne Baptista Zileto . . . collectus. Francofurti ad Moenum.

— — [another edition]. Index librorvm omnivm ivris tam pontifici qvam cæsarei. 1566. ff.[xii].66.[iii].116. [4000.]

— — Iam verò denuò multorum accessione locupletatus. 1579. ff.[iv].113.[x]. [4000.]

— — [another edition]. Elenchus [&c.]. 1585. pp.viii.ff.113.pp.17. [4000.]

ALBERICO GENTILI, De iuris interpretibus dialogi sex. Londini 1582. ff.ii.76. [200.]

MELCHIOR ADAM, Vitæ germanorum jureconsultorum et politicorum: qvi superiori seculo, et quod excurrit, floruerunt. Haidelbergæ 1620. pp.[xxxii].488.[xxxi]. [1500.]

GUIDO PANZIROLI [PANCIROLI], De claris legum interpretibus libri qvatvor. Venetiis 1637. pp. [xvi].509.[liv]. [1000.]

reissued in 1655 as a so-called 'editio secunda'.

— — [another edition]. Accessere: Joannis Fichardi . . . Vitæ recentiorum jctorum. Marci Mantuæ . . . Epitome virorum illustr. Joan. Baptistæ de Gazalupis Historia interpretum et glossatorum juris. Catellani Cottæ Recensio brevis insignium juris interpretum et doctorum. Matth. Gribaldi Mophæ Catalogus interpretum juris civilis. Alberici Gentilis De juris interpretibus dialogi sex. . . . Cura Christiani Godofr. Hoffmanni. Lipsiæ 1721. pp.[xxxii].660.[xx]. [500.]

PETER MÜLLER, De studio juris tractando diatribe. Annexis I. tribus centuriis regularum juridicarum, II. legibus in ff. concordantibus, III. legibus in ff. et c. geminatis, IV. scriptorum in jure privato, et V. scriptorum in jure publico sylloge. Editio secunda. Jenae 1678. pp.175. [1250.]

MARTINUS LIPENIUS, Bibliotheca realis juridica, omnium materiarum, rerum, et titvlorvm, in universo universi juris ambitu occurrentium. Francofurti ad Moenum 1679. pp.[xii].560.[li]. [20,000.]

— — [another edition]. Recensuit . . . et accuratum scriptorum indicem adjecit Gottlob Augustus Ienichen. Lipsiae 1736. pp.[viii].580. 54.282. [32,500.]

— — — Gottlieb Augusti Ienichen Supplementa, emendationes et illustrationes ad Bibliothecam juridicam Lipenio-Ienichianam. 1743. pp. 419.15. [7000.]

— — [another edition]. Post . . . Friderici Gottlieb Strvvii et Gottlob Avgvsti Ienichenii cvras emendata . . . et locvpletata. Lipsiae 1757. pp. [iii].x.860+[iii].476.351. [65,000.]

— — — Supplementa ac emendationes. Collegit et digessit Avgvstvs Fridericvs Schott [vol.ii: Renatvs Carolvs . . . de Senkenberg; iii–iv: Auctore d. Lvd. God. Madihn]. Lipsiae [vols.iii–iv: Vratislaviæ] 1775–1823. pp.[iv].504.138+viii.418.99.74 + [ii].vi.coll.1378.228 + pp.[ii].coll.1176.176. [100,000.]

CORNELIUS À BEUGHEM, Bibliographia juridica & politica novissima: perpetuo continuanda, sive conspectus primus catalogi librorum juridicorum . . . politicorum, quotquot . . . ab anno . . . 1651 . . . in quavis lingua . . . typis prodierunt. Amstelædami 1680. pp.[xvi].389. [3000.]

no more published.

AGOSTINO FONTANA, Amphiteatrvm legale, in quo quilibet operum legalium avthor habet suam sedem ordine alphabetico collocatam, sev bibliotheca legalis amplissima. [Edited by Carlo Maria Gabrielli]. Parmæ 1688. pp.[xl].coll.46.710+

pp.[ii].coll.480+pp.[vi].442.14+pp.[ii].coll.820.18+pp.[ii].840.20. [75,000.]

—— Bibliothecæ legalis amplissimæ continvatio. 1694. pp.[vi].283[*sic*, 282]+pp.[iv].coll.482. [25,000.]

DENIS SIMON, Nouvelle bibliothèque historique et chronologique des principaux auteurs & interprètes du droit civil, canonique & particulier, depuis Irnerius. Nouvelle édition. 1692–1695. pp.[xl].390+[x].334. [2000.]

SELECTA bibliotheca juridica . . . ex Compendio juris [Wolfgang Adam] Lauterbachiano collecta. Stutgardiæ 1698. pp.[xiii].224. [750.]

GEORG BEYER, De utili & necessaria autorum juridicorum et juris arti inservientium notitia schediasma. . . . Lipsiae 1698. pp. .137.

—— Notitiae autorum juridicorum . . . specimen II. 1701. pp. .144.

—— Notitiae . . . specimen III. 1705. pp. 151.

—— Secunda editio. Lipsiæ 1726. pp.[viii].144+[ii].144+[ii].140.[xviii]. [1000.]

—— Gottlob Avgvsti Ienichen Continvatio Notitiæ [&c.]. 1738. pp.[xvi].168. [25.]

—— Continuatio II. [By] Carolvs Ferdinandvs

Hommelivs. 1749. pp.[xx].169–356. [50.]

— — Continuatio III. 1750. pp.24.357–509. [50.]

CHRIST[IAN] GUEINZ, Pharos ad Themidos montem, sive de libris juris universi eosdemque allegandi ratione . . . commentatio. . . . Denuo edita . . . a Chr. Wildvogelio. Ienae 1700. pp.35. [50.]

J. G. SULPICIUS [*pseud.* JOHANN GEORG KULPIS], De studio juris publici recte instituendo, & de scriptoribus eo pertinentibus dissertatio. . . . Editio secunda. [*s.l.*] 1700. pp.[viii].207. [100.]

— — [another edition]. Wittebergae 1708. pp. [viii].78. [100.]

— — [another edition]. Halae Magdeburgicae. 1739. pp.[ ].78. [100.]

CATALOGUS Bibliothecæ Summi regii tribunalis wismariensis, qvam . . . à b. dn. Davidis Mevii . . . inchoatam, & ab . . . dn: Christiani Troyelii . . . auctam, novis rarisq; libris coemptis exornavit . . . Henning Joachim Berdes. Wismariæ 1703. pp. [222]. [5000.]

INTRODVCTIO in notitiam scriptorvm ivris civilis, saxonici et cameralis. Nordhvsæ 1703. pp. [viii].374. [4000.]

BURCARD GOTTHELF STRUVE, Bibliotheca ivris

selecta. . . . Accessit selectissima bibliotheca juris. . . . Editio altera. Ienae 1705. pp.[ ].480. [.]

— — Editio tertia. 1710. pp.[ ].592. [.]

— — Editio qvinta auctior longe et emendatior cvrante Christiano Gottlieb Bvdero. 1720. pp. [xlviii].931.[lxxvi]. [4000.]

— — Editio sexta. 1725. pp.[xxxvi].840.[lxvi]. [500.]

— — Editio septima. 1743. pp.[xxx].902.[cxxii]. [7000.]

— — Editio octava. 1756. pp.[xxxii].995.[cxvii]. [10,000.]

JOHANN CASPAR ZEUMER, Vitæ professorvm ivrivm, qvi in illvstri acadmia [*sic*] Jenensi ab ipsivs fvndatione ad nostra vsqve tempora vixervnt, vna cvm scriptis ab ipsis editis recensitæ. Ienæ [1706]. pp.[ii].197. [1000.]

JOH. JODOCUS BECKIUS [JOHANN JOST BECK], Prolegomena juris universi, quibus libri juris civilis, canonici et ecclesiastici protestantium, feudalis atque publici eorum omnium et singulorum in imperio nostro romano-germanico autoritas jurisque universi historia brevitur exhibentur. . . . Accesserunt . . . huic editioni sciagraphia potiorum scriptorum. Norimbergae 1712. pp.[viii].208.22.10. [580.]

VITAE tripartitae jurisconsultorum veterum a Bernardino Rutilio, Joanne Bertrando et Guilielmo Grotio conscriptae. . . . Edidit ac Βιοις νομιχων Bertrandi, vita ipsius auctore filio cum adnotationibus Friderici Jacobi Leckheri praemissa, notas Menagii, editoris Lugdunensis, et adhuc ineditas Thomae Reinesii . . . subjecit Jo. Christoph. Franck. Halae Magdeburgicae 1718.

GEORG ANDREAS VINHOLD, Notitia scriptorum juris naturæ. Lipsiæ 1723. pp.[xiv].108. [400.]

CARL JOHANN FOGEL, Antiqua et nova bibliotheca disputationum dnn. hamburgensium literatorum juridica. Hamburgi 1730. pp.94. [800.]

GOTTLOB AUGUST JENICHEN, Unpartheyische nachrichten von dem leben und denen schriften der ietztlebenden rechtsgelehrten in Teutschland. Leipzig 1739. pp.[xvi].240. [2000.]

GOTTLIEB STOLLE, Anleitung zur historie der juristischen gelahrheit. Jena 1745. pp.[xii].3–30. 96.648.[lxxx]. [2500.]

CHRISTOPH WEIDLICH, Geschichte der jetztlebenden rechts-gelehrten in Teutschland, und zum theil auch ausser demselben, als ein rechtsgelehrten-lexicon . . . herausgegeben. Merseburg

1748–1749. pp.[xvi].360+[xiv].708. [2500.]

— — [another edition]. Zuverlässige nachrichten von denen ietztlebenden rechtsgelehrten. Halle 1757–1765. pp.[xxiv].424+[xiv].432+[xii].483+[xiv].399+[iv].419+[xvi].419.[x]. [5000.]

CATALOGUE des livres imprimés de la Bibliothèque du roy. Jurisprudence. Tome I. Paris 1753. pp.viii.4.32.98.113. [8500.]

no more published.

BURCARD GOTTHELF STRUVE, Bibliotheca selectissima jvris. Accedvnt Hen. Contelmanni adnotationes. Editio secvnda. Lavsannae 1762. pp.[ii].vii.100. [200.]

the text is the same as that of the last chapter of Struve's Bibliotheca juris selecta, *above.*

DANIEL NETTELBLADT, Initia historiae litterariae ivridicae vniversalis. Halae Magdebvrgicae 1764. pp.[xxiv].560.[xxxii]. [2500.]

— — Editio secunda. 1774. pp.[xxxii].632.80.[xxx]. [4750.]

[ARMAND GASTON CAMUS], Lettres sur la profession d'avocat et sur les études nécessaires pour se rendre capable de l'exercer. On y joint un catalogue raisonné des livres utiles à un avocat. 1772. pp.vi.206.200. [1000.]

reissued in 1774.

— — [second edition]. 1777. pp.xvi.168.202. [1158.]

— — Troisième édition. [Edited by A. M. H. Boulard]. 1805. pp.432. [1753.]

— — Quatrième édition . . . revue . . . par [André Marie Jean Jacques] Dupin. 1818–1819. pp.[iii].xlviii.536+[iii].xii.691. [2348.]

— — [cinquième édition]. Profession d'avocat. 1830–1832. pp.[iii].xx.740+[iii].xvi.879. [4000.]

the subtitle varies; there is a further 'cinquième édition', Bruxelles 1833, the bibliographical (second) part of which does not appear to have been published.

JOHANN FRIEDRICH JUGLER, Beyträge zur juristischen biographie. Oder genauere litterärische . . . nachrichten von dem leben und den schriften verstorbener rechtsgelehrten auch staatsmänner. Leipzig 1773–1779. pp.[xxiv].208+[ii].209–442+[ii].222 + [ii].223–412 + [viii].184 + [iv].185–372 + [iv].187 + [iv].189–373 + [iv].187 + 189–379. [4000.]

[JEREMIAS NICOLAUS EYRING], Litterarischer almanach der Deutschen . . . litteratur der rechtsgelehrsamkeit. Göttingen.

1775. pp.58. [250.]
1776. pp.124. [425.]
1777. pp.126.[x]. [310.]
no more published.

CARL FERDINAND HOMMEL, Litteratvra ivris. Editio secvnda. Lipsiae 1779. pp.[xvi].366.[xxxvi]. [1000.]

ERNST CHRISTIAN WESTPHAL, Systematische anleitung zur kenntnis der besten bücher in der rechtsgelahrtheit und in den damit verbundenen wissenschaften. Zwote . . . auflage. Leipzig 1779. pp.16.199. [3000.]

—— Dritte . . . auflage, herausgegeben von Joh. Sigmund Gruber. 1791. pp.[ii].iv.[xii].580. [cxxviii]. [5250.]

[MOUTARD], Manuel bibliographique des amateurs, contenant l'état général de tous les objets . . . qui se vendent journellement dans Paris. . . . I. Jurisprudence. Paris 1780. pp.xx.56. [314.]

[MARQUIS A. R. DE VOYER D'ARGENSON DE PAULMY and A. G. CONTANT D'ORVILLE], De la lecture des livres françois. Sixième partie. Livres de théologie & de jurisprudence du seizième siècle. Mélanges tirés d'une grande bibliothèque (vol.I): 1780. pp.viii.449. [100.]

ALLGEMEINE juristische bibliothek. Herausgegeben von zweyen altdorfischen professoren [Julius Friedrich Malblanc and Johann Christian Siebenkees]. Nürnberg.

i. 1781. pp.[vi].472. [200.]
ii. 1782. pp.486[*sic*, 496]. [200.]
iii.
iv. 1784. pp.480. [200.]
v. 1785. pp.470. [200.]
vi. 1786. pp.236. [100.]

no more published.

AUGUST FRIEDRICH SCHOTT, Bibliothek der neuesten juristischen litteratur für das jahr 1783. Erster[-zwelter (*sic*)] theil. Leipzig 1783–1784. pp. [xx].227+[ii].229–481.[xvii]. [455.]

no more published?

HEINRICH JOHANN OTTO KÖNIG, Lehrbuch der allgemeinen juristischen litteratur. Halle 1785. pp. xvi.399+xvi.778.[ii]. [7500.]

JOHANN CHRISTIAN HELLBACH, Entwurf einer auserlesenen bibliothek für rechtsgelehrte. Erfurt 1787–1794. pp.[xxxii].288+xxiv.290. [5000.]

CHRISTOPH WEIDLICH, Vollständiges verzeichniss aller auf der Königl. preussl. Friedrichs-universität zu Halle . . . herausgekommenen juristischen disputationen und programmen. Halle 1789. pp.xii. 151.74. [1500.]

JUDAS THADAUS ZAUNER, Biographische nachrichten von den salzburgischen rechtslehrern von der stiftung der universität an bis auf gegenwärtige zeiten. Salzburg 1789. pp.[xvi].144. [500.]

JOHANN JAKOB PALM, Versuch einer handbibliothek der juristischen litteratur. Erlanger 1791. pp.[vi].823. [7000.]

[JOHANN SAMUEL ERSCH], Allgemeines repertorium der literatur für die jahre 1785 bis 1790. IV. Iuristische literatur. Jena 1793. pp.[96]. [2158.]

[—] — 1791–1795. Weimar 1799. pp.[110]. [2150.]

[—] — 1796–1800. Weimar 1807. pp.[90]. [1578.]

no more published.

KARL SALOMO ZACHARIÄ, Enzyklopädisch-szientifische literatur. Achtes heft, die enzyklopädisch-juristische literatur enthaltend. Leipzig &c. 1806. pp.v–x.61. [600.]

JOHANN SAMUEL ERSCH, Handbuch der deutschen literatur seit der mitte des achtzehnten jahrhunderts. . . . Ersten bandes dritte abtheilung, die literatur der jurisprudenz und politik enthaltend. Amsterdam &c. 1812. coll.464. [law: 2500.]

— — Literatur der jurisprudenz und politik, mit einschluss der cameral-wissenschaften. . . . Neue fortgesetzte ausgabe von Johann Christian Koppe. Leipzig 1823. pp.[vi].coll.712. [law: 3500.]

JULIEN MICHEL DUFOUR, Questions illustres, ou bibliothèque des livres singuliers en droit; Analyse d'un très-grand nombre de ces livres, et recueil d'arrêts sur les question de droit singulières. 1813. pp.viii.342. [1000.]

[— BRETON], Catalogue des livres composant la bibliothèque de la Cour de cassation. Deuxième partie. Jurisprudence. 1819. pp.[iii].537. [6000.]
— [supplément]. 1825. pp.98. [1000.]

JOHANN HEINRICH STEPF, Gallerie aller juridischen autoren von der ältesten bis auf die jetzige zeit, mit ihren vorzüglichsten schriften. Leipzig 1820–1825. pp.[ii].318 + [ii].308 + [ii].384 + [ii].546. [10,000.]
A–K only; no more published.

T[HEODOR] C[HRISTIAN] F[RIEDRICH] ENSLIN, Bibliotheca juridica, oder verzeichniss aller brauchbaren . . . besonders vom jahre 1700 . . . in Deutschland erschienenen werke über alle theile der rechtsgelehrsamkeit. Berlin 1824. pp.[ii].220. [5000.]

— — Zweite auflage, von Wilhelm Engelmann. Leipzig 1840. pp.viii.600. [10,000.]

— — — Supplement-heft. 1849. pp.iv.296. [5000.]

CATALOGUE of . . . books in the library of the Legislative council. Quebec [1822]. pp.[ii].64. [300.]

— [another edition]. 1832. [*sic*, 1834]. pp.ii.70. [750.]

printed on one side of the leaf.

[GUSTAV] HUGO, Beyträge zur civilistischen bücher kenntniss der letzten vierzig jahre. Berlin 1828–1829. pp.viii.540+xii.755. [500.]

— — Dritter band. Letzter beytrag. 1844. pp. xvi.87. [25.]

[JEAN BAPTISTE HENRI MONBALON], Catalogue des livres composant la bibliothèque de la ville de Bordeaux. Jurisprudence. 1834. pp.x.338. [3800.]

[CHARLES SUMNER], A catalogue of the law library of Harvard university. [Second edition]. Cambridge [Mass.] 1934. pp.viii.80. [1750.]

— — Catalogue of the library of the Law school of Harvard university. 1909. pp.viii.1216+[iii].1248. [100,000.]

R. SICKEL, Repertorium über die in den jahren 1802 bis mit 1834 erschienenen Sammlungen juristischer aufsätze und rechtlicher entscheidungen. Leipzig 1835. pp.xxiv.388 + [ii].353. [10,000.]

[GOTTFRIED LEBRECHT GOETHE and CARL GOTTLOB RICHTER], Lexicon literaturae academico-iuridicae, quo tituli dissertationum, programmatum aliarumque commentationum iuridicarum ab academiarum initiis usque ad finem anni 1835 editarum. Lipsiae 1836–1838. pp.xiii.394+[ii]. 548. [20,000.]

FRIEDRICH KAPPLER, Juristisches promtuarium; ein repertorium über alle in den jahren 1800 bis 1837 erschienenen abhandlungen über einzelne materien aus der gesammten rechtswissenschaft, (mit anschluss des criminalrechts). . . . Mit einem supplementhefte vermehrte ausgabe. Stuttgart 1837. pp.vi.938. [15,000.]
limited to german writings.

AUG. VOISIN, Bibliotheca gandavensis. Catalogue méthodique de la bibliothèque de l'université de Gand. . . . Jurisprudence. Gand 1839. pp.[v].lxxxii.394. [4359.]

HERMANN [ERNST] LUDEWIG, Zur bibliothekonomie. Dresden 1840. pp.xxx.41. [100.]

the text consists of a 'Fragment eines juristischen real-catalogs der Königlichen öffentlichen bibliothek zu Dresden'.

HERM[ANN] THEODOR SCHLETTER, Handbuch der juristischen literatur. Grimma [1840–]1843. pp. xix.328. [12,856.]

КАТАЛОГЪ библіотеки II-го отдѣленія собственной его Императорскаго величества Канцеляріи. Санктпетербургъ 1849. pp.[iii]. 281.xxix. [1132.]

— Прибавленіе. 1853. pp.[iii].450. [4874.]

ÍNDICE de las obras existentes en la bibliotheca de la Academia matritense de jurisprudencia y legislación. Madrid 1850. pp.[iv].40. [500.]

— Lista de las obras que han entrado en la bibliotheca desde la impresión del catálogo. [1851]. pp.6. [75.]

CATALOGUE of the library of the Law society of the United Kingdom. 1851. pp.[iii].222. [4000.]

— [another edition]. Catalogue of the printed books in the library of the Incorporated law society. By Frederic Boase. 1891. pp.iv.1084. [10,000.]

— — Supplement . . . by Waller M. Sinclair. 1906. pp.632. [6000.]

REVUE bibliographique et critique de droit français et étranger. [Edited by] Charles Ginoulhiac.

i. 1853–1854. pp.208. [400.]
ii. 1854–1855. pp.144. [250.]
iii. 1855–1856. pp.192. [275.]
iv. 1857. pp.48. [50.]

no more published.

O. A. WALTHER, Hand-lexicon der juristischen literatur des neunzehnten jahrhunderts. Weimar 1854. pp.vii.934. [20,000.]

CATALOGUE of law books, in the library at Hartwell. 1855. pp.[iii].122. [1750.]

— William Henry McAlpine, A catalogue of the law library at Hartwell house, Buckinghamshire. 1865. pp.vii.272. [2000.]

CATALOGUE of the library of the Supreme court of Victoria. Part I. Bibliotheca legis. Melbourne 1855. pp.[iii].102. [1000.]

— [another edition]. 1861. pp.vii.[xxiv].202. [xi]. [2000.]

— Second [*sic*] edition. 1875. pp.xvi.xvia–l. xvii.xxviii.xxxvi.309. [10,000.]

CATALOGUS der boekerij van den Hoogen raad der Nederlanden. [*s.l.*] 1856. pp.viii.142. [1254.]

WILLIAM IVORY, Catalogue of the law books in the library of the Society of writers to her majesty's signet in Scotland. Edinburgh 1856. pp.xi.268. [1985.]

CATALOGUE of the New-York state library . . . Law library. Albany 1856. pp.x.402. [5500.]

— First supplement. 1865. pp.[iii].180. [3000]

F. L. BOESIGK, Systematisches verzeichniss von buechern, zeitschriften, zerstreuten abhandlungen und einzelnen aufsaetzen betreffend die literatur und geschichte der privatunterthansverhältnisse. Dresden 1857. pp.[ii].66. [578.]

[COUNT] A[DOLPHE CHARLES THÉODORE] DE FONTAINE DE RESBECQ, Notice sur le doctorat en droit, avec . . . une analyse chronologique des lois, statuts, décrets . . . relatifs à cet enseignement, de 1791 à 1857, suivie . . . du catalogue raisonné des thèses soutenues de 1851 à 1857. 1857. pp.[iii]. lxiii.199. [500.]

WILLIAM H. SPILSBURY, Catalogue of the printed books in the library of the Hon. society of Lincoln's inn. 1859. pp.viii.972. [10,000.]

— — Supplementary volume, 1859–1890. By

John Nicholson. 1890. pp.[iii].468. [4000.]

TABLES analytiques de la Revue de législation et de la Revue critique de législation et de jurisprudence, précédées des tables de la Thémis et de la Revue du droit français et étranger, par mm. [J. B. C.] Coin-Delisle . . . Ch[arles] Million, suivies d'une liste des principaux travaux de droit et de législation contenus dans les séances et travaux de l'Académie des sciences morales et politiques, par Ch. Vergé. 1860. pp.[iii].lxiv.135.81. 127. [6000.]

W. C. STRATTON, Catalogue of the California state library. [Part I. Law books]. Sacramento 1860. pp.[iv].210. [2500.]

[F. A. VON AMSBERG], Katalog der bibliothek des Königlich-hannoverschen ober-appellationsgerichts zu Celle. Hannover 1862. pp.xxiv.659. [5000.]

AM. WILBAUX, Catalogue de la bibliothèque de la ville de Tournai. . . . Tome deuxième. [Jurisprudence]. Tournai 1863. pp.[iii].828. [3519.]

[J. J. B. A. GARNIER], Catalogue méthodique de la Bibliothèque communale de la ville d'Amiens. Jurisprudence. Amiens 1864. pp.400. [1597.]

VERZEICHNISS der von dem verewigten herrn staatsminister Carl Friedrich von Savigny . . . der Königlichen bibliothek zu Berlin vermachten werke. Berlin 1865. pp.[iii].95. [550.]

V[LADIMIR] I[ZMAILOVICH] MEZHOV, Литература русскаго правовѣдѣнія за 1859–1866 г. включительно . . . Томъ 1. С.-Петербургъ 1867. pp.[iii].249–360.1–56.ii.74.174. [6349.]

made up of offprints bearing the title of Библіографическій указатель книгъ . . . по правовѣдѣнію вышедшихъ; *in some copies pp.249–360 do not appear; no more published.*

GUSTAV WILHELM WUTTIG [vol.ii: LUDWIG ROSSBERG], Bibliotheca juridica. Handbuch der gesammten neueren juristischen und staatswissenschaftlichen literatur. Eine zusammenstellung aller . . . seit 1849 in Deutschland und den benachbarten staaten erschienenen schriften. Leipzig 1867–1877. pp.vi.330+[iv].249. [10,000.]

UEBERSICHT [*afterwards:* Übersicht] der gesammten staats- und rechtswissenschaftlichen literatur. Berlin.

[i]. 1868. Zusammengestellt von Otto Mühlbrecht. pp.xx.208. [3204.]
ii. 1869. pp.xx.186. [3051.]
iii. 1870. pp.xxii.206. [3129.]

iv. 1871. pp.xix.181. [2788.]
v. 1872. pp.xix.170. [2512.]
vi. 1873. pp.xx.180. [2594.]
vii. 1874. pp.xxix[*sic*, xix].192. [2749.]
viii. 1875. pp.xx.226. [3187.]
ix. 1876. pp.xxi.240. [3407.]
x. 1877. pp.xx.236. [3390.]
xi. 1878. pp.xix.234. [3393.]
xii. 1879. pp.xxii.290. [4071.]
xiii. 1880. pp.xx.264. [3756.]
xiv. 1881. pp.xxii.274. [3975.]
xv. 1882. pp.xx.252. [3535.]
xvi. 1883. pp.xxii.244. [3761.]
xvii. 1884. pp.xxiii.278. [4393.]

nos.4100–4999 are omitted in the numbering.

xviii. 1885. pp.xxiv.264. [4192.]
xix. 1886. pp.xxxiv.258. [4051.]
xx. 1887. pp.xxix.236. [3621.]
xxi. 1888. pp.xxviii.252. [3872.]
xxii. 1889. pp.xxviii.250.16.8. [4000.]
xxiii. 1890. pp.xxviii.244.8.8. [3750.]
xxiv. 1891. pp.xxxii.254.14. [4000.]
xxv. 1892. pp.xxxi.242. [3761.]
xxvi. 1893. pp.xxxii.256. [4003.]
xxvii. 1894. pp.xxxii.270. [4125.]
xxviii. 1895. pp.xxxii.266. [4139.]
xxix. 1896. pp.xxxi.278. [4136.]

xxx. 1897. pp.xxxi.267. [3992.]
xxxi. 1898. pp.xxx.274. [4147.]
xxxii. 1899. pp.xxxii.286. [4292.]
xxxiii. 1900. pp.xxxii.300. [4340.]
xxxiv. 1901. pp.xxxii.280. [3968.]
xxxv. 1902. pp.xxxii.276. [3917.]
xxxvi. 1903. pp.xxxii.296. [4259.]
xxxvii. 1904. pp.xxxii.304. [4466.]
xxxviii. 1905. pp.xxxii.294. [4191.]
xxxix. 1906. Fortgeführt von Hermann Mühlbrecht. pp.xxxvi.334. [4882.]
xl. 1907. pp.xxxvi.346. [5316.]
xli. 1908. pp.xliii.390. [5973.]
xlii. 1909. pp.xlvi.410. [5836.]
xliii. 1910. pp.xliv.409. [6101.]
xliv. 1911. pp.xliii.360. [5438.]
xlv. 1912. pp.xlvi.375. [6359.]
xlvi. 1913. pp.xlvi.345. [5436.]
xlvii. 1914. pp.355. [5165.]

no more published; issued bi-monthly under the title Allgemeine bibliographie der staats- und rechtswissenschaften *and collected annually, with an index, as above; the index for the last volume was not published.*

REVUE bibliographique de droit et de jurisprudence.

i. 1868–1869. pp.[iii].267. [2500.]
ii. (nos.1–10). 1869–1870. pp.204. [2000.]
no more published.

CATALOGUE méthodique des imprimés de la Bibliothèque publique de Douai. . . . Droit. Douai 1869. pp.8.lx.147. [1971.]

AMBROSE P. DIETZ, Bibliotheca Californiæ. A descriptive catalogue of books in the State library of California. Volume I. — Law library. Sacramento 1870. pp.xxxi.632. [8750.]

CATALOGUE of law books of the Department of justice. Washington 1873. pp.251. [3000.]

— [another edition]. 1904. By James A. Finch. pp.xlviii.1135. [15,000.]

KATALOG der juristischen abtheilung der Rigaschen stadtbibliothek. Riga 1874. pp.viii.276. [3600.]

SYSTEMATISCHE catalogus der Provinciale bibliotheek van Friesland. . . . Derde gedeelte. Rechtsgeleerdheid. Leeuwarden 1875. pp.vi.863–1226. [5000.]

CHR[ISTIAN] V. BRUUN, Bibliotheca danica. Systematisk fortegnelse over den danske literatur fra 1482 til 1830. . . . Andet hefte: rets- og lægevidenskab. Kjøbenhavn 1875. coll.xxi–lviii.597–878. [law: 2250.]

CATALOGUE de la bibliothèque de la ville de Montpellier. . . . Jurisprudence. Montpellier 1875. pp.vi.93. [544.]

GEO[RGE] M[ELVILLE] SEIDERS, A catalogue of [Simon] Greenleaf law library. Portland, Me. 1877. pp.61. [800.]

HILDEBRANDT's bibliographie der staats- und rechtswissenschaften. Die erscheinungen des deutschen buchhandels. Leipzig [Berlin].

i. Von der gründung des deutschen Kaiserreiches bis September 1876. 1877.

ii. 1876–1881. 1882.

no more published.

O. H. MILLER and J. R. ORWIG, Catalogue of the Pennsylvania state library . . . Part I. — Law books and state papers. Harrisburg 1878. pp.[viii].332. [4000.]

CH[ARLES] LE FORT, Catalogue des thèses soutenues devant la Faculté de droit de Genève de 1821 à 1877. Genève 1878. pp.32. [208.]

CATÁLOGO de las obras que contiene la biblioteca del tribunal superior del distritto [of Mexico]. México 1879. pp.64. [1200.]

FRANCESCO BUFALINI, Repertorio alfabetico per materia di oltre duemila opere di diritto costituzionale, amministrativo e internazionale di autori italiani e stranieri antichi e moderni. Milano 1879. pp.107. [2000.]

BIBLIOTHÈQUE du Comité de législation étrangère. Catalogue. Ministère de la justice. 1879. pp. xxviii.319. [1664.]

— [another edition]. 1889. pp.xl.719. [4062.]

— Deuxième [*sic*] édition. [By] Christian Daguin . . . Maurice Dufourmantelle. Société de législation comparée: 1899. pp.xl.599. [5469.]

CATALOGUE of the contents of the library of the Incorporated law society of Liverpool. Liverpool 1880. pp.[iii].95. [1500.]

CATALOGUS der boekerij van den Hoogen raad der Nederlanden. [*s.l.*] 1880. pp.viii.184.2. [3000.]

— [another edition]. 's-Gravenhage 1912. pp. iii–xxiv.311. [4000.]

[FÉNELON GUÉRIN], Catalogue de la bibliothèque de la ville du Mans. Jurisprudence. Le Mans 1881. pp.xiv.388. [3036.]

Law

CATALOGUE of the books of the Manchester law library society. 1881. pp.vi.182. [2500.]

— [another edition]. 1935. pp.x.316. [14,261.]

— — Supplements.

1938. pp.[ii].15. [200.]

there are numerous intermediate editions and supplements.

K. SCHULZ, Katalog der bibliothek des Reichsgerichts. Leipzig 1882. pp.lxv.coll.3038. [15,000.]

CENTRALBLATT [Zentralblatt] für [der] rechtswissenschaft. Stuttgart [Berlin; Leipzig; Berlin].

i. Herausgegeben von [Arthur] von Kirchenheim 1882. pp.[ii].476. [2000.]
ii. 1883. pp.[ii].476. [2000.]
iii. 1884. pp.[ii].488. [2000.]
iv. 1885. pp.[ii].470. [2000.]
v. 1886. pp.[ii].484. [2000.]
vi. 1887. pp.[ii].493. [2000.]
vii. 1888. pp.[ii].500. [2000.]
viii. 1889. pp.[ii].484. [2000.]
ix. 1890. pp.[ii].486. [2000.]
x. 1891. pp.[ii].470. [2000.]
xi. 1892. pp.[ii].470. [2000.]
xii. 1893. pp.[ii].446. [2000.]
xiii. 1894. pp.[ii].446. [2000.]
xiv. 1895. pp.[ii].430. [2000.]

xv. 1896. pp.[ii].400. [2000.]
xvi. 1897. pp.[ii].404. [2000.]
xvii. 1898. pp.[ii].418. [2000.]
xviii. 1899. pp.[ii].408. [2000.]
xix. 1900. pp.[ii].408. [2000.]
xx. 1901. pp.[ii].384. [2000.]
xxi. 1902. pp.[ii].376. [2000.]
xxii. 1903. pp.[ii].388. [2000.]
xxiii. 1904. pp.[ii].408. [2000.]
xxiv. 1905. pp.[ii].414. [2000.]
xxv. 1906. pp.[ii].374. [2000.]
xxvi. 1907. pp.[ii].220.104. [3000.]
xxvii. 1908. pp.[ii].220.104. [3000.]
xxviii. 1909. pp.[ii].214.104. [3000.]
xxix. 1910. pp.[ii].214.108. [3000.]
xxxi [*sic*]. Bearbeitet von Otto Waldschütz. pp.xxxiv.510. [15,000.]
xxxii [*sic*]. 1912. pp.600. [17,500.]
xxxiii [*sic*]. January–March 1913. pp.168. [5000.]

no more published.

MANUEL TORRES CAMPOS, Bibliografía española contemporánea del derecho y de la política, 1800–1880 [1881 a 1896]. Parte primera. Bibliografía española. Madrid &c. 1883, 1897 [*on cover:* 1898]. pp.208+168. [5500.]

[C. TESTER], Catalogue of the library of the Supreme court of South Australia. Adelaide 1883. pp.iv.114. [1000.]

CATALOGUE d'une collection de thèses publiées dans les Pays-Bas donnée à la Bibliothèque nationale par le Service des échanges internationaux. I. Droit. 1884. pp.69. [750.]

HENRY TENNYSON FOLKARD, Catalogue of the law books preserved in the Reference department of the Wigan public library. Wigan 1884. pp.16. [300.]

BIBLIOTHECA JURIDICA. Systematisches verzeichniss der neueren und gebräuchlicheren auf dem gebiete der staats- u. rechtswissenschaft erschienenen lehrbücher, . . . etc. Leipzig 1885. pp.xii.61. [1250.]

G[EORG] MOLLAT, T. O. Weigel's systematisches verzeichniss der hauptwerke der deutschen literatur aus dem gebiete der rechts- und staatswissenschaften [aus den jahren 1820–1882]. Leipzig 1886. pp.[vi].106. [law: 2500.]

OTTO MÜHLBRECHT, Wegweiser durch die neuere literatur der staats- und rechtswissenschaften. Berlin 1886. pp.xvi.429. [11,500.]

— — Zweite . . . auflage. Berlin 1893. pp.[ii]. xxviii.748. [34,000.]

— — — [supplement]. Band II, enthaltend die litteratur der jahre 1893–1900. 1901. pp.xvi.651. [15,000.]

KATALOG der bibliothek des Reichs-justizamts. Berlin 1887. pp.xlvii.761. [12,000.]

— — Zweite ausgabe. [By Rudolf Kaiser]. 1897. pp.lxv.1308. [20,000.]

CATALOGUE of the books in the library of the Faculty of procurators. Glasgow 1887. pp.xxxii. 497. [7500.]

— [another edition]. 1903. By John Muir. pp. liv.1049. [10,000.]

— — Supplement . . . 1903 to . . . 1922. pp. xviii.398. [3500.]

ÉMILE SOCARD, Catalogue de la bibliothèque de la ville de Troyes . . . [tome quinzième(–seizième)]. Jurisprudence. Troyes 1888–1889. pp.[iii].iv.523 +[iii].vi.532. [4350.]

KATALOG der Bernischen hochschulbibliothek. II. abteilung. Jus. Bern 1890. pp.250. [5000.]

PAUL ERTEL, Die quellen des römischen-gemeinen, kirchlichen und deutschen rechtes. Berlin 1890. pp.[iii].vi.171. [1000.]

SOMMAIRE périodique des revues de droit. Tables mensuelles de tous les articles et études juridiques publiés dans les périodiques belges et étrangers. Bruxelles.

[i]. 1891. pp.xiii.[176]. [728.]
ii. 1892. pp.[512]. [3456.]
iii. 1893. pp.[182]. [1481.]

[*continued as:*]

Sommaire méthodique des traités, monographies et revues de droit. Office international de bibliographie: Bruxelles.

[iv]. 1894. pp.220. [4532.]

[*continued as:*]

Bibliographia sociologica.

[v]. [1895]. pp.xiii.[xvi].268. [6655.]

no more published.

[WILLIAM J. C. BERRY], Catalogue of the library of the Association of the bar of the city of New York. New York 1892. pp.[iii].1135. [20,000.]

A[UGUSTE MARIE LOUIS] and P. L. TISSOT, Catalogue de la Bibliothèque communale de Brest.... Théologie et jurisprudence. Brest 1893. pp. lxxxiii.157. [law: 887.]

[ERNEST CUSHING RICHARDSON], Library of political science and jurisprudence. Finding list. College of New Jersey: Princeton 1893. pp.44. [3000.]

THE LAW book adviser. A journal of legal bibliography. Volume I. Washington 1893–1897. pp.12.80.

no more published.

FRATELLI BOCCA, Catalogo delle opere di diritto, giurisprudenza e scienze sociali pubblicate in Italia dal gennaio 1891 al giugno 1894. Torino 1894. pp.xiv.93. [1250.]

— — dal luglio 1894 al giugno 1898. 1898. pp.xvi.83. [1200.]

CATALOGUE de la bibliothèque des avocats près la Cour d'appel de Bruxelles. 3me Édition. 1894. pp.xxxiv.707. [4824.]

MANUEL CRUZADO, Memoria para la bibliografía jurídica mexicana. México 1894. pp.139. [175.]

DEODATO C. VILELLA DOS SANTOS, Catálogo da esposição de trabalhos jurídicos realizado pelo Instituto da ordem dos advogados brazileiros. Rio de Janeiro 1894. pp.vii.223. [970.]

KATALOG der bibliothek des Königlichen oberverwaltungsgerichts. Berlin 1894. pp.x.307. [2000.]

CATALOGUE of the Owens college library. Class v. Legal sciences. Manchester 1894. pp.[ii]. 133. [2500.]

MATTHIAS LEVY, Catalogue of the books in the library of the Institute of shorthand writers, practising in the Supreme court of judicature. 1895. pp.24. [250.]

— — Addenda. [1895]. single leaf. [20.]

— — — 1899. pp.6. [75.]

JURISTISCHER litteraturbericht, 1884 bis 1894.... Herausgegeben von A[rthur] v. Kirchenheim. Centralblatt für rechtswissenschaft (ergänzungsband): Leipzig [1895–]1896. pp.[iii].366. [2500.]

BIBLIOGRAPHIE générale et complète des livres de droit et de jurisprudence publiés jusqu'au 23 octobre 1897. 1898. pp.xxxii.154. [4000.]

— [another edition]. 1924. pp.xlii.194. [5000.]

there are several intermediate editions.

HENRY TENNYSON FOLKARD, Law books . . . in the . . . Wigan free public library. Wigan 1899. pp.36. [1000.]

25 copies printed.

RIVISTA delle riviste giuridiche italiane ed estere. Roma.

i. 1899. pp.704. [2800.]

no more published?

LEGAL literature.

i–ii. 1899. pp.32. [100.]

iii–v. 1900. pp.33–80. [150.]
vi. 1901. pp.81–92. [20.]
vii–viii. 1902. pp.93–116. [50.]
ix. 1903. pp.117–128. [20.]
x. 1904. pp.129–152. [30.]

new ser.

i–ii. 1905. pp.16+16. [50.]
iii. 1906. pp.16. [25.]
iv–v. 1907. pp.16+16. [50.]
vi–vii. 1908. pp.16+16. [50.]
viii. 1909. pp.16. [25.]
ix. 1910. pp.16. [25.]
x–xi. 1911. pp.16+16. [50.]

no more published.

FRANK N[ELLIS] BEEBE, Catalogue of the law library of the Supreme court of Ohio. Columbus 1901. pp.[ii].589[*sic*, 601.]

[ANNA PARKER PRUYN], Catalogue of books relating to the literature of the law collected by the late John V. L. Pruyn. Albany, N.Y. 1901. pp.[vii].300. [2000.]

125 copies printed.

АЛФАВИТНЫЙ СПИСОКЪ КНИГЪ библіотеки Юридическаго факультета Императорскаго Казанскаго университета. Казань 1901. pp.[ii].133. [1464.]

KATALOG der fremdsprachigen bücher in der bibliothek der Juristischen fakultät der Kaiserlichen universität zu Kyoto. Kyoto 1903. pp.[ii].viii.20.[ff.2].coll.846.pp.847–953. [10,000.]

— — Zweite ausgabe. 1913. pp.[ii].ix.50.coll. 2645. [45,000.]

[UNO THERMAN], Katalog öfver juridiska föreningens i Finland. Helsingfors 1904. pp.95. [1500.]

CHIEF court library catalogue. Rangoon 1904, 1924. ff.[ii].76+[v].277.152. [3000.]

vol.ii is entitled Catalogue of the High court library, Rangoon.

G. ZIELER and TH. SCHEFFER, Das akademische Deutschland. Biographisch - bibliographisches handbuch für die universitäten des Deutschen reiches, als ergänzung zum Deutschen universitäts-kalender. Band II. Die juristischen fakultäten. Leipzig 1905. pp.[ii].iv.86. [1500.]

[PETER JOHN ANDERSON], Subject catalogue of the law library in Marischal college. University of Aberdeen: University studies (no.23): Aberdeen 1906. pp.111. [1250.]

M. D. SEVERN, Catalogue of the books in the library of the Honourable society of Gray's inn. 1906. pp.viii.959. [7500.]

GOJKO NIKETIĆ, Правна библиографија чланака и књига у српској књижевности до краја 1905 године. Београд 1906. pp.[vii].234. [2800.]

[JOSÉ MARIA VIGIL], Catálogos de la Biblioteca nacional de México. Cuarta división. Jurisprudencia. México 1908. pp.508. [10,000.]

INDEX to legal periodicals. Published in conjunction with the Law library journal. American association of law libraries: New York.

i. 1908. [4200.]
ii. 1909. [5500.]
iii. 1910. [7000.]
iv. 1911. [4500.]
v. 1912. [4500.]
vi. 1913. [4300.]
vii. 1914. [6750.]
viii. 1915. Gertrude Elstner Woodard, editor. pp.70.91.76. [4000.]
ix. 1916. pp.56.244. [6000.]
x. 1917. pp.28.147. [4000.]
xi. 1918. pp.160. [4500.]
xii. 1919. pp.181. [5500.]
xiii. 1920. Elsie Basset, editor. pp.211. [6500.]
xiv. 1921. pp.188. [6000.]
xv. 1922. G. E. Woodard, editor. pp.264. [8000.]

xvi. 1923. pp.223. [6500.]
xvii. 1924. pp.228. [6500.]
xviii. 1925. Eldon R. James, editor. pp.324. [9000.]
xix. 1926. pp.295. [8000.]
xx. 1927. pp.302. [9000.]
— 1926–1928. pp.779. [24,000.]
xxii. 1929. pp.328. [10,000.]
xxiii. 1930. pp.364. [10,000.]
— 1928–1931. pp.1009. [30,000.]
xxv. 1932. pp.439. [12,500.]
xxvi. 1933. pp.396. [12,500.]
— 1931–1934. pp.1135. [35,000.]
xxviii. 1935. pp.405. [12,500.]
xxix. 1936. pp.424. [12,500.]
— 1934–1937. pp.1071. [32,500.]
xxxi. 1937–1938. pp.412. [12,500.]
xxxii. 1938–1939. pp.457. [12,500.]
— 1937–1940. pp.1174. [35,000.]
xxxiv. 1940–1941. pp.387. [10,000.]
xxxv. 1941–1942. pp.382. [10,000.]
— 1940–1943. [Edited by E. R. James and others]. pp.1045. [25,000.]
xxxvii. 1943–1944. pp.275. [7500.]
xxviii. 1944–1945. pp.275. [7500.]
— 1943–1946. [Edited by] John M. Maguire . . . Jessie I. Wharton. pp.799. [20,000.]

xl. 1946–1947. pp.372. [10,000.]
xli. 1947–1948. pp.429. [12,500.]
— 1946–1949. pp.1282. [32,500.]
— 1949–1952. [Edited by] J. M. Maguire . . . Iris V. Azian. pp.968. [30,000.]
— 1952–1955. [Edited by] Dorothea A. Flaherty. pp.898. [27,000.]
— 1955–1958. pp.830. [25,000.]
— 1958–1961. pp.915. [27,500.]
— 1961–1962. Edited by Mildred Russell. pp.297. [9000.]
— 1962–1963. pp.407. [12,000.]

in progress; only the final cumulative issue in each year and the triennal cumulations are set out.

CATÁLOGO de los principales artículos publicados en las revistas de la biblioteca. Colegio de abogados: [Barcelona] 1909. pp.xxix.471. [15,000.]

CATALOGUS van boeken in noord-Nederland verschenen van de vroegsten tijd tot op heden. [IV. Rechten, staatswetenschappen en staatshuishoudkunde]. Samengesteld door de Tentoonstellings-commissie der nationale tentoonstelling van het boek . . . 1910. Vereeniging ter bevordering van de belangen des boekhandels: 's-Gravenhage. 1911. pp.[ii].coll.248.[xxxiv]. [3000.]

ELLEN M. SAWYER, Catalogue of the laws of foreign countries in the State library of Massachusetts. Boston 1911. pp.311. [4000.]

RÉPERTOIRE des thèses de droit soutenues dans les facultés françaises. Période 1911–1920.
details of this work are entered under Academic writings: Law, above.

KATALOG der Grossherzoglich badischen hof- und landesbibliothek. . . . Vierte abteilung. Fachübersichten 1886 bis 1907. Recht. Karlsruhe 1912. pp.viii.115. [3500.]

FREDERICK C[HARLES] HICKS, Aids to the study and use of law books. A selected list . . . of publications relating to law literature, law study and legal ethics. New York 1913. pp.129. [750.]
— — [second edition]. Materials and methods of legal research. With bibliographical manual. Rochester, N.Y. 1923. pp.626. [3500.]
— — Second [*sic*] edition. 1933. pp.xvi.651. [4000.]

INTERNATIONALES und ausländisches recht. Gesamtkatalog der bestände von 30 berliner bibliotheken. Internationale vereinigung für vergleichende rechtswissenschaft: Berlin 1914. pp.lxxvii. 1684.

[GUSTAVO OLIVERA and JUAN SCHREIBER], Catálogo de la colección de tesis jurídicas. Universidad nacional de la Plata: Buenos Aires 1914. pp.101. [1000.]

C. E. A. BEDWELL, A catalogue of the printed books in the library of the Honourable society of the Middle temple. Glasgow [printed] 1914. pp.xiv.694+[iv].695–1336+[iv].521. [22,500.]

THE ATHENÆUM subject index to periodicals, 1915. . . . Economic and political sciences, law. 1916. pp.28. [750.]
no more sections devoted to law published.

KATALOG över Stockholms högskolas juridiska fakultets bibliotek. Stockholm 1918. pp.xviii.709.

BULLETIN sommaire des principaux documents parlementaires étrangers transmis à la présidence de la Chambre des députés. 1924–1928.

[*continued as:*]

Bulletin de l'information parlementaire étrangère. 1928–1932.

[*continued as:*]

Bulletin de l'information parlementaire française et étrangère. 1932–1939.

WILHELM FUCHS, Juristischer literaturführer.

Münster 1924. pp.68. [250.]

— — Dritte . . . auflage. Juristische bücherkunde. [Archiv für bibliographie (beiheft 7):] Linz a. d. Donau 1928. pp.vii.245. [1000.]

— — Fünfte . . . auflage. 1953. &c. *in progress.*

M. ALCOCER [Y MARTÍNEZ] and SATURNINO RIBERA, Historia de la universidad de Valladolid. Bio-bibliografías de juristas notables. Anales universitarios (vol.v): Valladolid 1924 [1925]. pp.100. [250.]

PAUL GÜNTZEL and HEINRICH TREPLIN, Rechtswissenschaft. Jahresberichte des Literarischen zentralblattes über die wichtigsten wissenschaftlichen neuerscheinungen des gesamten deutschen sprachgebietes (1924, vol.iv): Leipzig 1925. pp. 146. [750.]

MARIANO ALCOCER [Y MARTÍNEZ] and SATURNINO RIBERA, Catálogo bibliográfico de las obras impresas en Valladolid hasta fin del siglo XVIII que hacen relación a ambos derechos. Anales universitarios: Historia de la universidad de Valladolid: Valladolid 1925. pp.[ii].ccxl. [1000.]

WALTER SCHUBERT, Katalog der bibliothek des

oberlandsgerichts in Celle. Celle 1926. pp.xxxix. 1930. [35,000.]

RASSEGNA bibliografica delle scienze giuridiche [vol.v–ix: sociale e politiche]. Napoli.

i. 1926. pp.xi.565. [250.]
ii. 1927. pp.xx.662. [1000.]
iii. 1928. pp.xxiii.692. [1500.]
iv. 1929. pp.xxi.439. [1000.]
v. 1930. pp.xxxiii.816. [1500.]
vi. 1931. pp.xxxviii.729. [1500.]
vii. 1932. pp.xxxi.668. [1500.]
viii. 1933. pp.xxxiii.628. [1500.]
ix. 1934. pp.xxxi.754. [2500.]

A. GRANDIN, Bibliographie générale des sciences juridiques, politiques, économiques et sociales. 1926 &c.

in progress; details of this publication are given above under Economics.

MIKLÓS NAGY, Közjog és közigazgatási jog, 1866–1928. Az Országgyűlés könyvtárának katalógusa (vol.i): Budapest 1929. pp.lxiii.517. [5000.]

KATALOG der Otto von Gierke-bibliothek in der Handels-universität, Tokio. Tokio 1930. pp.[v]. coll.612.238.28. [8000.]

[RUDOLF KEYDELL], Verzeichnis der lesesaalbibliothek. Abteilung 7. Rechts- und staatswissenschaften. Universitäts-bibliothek: Berlin 1930. pp.viii.96. [1500.]

LAW book review digest and current legal bibliography. [Edited by William Lawrence Friend]. Volume I, number I[-4]. Philadelphia 1931-1932. pp.104. [500.]
no more published.

SALVATORE GALGANO, Repertorio della legislazione mondiale, anno 1932. Istituto di studi legislativi: Roma 1933 &c.
in progress?

BIBLIOGRAFIA giuridica internazionale (volumi ed articoli). Istituto di studi legislativi: Roma.
i. 1932. A cura del prof. Salvatore Galgano. [1935-]1938. pp.xxiv.475. [11,608.]
ii. 1933.
iii. 1934.
iv. 1935. [1937-]1940. pp.viii.806. [19,972.]
v. 1936.
vi. 1937. 1941. pp.xii.508. [14,364.]

CATALOGUE des thèses de droit soutenues devant les facultés de France. Université de Paris: Faculté de droit: 1933 &c.

GLADYS WELLS RINGER, Catalog of the law library of Indianapolis bar association. Indianapolis 1935. pp.iii.328.

[—] — Cumulated supplement. 1938. pp.101. [1500.]

A LIST of selected books from the tercentennial exhibition of the Harvard law school library. Cambridge 1936. pp.[ii].18. [164.]

CATÁLOGO metódico de la biblioteca. Universidad nacional del litoral: Facultad de ciencias jurídicas y sociales: Santa Fe 1937–1938. pp.616+110. [10,000.]

— Suplemento.

i. 1938–1939. pp.[ii].294. [5000.]

ii. 1940–1943. pp.270. [3500.]

RECUEIL universel de lois et decrets. Centre d'information législative internationale: Genève.

i–iii/iv. Mars–mai/juin 1938. pp.739+736+626. [7500.]

no more published.

CATÁLOGO de derecho civil. Universidad: Facultad de derecho y ciencias sociales: Biblioteca: Montevideo 1939. pp.3–187. [7000.]

FRANCISCO COUTO DE OLIVEIRA, Catálogo da

biblioteca. Supremo tribunal federal: Rio de Janeiro 1940. pp.lxxvii.332. [6000.]

CATÁLOGO de la biblioteca Dalmacio Vélez Sársfield. [Universidad nacional:] Biblioteca mayor: Publicaciones de la nueva serie (vol.ii): Córdoba 1940. pp.iii–xxxi.231. [900.]

CATÁLOGO de la Biblioteca de ciencias jurídicas y sociales. Universidad de Chile: Facultad de ciencias jurídicas y sociales: [Santiago 1940]. pp.228.

[JEAN MARIE CHRISTMAS], A catalog for a law library of 15,000 volumes. [Edited by Elsie Basset]. Columbia university: School of library service: New York 1942. pp.[vi].305. [5000.]

on the titlepage the author is given as Miles O[scar] Price, the above names being taken from the preface.

LISTE des acquisitions [des accroissements]. Ministère de la justice: Bibliothèque: Bruxelles.

1940–1942. pp.188. [1000.]
1944–1946. pp.239. [1500.]
1947. pp.160. [1000.]
1948. pp.239. [1500.]
1949.
1950.

1951. pp.[ii].55.vi+[iv].38. [1000.]*
1952. pp.[vi].41+[v].29. [750.]*
1953. pp.[v].48+[v].29. [750.]*
1954. pp.[iv].57+[viii].58.xxi. [750.]*
no more published?

CATÁLOGO de tesis de la Facultad de derecho. Universidad nacional mayor de San Marcos: [Lima] 1944. pp.149. [2800.]

SUBJECT index, January 1, 1902–December 31, 1943. Chicago law institute: [Chicago 1944]. pp.495.

PAUL LIPPA, Führer durch die juristische literatur. Die neuerscheinungen und neuauflagen seit dem 8. Mai 1945. Berlin 1948. pp.84. [657.]
— — [another edition]. 1950. pp.251. [1961.]

L[OUIS] TH. MAES, La bibliothèque du grand conseil à Malines. Ville de Malines: 1949. pp.131. [699.]
500 copies printed.

[K. R. THOMSON], Catalogue of a collection of civil and canon law books in the university of Glasgow. Glasgow university: Publications: [Glasgow 1950]. ff.[11]. [262.]

CATALOGUE of foreign books in the Tôkyô university, 1923–1935. Vol.v. Law and politics. Part I. Law books in english. Imperial university: Library [Tokyo 1950]. pp.207. [7500.]

CATÁLOGO de la biblioteca 1850–1950. Autores. Ilustre colegio de abogados: Barcelona 1952 [1953]. pp.895. [30,000.]

JULIUS J. MARKE, A catalogue of the law collection at New York university, with selected annotations. University of the city of New York: School of law: New York 1953. pp.xxxi.1372. [15,000.]

CATALOGUE des sources de documentation juridique dans le monde. Unesco: [1953]. pp.362. [3500.]

— Seconde édition. 1957. pp.424. [4000.]

BIBLIOGRAPHY on foreign law of China, Japan, Korea, Philippine islands, and USSR. Department of the army: Army library: Law branch: Washington 1953. ff.9.*

BIBLIOGRAPHY on foreign law of Europe, Africa, Iceland, and USSR. Department of the army: Army library: Law branch: Washington 1953. ff.25.*

KONRAD STOLLREITHER, Internationale bibliographie der juristischen nachschlagewerke. Frankfurt am Main [1955]. pp.xvi.595. [10,000.]

. INDEX to foreign legal periodicals. Volume 1, number 1. University of London: Institute of advanced legal studies, and American association of law libraries: February 1960. pp.64. [1250.]
no more published.

HELMUT DAU, Bibliographie juristischer festschriften und festschriftenbeiträge 1945–1961, Deutschland-Schweiz-Österreich. Karlsruhe 1962. pp.[vii].166. [2290.]

CAHIERS de bibliographie juridique. Série A. Europe occidentale: Allemagne, Belgique, Espagne, France, Grande-Bretagne, Italie, Luxembourg, Pays-Bas, Portugal, Suisse. Conseil supérieur de la recherche scientifique de l'Espagne: Institut de droit comparé: Barcelone &c.

i. 1962. pp.71. [1000.]
ii. 1963. pp.73. [1000.]

in progress.

6. *Comparative law*

SELECT list of references on comparative legislation. Library of Congress: Washington 1906. ff.10. [51.]*

ERICH HANS KADEN, Bibliographie der rechtsvergleichenden literatur des zivil- und handelsrechtes in Zentral- und Westeuropa und in den Vereinigten Staaten von Amerika 1870 bis 1928. Institut für ausländisches und internationales privatrecht [and] Internationale vereinigung für vergleichende rechtswissenschaft und volkswirtschaftslehre: Berlin 1930. pp.xvi.coll.276. pp.277–295. [4500.]

RÉPERTOIRE des thèses de droit comparé soutenues à la Faculté de droit de Paris pendant les années 1900 à 1930. Université de Paris: Faculté de droit: Bulletin de documentation législative et sociale (no.23): [1931]. pp.70. [1300.]

CHARLES [KÁROLY] SZLADITS, A bibliography on foreign and comparative law. Books and articles in english. Parker school of foreign and comparative law: New York 1955. pp.xx.508. [13,742.]

TEXTOS constitucionais na Biblioteca de Rui Barbosa. Colecção de estudos jurídicos (no.3): [Rio de Janeiro] 1960. pp.xvi.379. [1302.]

7. *Miscellaneous*

VINCENZO ARIANI, Commentarius de claris jureconsultis neapolitanis ac de iis praesertim qui superiore saeculo et hac nostra aetate floruerunt. Neapoli 1769. pp.viii.cviii. [100.]

[JOHANN CHRISTOPH SIEBENKEES], Apocalypsis CL iureconsultorum et scriptorum iuris pseudonymorum collecta a Philalethe. Solisbaci 1806. pp.47. [150.]

LIST of references on primitive and customary law. Library of Congress: Washington 1905. ff.6. [48.]*

SELECT list of references on judicial reform. Library of Congress: Washington 1911. ff.4. [26.]*

SELECT list of references on legal aid. Library of Congress: Washington 1912. ff.2. [17.]*

SELECT list of references on reform in civil law and procedure. Library of Congress: [Washington] 1913. ff.16. [166.]*

LIST of references on respect for law, including public opinion as an aid to enforcement. Library of Congress: [Washington] 1922. ff.5. [46.]*

LEGAL aid. Russell Sage foundation: Library: Bulletin (no.91): New York 1928. pp.4. [75.]

THE LAWYER and his relation to government. A

brief bibliographical list. Library of Congress: [Washington] 1928. ff.5. [50.]*

VERZEICHNIS jüdischer verfasser juristischer schriften. Stuttgart 1936. pp.[iv].53.

C[HARLES] K[INGSLEY] MECK, Colonial law. A bibliography with special reference to native african systems of law and land tenure. Nuffield college [Oxford]: 1948. pp.xiii.59. [813.]

BIBLIOGRAFIA de direito constitucional. Fundação Getulio Vargas: Rio de Janeiro 1949. pp.54.

MARC DE SMEDT, Essai de bibliographie médicolégale et criminologique. Liège 1953. pp.124. [1500.]

JUDICIAL salaries. House of Commons: Library: Bibliographies (no.80): 1953. ff.7. [32.]*

ПРЕДВАРИТЕЛЬНЫЙ КАТАЛОГ по отделу государства и права. Институт по изучению истории и культуры СССР: Сообщения библиотеки института (no.1): Мюнхен 1954. pp.60. [600.]*

BIBLIOGRAPHIE des gesamten rechts der presse, des buchhandels, des rundfunks und des fernsehens. Bucharchiv München: Institut für buchwissenschaften: Berlin &c. 1957. pp.vii.297. [1700.]

International law and relations.

1. *Bibliographies*

EDWIN M[ONTEFIORE] BORCHARD, The bibliography of international law and continental law. Library of Congress: Washington 1913. pp.93. [350.]

CHECKLIST of bibliographies compiled by the Division of library and reference services. A selected list. Department of state: Division of library and reference services: Bibliography (no. 75): Washington 1953. ff.ii.pp.17. [62.]*

HELEN F[IELD] CONOVER, A guide to bibliographic tools for research in foreign affairs. Library of

Congress: General reference and bibliography division: Washington 1956. pp.[v].145. [792.]*

2. *Periodicals*

[ELIZABETH HALDEMAN and ELSIE BASSET], Serials of an international character. Tentative list. Institute of international education: Bulletin (2nd ser., no.3): New York 1921. pp.61. [750.]

THE UNITED NATIONS and international events: some pertinent periodicals. Library of Congress: Washington 1950. ff.5. [26.]*

[JEAN MEYRIAT], Liste mondiale des périodiques spécialisés dans les relations internationales. Conférence permanente des hautes études internationales: [1953]. pp.[ii].30. [125.]
also issued in English.

— Second edition. Directory of periodicals published by international organizations. Union of international associations: Publication (no.162): [1959]. pp.x.241. [1340.]

CATALOGUE of periodicals currently received in Chatham house library. Royal institute of international affairs: 1960. pp.[ii].16. [539.]*

PERIODICALS related to international understanding. Office of education: Educational materials laboratory: Report (vol.4, no.4): Washington 1962. pp.6. [40.]*

3. *History*

WALTER BRAEUER, Handbuch zur geschichte der volkswirtschaftslehre. Ein bibliographisches nachschlagewerk. Frankfurt am Main [1952]. pp.224. [2500.]

4. *General*

JOHANN TOBIAS RAUSCHELBACH, Dissertatio in qva judicium de præcipuis nonnullis scriptoribus juris naturæ . . . proponit Joh. Tobias Rauschelbach. Lipsiæ 1699. pp.20. [100.]

JOHANN GRÖNING, Bibliotheca juris gentium communis, qua præcipuorum, Asiæ, Africæ, et Americæ, populorum de juris naturæ & gentium principiis instituta, nec non scriptorum . . . sententiæ. .. recensentur. Hamburgi 1701. pp.[ii].150. [500.]

JOHANN GRÖNING, Bibliotheca juris gentium Europæ. Hamburgi 1703. pp.16.368. [500.]

JOHANN GRÖNING, Bibliotheca juris gentium exotica, seu de juris naturæ, & gentium principiis juxta doctrinam asiaticorum, africanorum & americanorum liber unus. Hamburgi [1703]. pp. 150. [250.]

CHRISTIAN FRIEDRICH GEORG MEISTER, Bibliotheca ivris natvrae et gentivm. Goettingae 1749–1757. pp.xvi.424 + [iv].300 + [ii].288.[xliv]. [5000.]

BARON DIED[RICH] HEINR[ICH] LUDW[IG] VON OMPTEDA, Litteratur des gesammten sowohl natürlichen als positiven völkerrechts. Regensburg 1785. pp.[xii].364+[iii].373–672.[xvi]. [3000.]
— — Dritter theil. Neue literatur des völkerrechts . . . von Carl [Christoph] Albert von Kamptz. Berlin 1817. pp.xxii.384. [3000.]

CARL HEINR[ICH] VON RÖMER, Handbuch für gesandte. Erster theil, die literatur des natürlichen und positiven gesandtschaftsrechts enthaltend. Leipzig 1791. pp.[viii].167. [750.]
no more published.

CAROLUS HENRICUS LUDOVICUS POELITZ, De mutationibus, quas systema iuris naturae ac gentium a Grotii temporibus hucusque expertim fuerit, commentatio literaria. Vitebergae [1805]. pp. 20. [176.]

A. L. J. MICHELSEN, Grundriss zu vorlesungen über positives völkerrecht. Kiel 1840. pp.16. [200.]

[JOHN L. CADWALADER], Digest of the published

opinions of the Attorneys-general, and of the leading decisions of the federal courts, with reference to international law, treaties, and kindred subjects. Washington 1877. pp.vii.268. [2000.]

• [—] — Revised edition. 1877. pp.vii.290. [2000.]

CATALOGUE of the works relative to the law of nations and diplomacy in the library of the Department of state. Washington 1881. pp.87. [1000.]

fragments of new editions were published in 1887 and 1897.

— [supplement]. A list of books [,pamphlets, and maps] received at the library of the Department of state with references to international treaties and articles on subjects relative to the law of nations and diplomacy. No.1[–11; new series, no.1–32]. July 1886–September 1887, May 1892–December 1905.

ALPHONSE RIVIER, Note sur la littérature du droit des gens avant la publication du Jus belli ac pacis de Grotius (1625). Bruxelles 1883. pp.75. [250.]

[T. F. DWIGHT], Catalogue of the works relative to the law of nations and diplomacy in the library of the Department of state. Washington 1886. pp.3–110. [1250.]

A–Cussy only; no more published; reissued in 1897.

FELIX STOERK, Die litteratur des internationalen rechts, 1884 bis 1894. Juristischer litteraturbericht (part 9): Leipzig 1896. pp.[ii].40. [250.]

[MARQUIS RAMÓN DE DALMAU Y DE OLIVART], Catalogue d'une [vol.ii: de ma] bibliothèque de droit international et sciences auxiliaires. 1899–1907. pp.xxiv.407+xxiv.296. [4819.]

236 (vol.ii: 62) copies privately printed.

— — Deuxième édition. Bibliographie du droit international. Bibliothèque internationale et diplomatique (vol.xli): 1905–1910. pp.[iv].iv.1278. [6235.]

the author's name, in the form of marquis de Olivart, appears in the second edition and in the second volume of the first.

— — — [supplement]. Liste des livres offerts en don à l'université de Harvard . . . par le marquis de Olivart. Madrid 1912. pp.39. [200.]

MONTHLY bulletin of books, pamphlets and magazine articles dealing with international relations. Association for international conciliation: New York 1908–1913.

INTERNATIONALES und ausländisches recht. Gesamtkatalog der bestände von 30 berliner bibliotheken. Internationale vereinigung für vergleichende rechtswissenschaft: Berlin 1914. pp.lxxvii. 1684. [22,000.]

A. DARRAS, Répertoire de droit international privé et de droit pénal international. . . . Tome premier, abandon–brevets d'invention. 1914. pp. [v].iii.1109. [5000.]
no more published.

HERMANN H[ENRY] B[ERNARD] MEYER, List of references on europe and international politics in relation to the present issues. Library of Congress: Washington 1914. pp.144. [1000.]

A FORTY YEARS' catalogue of the books, pamphlets & papers in the library of the International law association. 1915. pp.70. [1500.]

BIBLIOGRAPHIE des publications parues . . . aux Pays-Bas sur le droit international, les relations internationales et la [grande] guerre et le mouvement de la paix. La Haye 1915 &.

D. P. HEATLEY, International relations. Historical association of Scotland: Pamphlet (no.8): [*s.l.*] 1916. pp.8. [75.]

LIST of references on internationalism. Library of Congress: [Washington] 1916. ff.2–8. [108.]*

P[HILIPPUS] C[HRISTIANUS] MOLHUYSEN and E[LSA] R[ACHEL] OPPENHEIM, Catalogue. Bibliothèque du Palais de la paix [The Hague]: Leyde 1916. pp.xlix.coll.5–1576. [12,000.]

— — Premier supplément. By P. C. Molhuysen and D. Albers. 1922. pp.xlvii.coll.5–1042. [10,000.]

— — — Index alphabétique du Catalogue (1916) et du Supplément (1922). 1922. pp.[iii]. coll.9–790.

— — Deuxième supplément. By J. Ter Meulen and A. Lysen. 1930. pp.xxi.coll.5–1554. [15,000.]

— — — Index alphabétique par noms d'auteurs ou mots d'ordre du Catalogue (1916) et des Suppléments (1922 et 1929). 1932. pp.[iv].coll.9–1466.

— — — Index sommaire par ordre alphabétique des matières du Catalogue (1906) et des Suppléments (1922 et 1929). 1933. pp.[iv].coll.76. pp.[ii].[iv].coll.80.

— — Troisième supplément. 1937. ff.xix.coll. 2744. [21,729.]

— — — Index alphabétique par noms propres du troisième supplément. 1937. pp.79.

also has english titlepage and text, beginning at the end of the volume, which has to be inverted.

— — Supplément 1937–1952. 1954–1961. pp.

viii.170 + vi.150 + viii.342 + iv.173 + vi.156. [8000.]*

DONATIVO BUSTAMENTE. Catálogo de derecho internacional. Biblioteca nacional: Habana 1917. pp.viii.48. [250.]

SELECT list of treatises in english on international law. Library of Congress: Washington 1917. ff.2. [14.]*

CATALOGO alphabetico da bibliotheca do Ministerio das relações exteriores. Tomo I. A–L. Rio de Janeiro 1917. pp.537. [4778.]
no more published.

D. P. HEATLEY, Diplomacy and the study of international relations. Oxford 1919. pp.xvii.292. [100.]

ANNUAL digest of public international law cases. London school of economics and political science: Department of international studies.
1919–1922. Editors: sir John Fischer Williams and [sir] H[ersh] Lauterpacht. 1932. pp. lv.510. [349.]
1923–1924. 1933. pp.xlviii.468. [247.]
1925–1926. Editors: Arnold D. McNair and H. Lauterpacht. 1929. pp.xlv.497. [371.]
1927–1928. 1931. pp.li.592. [389.]

1929–1930. Edited by H. Lauterpacht. 1935. pp.xxxvi.534. [302.]

1931–1932. 1938. pp.xlv.464. [233.]

[*continued as:*]

Annual digest and reports of public international law cases.

1933–1934. 1940. pp.xlv.527. [223.]

1935–1937. 1941. pp.xlix.514. [232.]

1938–1940. 1942. pp.xxxiv.607. [223.]

1941–1942. 1945. pp.xxxvi.651. [182.]

— 1919–1942 (supplementary volume). Including consolidated index and tables of cases. 1947. pp.xxvi.550. [171.]

1943–1945. 1949. pp.xxxii.584. [207.]

1946. 1951. pp.xxii.437. [186.]

1947. 1951. pp.xxiv.335. [138.]

1948. 1953. pp.xxviii.706. [226.]

1949. 1955. pp.xxiv.613. [219.]

1950. 1956. pp.xxvii.460. [151.]

1951. 1957. pp.xliii.744. [223.]

1952. 1957. pp.xxxix.651. [149.]

1953.

1954.

1955. 1958. pp.xliv.1042. [250.]

1956. 1960. pp.xxxix.871. [200.]

1957. Edited by sir Hersch Lauterpacht and E. Lauterpacht. pp.xlv.1013. [300.]

1958. Edited by E. Lauterpacht. pp.xli.754+xxvii.571. [300.]
xxvii. 1963. pp.xxxiii.664. [75.]
xxviii. 1963. pp.xlii.679. [175.]
in progress.

LIST of references on diplomacy. Library of Congress: [Washington] 1923. ff.17. [175.]*

A BRIEF list of references on international relations. Library of Congress: Washington 1923. ff.3. [31.]*

B. M. HEADICAR, Edward Fry library of international law. Catalogue of the books, pamphlets, and other documents in the library. Together with other works bearing on the subject of international law in the library of the London school of economics. 1923. pp.[iii].viii.174. [2500.]
— — First supplement. [1925]. pp.54. [800.]

BULLETIN de l'Office de documentation internationale contemporaine. 1925. ff.[316]. [3329.]*
[*continued as:*]
Bulletin bibliographique de documentation internationale contemporaine. Office de documentation internationale contemporaine [Bibliothèque de documentation internationale contemporaine] and Institut international de coopération

intellectuelle [n.s.: and Centre européen de la Dotation Carnegie pour la paix internationale].

i. 1926. pp.[204]. [3906.]
ii. 1927. pp.[209]. [4031.]
iii. 1928. pp.[212]. [4019.]
— Tables de la première série. [1929]. pp.23.
iii [*sic*, iv]. 1929. pp.[219]. [4093.]
iv. [*sic*, v]. 1930. pp.[266]. [4895.]
v [*sic*, vi]. 1931. pp.[284]. [5279.]
— Tables de la deuxième série. [1932]. pp.24.
vii. 1932. pp.[279]. [5286.]
viii. 1933. pp.[269]. [4714.]
ix. 1934. pp.[286]. [5163.]
— Table de la troisième série. [1935]. pp.29.
x. 1935. pp.[242]. [4510.]
xi. 1936. pp.[264]. [4874.]
xii. 1937. pp.[261]. [4765.]
— Table de la quatrième série. [1938]. pp.26.
xiii. 1938. pp.[243]. [4766.]
xiv. 1939. pp.[189]. [4370.]

ANNUAIRE de la vie internationale: politique, économique, juridique. [Edited by Lapradelle].

1927. pp.3–289. [6000.]
1928. pp.3–311. [6000.]
no more published.

AIDS to international understanding. A book list

with notes. [Compiled by the Newark public library]. New Jersey federation of women's clubs: Committee on international relations: [Newark 1928]. pp.16.

INTERNATIONAL books news. Number 1[–(25)]. World peace foundation: Boston January 1928–May 1934. [2000.]

INTERNATIONAL law. A list of books. Library of Congress: [Washington] 1929. ff.11. [85.]*

SUGGESTED topics for club studies in foreign affairs. Library of Congress: Washington 1929. ff.2. [34.]*

LISTE bimensuelle [mensuelle] d'articles sélectionnés. . . . Fortnightly [Monthly] list of selected articles. Société des nations [Nations unies]: Bibliothèque: Genève.

i. 1929. pp.[viii].273. [7500.]
ii. 1930. pp.8.287. [8500.]
iii. 1931. pp.9.383. [12,500.]
iv. 1932. pp.8.293. [10,000.]
v. 1933. pp.7.202. [7500.]
vi. 1934. pp.8.213. [7500.]
vii. 1935. pp.8.260. [9000.]
viii. 1936. pp.8.278. [9000.]
ix. 1937. pp.7.289. [10,000.]

x. 1938. pp.[iii].7.276. [10,000.]
xi. 1939. pp.[iii].258. [9000.]
xii. 1940. pp.[iii].102. [3500.]
xiii. 1941. pp.[iii].84. [3000.]
xiv. 1942. pp.[iii].106.[3500.]
xv. 1943. pp.[iii].91. [3500.]

xvi. 1944. pp.[iii].104. [4000.]
xvii. 1945. pp.[iii].98. [3500.]
xviii. 1946. pp.[iii].124. [4500.]
xix. 1947. pp.[iii].125. [4500.]
xx. 1948. pp.[iii].164. [6000.]
xxi. 1949. pp.[iii].180. [7000.]
xxii. 1950. pp.[iii].193. [7500.]
xxiii. 1951. pp.[iii].215. [8000.]
xxiv. 1952. pp.[iii].228. [8500.]
xxv. 1953. pp.[iii].201. [7500.]
xxvi. 1954. pp.[iv].225. [8000.]
xxvii. 1955. pp.[iv].254. [9000.]
xxviii. 1956. pp.[iv].244. [8500.]
xxix. 1957. pp.[iv].250. [9000.]
xxx. 1958. pp.[iv].258. [9000.]
xxxi. 1959. pp.[iv].231. [8000.]
xxxii. 1960.
xxxiii. 1961. pp.[iv].226. [8000.]
xxxiv. 1962. pp.[iv].216. [7500.]

in progress.

International Law

H. A. C. STURGESS, A catalogue of books, chiefly on foreign and international law, collected by the late baron Phillimore . . . and presented to the library of the . . . Middle temple. 1930. pp.90. [1200.]

WILLIAM L[EONARD] LANGER, Recent books on international relations. Foreign affairs: New York 1930–1936.
issued quarterly.

BEGINNINGS of a library on international relations. Carnegie endowment for international peace: Division of intercourse and education: New York [1931]. pp.11. [35.]

M[ARY] ALICE MATTHEWS, The American institute of international law and the codification of international law. Carnegie endowment for international peace: Library: Select bibliographies (no.2): Washington 1933. ff.17. [175.]*

M[ARY] ALICE MATTHEWS, The international commission of jurists (Rio de Janeiro) and the codification of international law. Carnegie endowment for international peace: Library: Select bibliographies (no.1): Washington 1933. ff.8. [80.]*

FOREIGN affairs bibliography. A selected and annotated list of books on international relations. Council on foreign relations: New York &c.

1919–1932. [By] William L[eonard] Langer and Hamilton Fish Armstrong. 1933. pp. xvii.551. [7500.]

1932–1942. [By] Robert Gale Woolbert. 1945. pp.xxi.705. [10,000.]

M[ARY] ALICE MATTHEWS, Diplomacy. Select list of works in English on diplomacy, diplomatic and consular practice, and foreign office organization. Carnegie endowment for international peace: Library: Select bibliographies (no.4): Washington 1936. pp.7. [100.]*

INTERNATIONAL AFFAIRS. A selected list of books. . . . Compiled by the National peace council. Fourth edition. [National book council:] Book list (no.21A): 1936. pp.8. [300.]

M[ARY] ALICE MATTHEWS, International law. Select list of works in English on public international law; with collections of cases and opinions. Carnegie endowment for international peace: Library: Select bibliographies (no.3): Washington 1936. pp.21. [250.]*

— — Revised . . . by Helen Lawrence Scanlon. 1946. pp.20. [200.]*

E[ARLE] H[OYT] KETCHAM, Preliminary select bibliography of international law. [Syracuse, N.Y. 1937]. ff.iii.69. [1500.]*

KARL STRUPP, Bibliographie du droit des gens et des relations internationales. Leyde 1938. pp.xix. 521. [2860.]
limited to works published in 1933–1936.

RALPH O. NAFZIGER, International news and the press. Communications, organization of news-gathering, international affairs and the foreign press. An annotated bibliography. New York 1940. pp.xxix.193. [5500.]

[F. L. SHPIGEL, *ed.*], Международное положение. Указатель литературы, 1939–. . . 1940. Москва 1940. pp.151. [1600.]

WALTER SCHIFFER, Répertoire des questions de droit international général posées devant la Société des nations, 1920–1940. . . . Publié sous la direction de A. C. Breycha-Vauthier. Geneva research centre: Genève 1942. pp.[v].2–391. [1237.]

E[VA] M[ARIAN] HUBBACK, How to lead discussion groups . . . with a bibliography of books on contemporary affairs. Association for education in citizenship: Unless we plan now (no.1): [1942]. pp.24. [450.]

ALEXIS ST. LÉGER LÉGER, A selection of works for an understanding of world affairs since 1914. Library of Congress: Division of bibliography: Washington 1943. pp.[viii].87. [882.]

PAUL KRUSE, List of books — basic collection — foreign service. Library of Congress: Washington 1944. pp.45. [500.]*

— Supplementary list, United States government publications. 1945. ff.7. [77.]*

SHORT TITLE classified catalog. UNCIO [United nations conference on international organization] conference library: [San Francisco 1945]. ff.[i].66. 1000.]*

E. STIFF, Reference library on international affairs. Basic list, works in english. Royal institute of international affairs: 1945. pp.19.*

THE WORLD in focus. A monthly index of selected materials on foreign affairs. Library of international relations: Chicago.*

i. 1945–1946. ff.[160]. [1000.]
ii. 1946–1947. ff.[193]. [1250.]
iii. 1947–1948. ff.[176]. [1000.]

[ROBERT PIERRE MARICHAL *and others*], Histoire et

diplomatie du IXe au XIXe siècles. Archives nationales: 1946. pp.viii.44. [250.]
an exhibition catalogue.

FOREIGN information services (exclusive of the U.S.): a list of serial references for the period July 1, 1945–March 15, 1946. I. General. Library of Congress: Washington 1946. ff.26. [73.]*
— II. Individual countries (Albania-Canada). Library of Congress: Washington 1946. ff.27–65. [130.]*

ANNOTATED bibliography of international politics. Central office of information: Reference division: 1947.*

BIBLIOGRAPHY on the codification of international law. United nations: General assembly (A/AC.10/6): [Lake Success] 1947. pp.14. [175.]*

MARGARET M. HEATON, Reading ladders for human relations. American council on education: Washington [1947]. pp.viii.67.
— — Fourth edition. Muriel [Estelle] Crosby, editor. [1963]. pp.xiii.242. [1500.]

FOREIGN office printed library. 1948 &c.
weekly accession leaflets.

CURRENT research in international affairs. A

selected bibliography of work in progress. Carnegie endowment for international peace: International conciliation (no.437 &c.): New York.

[i]. [Compiled by Helen Lawrence Scanlon] ... (no.437): 1948. pp.[ii].69. [327.]

[ii]. [Compiled by Ruth E. Stanton and Agnese Nelms] ... (no.446): 1948. pp.684–762. [484.]

[iii]. [Compiled by H. L. Scanlon] ... (no. 456): 1949. pp.875–978. [640.]

[iv]. [Compiled by R. E. Stanton] ... (no. 466): 1950. pp.585–668. [809.]

[v]. [1952]. pp.[xiii].193. [988.]

no more published.

WORLD affairs. A selected list of publications. National peace council.

i. 1948. pp.[8]. [125.]

ii. 1949. pp.[8]. [125.]

BIBLIOGRAFÍA mensal. Ministerio das relações exteriores: Serviço de documentação: Biblioteca: [Rio de Janeiro] 1950 &c.

PIER FAUSTO PALUMBO, Bibliografia storica internazionale 1940–1947. Biblioteca storica (no.2): Roma 1950. pp.lxiii.244. [3572.]

FOREIGN relations library. Basic collection guide.

Department of state: Division of library and reference services: Bibliography (no.63): Washington 1952. pp.[v].56. [600.]*

B[ARTHOLOMEUS] LANDHEER and J[AN] L[OUIS] F[REDERIK] VAN ESSEN, Fundamentals of public international law. Peace palace: Library: Selective bibliographies (no.i): Leyden 1953. pp.[ii].85. [750.]

UNPUBLISHED research on international affairs . . . completed and in progress. Department of state: External research list (no.11.1): Washington 1953.*

A. General and political. pp.[iii].51. [1250.]
B. Economic, social, organizational and informational. pp.[iv].31. [750.]

WORLD politics. A selected and annotated bibliography of books in the english language. Department of state: Division of library and reference services: Bibliographic list (no.89): [Washington] 1953. ff.7. [45.]*

LEONARD S[TOUT] KENWORTHY, Free and inexpensive materials on world affairs. Washington [1954]. pp.94. [1500.]

RUTH SAVORD and DONALD WASSON, World affairs. A foreign service reading list. Foreign service journal: [Washington] 1954. pp.[23]. [600.]

CALENDAR and texts of documents on international affairs. Royal institute of international affairs: 1954 &c.*

in progress.

CATALOGUE of the combined book exhibit. International affairs [World affairs] book fair. Carnegie endowment for international peace: New York.

i. 1954. [Edited by Thomas J. McLaughlin]. pp.[iii].27. [900.]
ii. 1955. pp.[iii].28. [800.]
iii. 1956. pp.[iii].36. [1000.]

MARY H[AYS] WEIK, Towards a new world. A bibliography of the United nations and world affairs. American federation of world citizens: World community series (no.7): Cincinnati [1955]. ff.5. [100.]*

SEYMOUR WILLIS BEARDSLEY, Human relations in international affairs. A guide to significant interpretation and research. Public affairs press: Washington [1956]. pp.vi.40.

INTERNATIONAL politics. A selective monthly bibliography. Department of state: Office of libraries and intelligence acquisition [1958 &c.: of intelligence resources and coordination]: Washington.*

i. 1956. pp.[320]. [4700.]

ii. 1957. pp.[434]. [7000.]

in progress.

SELECT articles on current affairs. Indian council of world affairs: Library: Bibliographical series: New Delhi.*

i. 1956. [By B. C. Tewari]. ff.[ii].xii.pp.149. [2000.]

ii. 1957. ff.[ii].xiii.pp.155. [2000.]

iii. 1958. ff.[i].xii.pp.236. [3000.]

iv. 1959. Compiled by B. C. Tewari and Shaukat Ashraf. ff.[ii].xix.pp.280. [3500.]

in progress.

VÖLKERRECHT, internationale beziehungen, zeitgeschichte. . . . Gemeinsamer katalog des arbeitskreises der deutschen institute für völkerrecht, internationale beziehungen und zeitgeschichte. Frankfurt am Main &c. 1957. pp.127. [700.]

МЕЖДУНАРОДНА ПОЛИТИКА. Библиографски списъци. София 1957. pp.44. [500.]

HANS WEHBERG, Tableau général des résolutions

(1873–1956). Institut de droit international: Bâle 1957. pp.xviii.404. [139.]

V[LADIMIR] E[MMANUILOVICH] GRABAR, Материалы к истории литературы международного права в России (1647–1917). Академия наук СССР: Институт права им. А. Я. Вышинского: Москва 1958. pp.492. [2000.]

DIE VÖLKERRECHTLICHEN dissertationen an den westdeutschen universitäten, 1945–1957. Deutsche gesellschaft für völkerrecht: Karlsruhe 1958. pp.52. [500.]

INTERCOM. World affairs center for the United States: New York 1958 &c.*
in progress.

V[SEVOLOD] N[IKOLAEVICH] DURDENEVSKY, Советская литература по международному праву. Библиография 1917–1957. Советская ассоциация международного права: Москва 1959. pp.304. [2500.]

PANORAMA of recent books, films, and journals on world federation, the United nations, and world peace. United world federalists: Washington 1960. ff.[27]. [75.]*

V. N. EGOROV, Международные отношения (библиографический справочник 1945–1960 гг.). Москва 1961. pp.408. [3000.]

INTERNATIONAL organizations and military security systems. Air force academy: Library: Special bibliography series (no.25): [*s.l.*] 1962. pp.28.

JUDITH WRAGG CHASE, Books to build world friendship. An annotated bibliography of children's books. Dobbs Ferry, N.Y. 1964. pp.xx.76. [296.]

5. *Federalism*

ANNE L[AURA] BADEN, Selected list of recent writings on internationalism (superstate). Library of Congress: [Washington] 1933. pp.30. [329.]*

M[ARY] ALICE MATTHEWS, Federalism. Carnegie endowment for international peace: Library: Select bibliographies (no.8): Washington 1938. pp.11. [125.]*

HELEN L[AWRENCE] SCANLON, The new world order. Select list of references on regional and world federation. Carnegie endowment for international peace: Library: Select bibliographies (no. 10): Washington 1940. pp.17. [200.]*

HANS AUFRICHT[-RUDA], World organization. An annotated bibliography. Woodrow Wilson memorial library: New York 1943. pp.16. [125.]

— — Seventh . . . edition. 1946. pp.28. [250.]

[ROBERT K. TURNER], Bibliography on world organization. Woodrow Wilson memorial library: New York [1947]. pp.18. [200.]

HELEN F[IELD] CONOVER, World government: a list of selected references. Library of Congress: General reference and bibliography division: Washington [1947]. ff.11. [65.]*

ERNEST MONPIED, GEORGES ROUSSOS and EUGÈNE ZALESKI, Bibliographie fédéraliste. Union fédéraliste universitaire: 1950. pp.87. [640.]

— — Deuxième édition. [1952]. pp.109. [1291.]

[ROBERT K. TURNER], Bibliography on world organization. Woodrow Wilson memorial library: New York [1950]. pp.13. [150.]

6. *Treaties*

VISCOUNT [CHARLES FRANÇOIS LEFÈVRE] DE LA MAILLARDIÈRE, Abrégé des principaux traités conclus, depuis le commencement du XIVe siècle jusqu'à présent, entre les différentes puissances de l'Europe. 1778. pp.[vi].xxxvi.384+xii.468. [150.]

TABLE générale chronologique et alphabétique du Recueil des traités, conventions et transactions des puissances de l'Europe et d'autres parties du globe, . . . commencé par Geo. Fréd. de [Georg Friedrich von] Martens et continué jusqu'à nos jours. Gottingue 1837–1843. pp.iv.383+iv.428. [7000.]

[ ] TÉTOT, Répertoire des traités de paix, de commerce, d'alliance, etc., conventions et autres actes conclus entre toutes les puissances du globe.

1493–1866 [1867]. 1866[–1867]. pp.x.483+ [iv].595. [7421.]

1867–1894 [1897]. 1895–1899. pp.viii.348+ [ii].364. [3755.]

GABRIEL DE RIBIER, Répertoire des traités de paix, de commerce, d'alliance, etc., conventions et autres actes conclus entre toutes les puissances du globe depuis 1867. 1895–1899. pp.viii.347+ 363. [5000.]

DENYS P[ETER] MYERS, List of arbitration treaties, pacts, to which pairs of nations are parties. World peace foundation: Pamphlet series (no.2, part i): Boston 1911. pp.16. [100.]

— — Revised list [&c.]. . . . (no.6, part v): 1912. pp.24. [163.]

LIST of references on the interpretation and enforcement of treaties. Library of Congress: Washington 1914. ff.4. [44.]*

LIST of references on recent treaties. Library of Congress: Washington 1915. ff.3. [34.]*

LIST of references on international agreements as distinguished from more formal treaties. Library of Congress: Washington 1917. ff.7. [55.]*

A TENTATIVE list of treaty collections. Washington 1919. pp.103. [1000.]

SELECT list of references on the treaty making power: United States and foreign countries. Library of Congress: Washington 1919. ff.9. [66.]*

DENYS PETER MYERS, Manual of collections of treaties and of collections relating to treaties. Harvard bibliographies: Library series (vol.ii): Cambridge [Mass.] 1922. pp.xlvii.685. [3468.]

LIST of references on the four-power treaty. Library of Congress: Washington 1922. ff.3. [36.]*

RÉPERTOIRE général des traités et autres actes diplomatiques conclus depuis 1895 jusqu'en 1920. Institut intermédiaire international: Harlem &c. 1926. pp.xix.516. [4412.]

V. M. BOULTER, Chronology of international affairs and treaties . . . 1920– . . . 1925. Royal institute of international affairs: Survey of international affairs (1925: supplement): 1928. pp.235. [1000.]

TRAITÉS internationaux et actes législatifs. (Suppléments à la Liste mensuelle d'articles sélectionnés). Société des nations: Bibliothèque: Genève.

i. 1930. pp.[iv].10[*sic*, 110]. [1000.]

[*continued as:*]

Répertoire de traités internationaux et d'actes législatifs.

ii. 1931. pp.[iv].126. [2250.]
iii. 1932. pp.[iv].127–221. [1500.]
iv. 1933. pp.[iv].223–300. [1000.]
v. 1934. pp.[iv].301–388. [1250.]
vi. 1935. pp.[iv].389–492. [1500.]
vii. 1936. pp.[iv].139. [2500.]
viii. 1937. pp.[iv].108. [1500.]
ix. 1938. pp.[iv].123. [1750.]
x. 1939. pp.[iv].132. [2000.]
xi. (no.1/2). 1940. pp.20. [500.]

no more published.

FRANCIS COLT DE WOLF, General synopsis of treaties of arbitration, conciliation, judicial settlement, security and disarmament, actually in force between countries invited to the disarmament conference. Carnegie endowment for international peace: Washington 1933. pp.xi.201. [8000.]

BIBLIOGRAPHIE de la théorie générale des traités. Nations unies: Assemblée générale: Commission du droit international: Lake Success 1950. pp.72. [700.]*

ÉTAT des conventions multilatérales pour lesquelles le secrétaire général exerce les fonctions de dépositaire. Nations unies: New York 1953 &c. loose-leaf.*

DEUTSCHES und ausländisches schrifttum zu den regionalen sicherheitsvereinbarungen 1945–1956. Europa-archiv: Aktuelle bibliographien (no.14): Frankfurt/Main 1957. pp.64. [1363.]

7. *Miscellaneous*

A[PPLETON] P[RENTISS] C[LARK] GRIFFIN, List of references on recognition in international law and practice. Library of Congress: Washington 1904. pp.18. [100.]

REFERENCES on certain considerations in international law as related to the Russo-Japanese war. Library of Congress: Washington 1905. ff.5. [50.]*

LIST of references on extraterritorial jurisdiction in non-christian states, with special references to Turkey and the capitulations. Library of Congress: Washington 1914. ff.11. [92.]*

LIST of references on the triple alliance and triple entente. Library of Congress: Washington 1914. ff.5. [60.]*

LIST of references on the recall or dismissal of foreign representatives by the executive. Library of Congress: Washington 1916. ff.6. [52.]*

LIST of references on secret diplomacy and a more democratic control of foreign policy. Library of Congress: [Washington] 1916. ff.2. [22.]*

LIST of references on international loans and their influence on international politics. Library of Congress: [Washington] 1919. ff.6. [66.]*

ROBERT DORÉ, Bibliographie des 'livres jaunes'. 1922. pp.28. [213.]

LIST of references on the codification of international law. Library of Congress: [Washington] 1923. ff.8. [87.]*
— A supplementary list. 1924. ff.5. [42.]*

REPORT of exhibit held for leaders of young people to suggest ways and means of cultivating ... ideas of international friendship and good will. League of nations non-partisan association: Educational committee: [New York 1925]. pp.[ii].22. [150.]

[PERCY] EVANS LEWIN, Select bibliography of recent publications ... illustrating the relations between europeans and coloured races. Royal colonial institute bibliographies (no.3): 1926. pp.62. [1300.]

LIST of recent references on women in international affairs. Library of Congress: [Washington] 1926. ff.7. [66.]*

WILLIAM ADAM SLADE, Democratic control of foreign affairs. A bibliographical list. Library of Congress: [Washington] 1927. pp.22. [234.]*

[FRANCES GARDINER DAVENPORT and] J[OHN] F[RANKLIN] JAMESON, A provisional list of printed lists of ambassadors and other diplomatic representatives. Paris [1928]. pp.16. [150.]

M[ARY] ALICE MATTHEWS, International police. Carnegie endowment for international peace:

Library: Select bibliographies (no.7): Washington 1937. ff.9. [125.]*

— — Revised . . . by Helen Lawrence Scanlon. 1944. pp.18. [225.]*

N. C. LEITES, Syllabus for . . . psychology of international relations. University of Chicago. Chicago 1940. ff.[i].37. [700.]*

POLITICAL developments and the war (April 1, 1942 [*sic*, 1941]–March 31, 1942). Selected and annotated bibliography on world politics under the impact of war. Library of Congress: Legislative reference series: Bibliographies of the world at war (no.1): Washington 1942. pp.238. [1683.]*

ALAIN [LE ROY] LOCKE, World view on race and democracy. A study guide in human group relations. American library association: Chicago 1943. ff.[iii].19. [100.]*

WILLIAM C[ECIL] ROGERS, International administration. A bibliography. Public administration service: Publication (no.92): Chicago 1945. pp. viii.32. [250.]*

THE LEAGUE of nations intellectual co-operation program. A list of references. Library of Congress: General reference and bibliography division: Washington 1945. pp.[ii].20. [70.]*

INTERNATIONAL police force. House of commons: Library: Bibliography (no.34): [1947]. ff.35. [185.]*

BOOKS to help build international understanding, selected for children and young people. Prepared by Nora Ernestine Beust. Office of education: Washington 1948.*

— [another edition]. Prepared by N. E. Beust and Gertrude G. Broderick. 1955. pp.37. [300.]*

WAYS and means of making the evidence of customary international law more readily available. United Nations (A/CN.4/6): Lake Success 1949. pp.v.114. [100.]

LEONARD S[TOUT] KENWORTHY, Free and inexpensive materials on world affairs for teachers. Columbia university: Teachers college: New York 1949. pp.100. [1000.]

— — [another edition]. Free and inexpensive materials on world affairs. 1963. pp.viii.83. [1000.]

EVA M. DRATZ, Aids to world understanding for elementary schoold children. An annotated bibliography. Public schools: Minneapolis 1950. pp. 47. [450.]

INTERNATIONAL economic and social development: a selective background reading list, prepared for the National conference on international economic and social development, April 7–9, 1952. Library of Congress: Washington 1952. ff.55. [314.]*

NORA E. BEUST and GERTRUDE G[OLDEN] BRODERICK, Books to help building international understanding. Revised. Selected for children and young people. Bureau of education: Washington 1954. pp.37. [300.]*

B[ARTHOLOMEUS] LANDHEER and J[AN] L[OUIS] F[REDERIK] VAN ESSEN, Recognition in international law. Peace palace: Library: Selective bibliographies (no.ii): Leyden 1954. pp.[ii].28. [300.]

L'ÉDUCATION de la jeunesse en vue de la compréhension et de la coopération internationales. Unesco: Revue analytique de l'éducation (vol.vi, no.6): 1954. pp.21. [80.]

ÉLÉMENTS de bibliographie sur l'éducation du sens international chez l'enfant. Bureau international catholique de l'enfance: [*s.l.* 1955]. pp.30. [250.]

International Law

V[LADIMIR] E[MMANUILOVICH] GRABAR, Материалы к истории литературы международного права в России, 1647–1917. Академия наук СССР: Институт права им. А. Я. Вышинского: Москва 1958. pp.492. [1200.]

Crime, criminal law.

1. *Bibliographies*

LIST of bibliographies on crime and criminals. Library of Congress: [Washington] 1922. ff.21. [206.]*

THORSTEN SELLIN and J. P. SHALLOO, A bibliographical manual for the student of criminology. Philadelphia 1935. pp.v.41. [250.]

HELEN F[IELD] CONOVER, Crime and criminal justice: a bibliography of bibliographies and a selected list of recent books 1937–1939. Compiled . . . under the direction of Florence S[elma] Hellman. Library of Congress: Division of bibliography: [Washington] 1940. pp.[ii].52. [470.]

2. *Periodicals*

[CHRISTINE KENNEDY], Survey of criminological journals. A handlist of periodicals of interest to students of criminology with their locations in certain London libraries. Institute for the study and treatment of delinquency: 1958. pp.[8]. [200.]

3. *General*

[HEINRICH BLÜMNER], Entwurf der litteratur des

criminalrechts in systematischer ordnung. Leipzig 1794. pp.xii.124. [1500.]

a copy in the Zentralbibliothek Zürich contains numerous additions in manuscript.

CHRISTOPH LORENZ BRUNNER, Handbuch der litteratur der criminalrechtswissenschaft. Erster band. Bayreuth 1804. pp.xxiv.264. [1500.]

a copy in the Zentralbibliothek Zürich contains additions in manuscript; no more published?

GEORG WILHELM BÖHMER, Handbuch der litteratur des criminalrechts in seinen allgemeinen beziehungen, mit besondrer rücksicht auf criminalpolitik. Göttingen 1816. pp.xlviii.888. [3200.]

FRIEDR[ICH] KAPPLER, Handbuch der literatur des criminalrechts und dessen philosophischer und medizinischer hülfswissenschaften. Stuttgart 1838. pp.xxxii.1218. [8879.]

J[EAN] J[ERVAIS] G[UILLAUME] NYPELS, Bibliothèque choisie du droit criminel (droit pénal et procédure criminelle) ou notice des ouvrages utiles à connaître, publiés dans les principales contrées de l'Europe et aux États-Unis d'Amérique, sur cette partie de la science du droit, avec l'indication des sources du droit criminel. Bruxelles 1864. pp.[vi].170. [1868.]

Criminal Law

A. BERGER, Systematisch-alphabetisches generalregister zu band I–XII der Zeitschrift [für die gesamte strafrechtswissenschaft] und sämmtlichen beilagen, Mitteilungen der Internationalen kriminalistischen vereinigung, band I–III, Mitteilungen ihrer deutschen landesgruppe, band I u. II, usw. Zugleich bibliographie aller in band I–XII der Zeitschrift und ihren beilagen enthaltenen litteratur- und gesetzgebungsberichte. Berlin 1893. pp. xvi.180.

ARTHUR VON KIRCHENHEIM, Die litteratur des strafrechts und der kriminalpolitik, 1884 bis 1894. Juristischer litteraturbericht (part 6): Leipzig 1896. pp.[ii].35. [150.]

LIST of references on penology. Library of Congress: Washington 1904. ff.4. [24.]*

CONSTANTE AMOR Y NEVEIRO, Bibliografía de los estudios penales. Madrid 1909. pp.567. [7500.]

JOHN H[ENRY] WIGMORE, A preliminary bibliography of modern criminal law and criminology. Northwestern university: Law school: Gary library of law: Chicago 1909. pp.xii.128. [2500.]

КАТАЛОГЪ библіотеки. Императорскій С.-Петербургскій университетъ: Кабинеть уголовнаго права: С.-Петербургъ 1909. pp.xii. 133. [5500.]

— Чатсь II. 1913. pp.ix.63. [2500.]

LIST of works relating to criminology. Public library: New York 1911. pp.[iii].362. [7500.]

A. DARRAS, Répertoire de droit international privé et de droit pénal international. . . . Tome premier, abandon-brevets d'invention. 1914. pp. [v].iii.1109. [5000.]

no more published.

[SIR] JOHN G[HEST] CUMMING, A contribution towards a bibliography dealing with crime. Calcutta 1914. pp.[v].ff.2.ii.33. [500.]

— — Third edition. London 1925. pp.xv.107. [1750.]

interleaved.

CRIME prevention and crime repression. Russell Sage foundation: Library: Bulletin (no.81): New York 1927. pp.4. [75.]

AUGUSTUS FREDERICK KUHLMAN, A guide to material on crime and criminal justice. Social science research council: New York 1929. pp.[ii]. 633. [13,276.]

— — Author index. . . . By Dorothy Campbell Culver. New York 1934. pp.32.

CRIME and criminal justice. A short list of books. Library of Congress: [Washington] 1930. pp.8. [84.]*

— [another edition]. Compiled by Helen F[ield] Conover under the direction of Florence S[elma] Hellman. 1940. pp.52. [470.]*

there was an intermediate edition.

CATALOGUE. John Howard library of criminal law and penology: 1931. pp.51. [750.]

DOROTHY CAMPBELL CULVER, Bibliography of crime and criminal justice. University of California: Bureau of public administration: New York.

1927–1931. 1934. pp.xl.413. [13,292.]

— [supplement]. Crime in foreign countries. A select list of references. Compiled by Helen F[ield] Conover under the direction of Florence S[elma] Hellman. Library of Congress: Division of bibliography: [Washington] 1935. pp.12. [158.]*

1932–1937. 1939. pp.xxxi.391. [9314.]

SELECT list of recent references on crime and criminal justice. Library of Congress: Washington 1935. ff.27. [346.]*

CRIME in foreign countries: a select list of recent

references. Library of Congress: Washington 1935. ff.11. [158.]*

LEOPOLD ENGELHARDT, Bibliographie des gesamten strafrechts einschliesslich der verwandten wissensgebiete, 1933–1935. München 1936. ff. xxxiii.350+[iv].121+ff.[vi].142. [3000.]*

CRIME, its cause and prevention. Russell Sage foundation: Library: Bulletin (no.138): New York 1936. pp.4. [75.]

BIBLIOGRAPHY of crime and kindred subjects. Federal bureau of investigation: Washington 1937. ff.17. [150.]*
limited to writings in english.

CRIME and the treatment of criminals. A selected list of books, compiled by the Howard league for penal reform. Fifth edition. National book council: Book list (no.53): 1937. pp.[4]. [150.]

[ADOLF] SCHÖNKE, Ausländisches strafrecht. Übersicht über die wichtigsten quellen und über das wichtigste schrifttum. Berlin [1937]. pp.36. [250.]

— — Dritte bearbeitung, 1948. pp.80. [600.]

CATÁLOGO de derecho penal. Universidad de Montevideo: Facultad de derecho y ciencias sociales: Montevideo 1942. pp.89. [3500.]

BIBLIOGRAFÍA de ciencias penales, formada con los trabajos publicados en la revista Criminalia de los años I al IX de septiembre de 1933 a agosto de 1943. Cuadernos 'Criminalia' (no.15): México 1943. pp.159.

HERMAN K. SPECTOR, Bibliography on criminology, penology & allied subjects. Department of correction: Penitentiary of the city of New York: [New York 1944]. pp.192. [2000.]*

HERMAN K. SPECTOR, Coordinated reference bibliography for the use of the California department of corrections, the Youth authority, the Adult authority, the Bureau of paroles. State board of corrections: Research committee: Sanamento 1952. ff.[i].100. [745.]*

MARC DE SMEDT, Essai de bibliographie médicolégale et criminologique. Liège 1953. pp.124. [1500.]

ÉLÉMENTS d'une documentation en criminologie. Unesco: Rapports et documents de sciences sociales (no.14): 1961. pp.116. [1158.]*

DOROTHY CAMPBELL TOMPKINS, The offender—a bibliography. University of California: Institute of governmental studies: [Berkeley] 1963. pp. viii.268. [3500.]*

4. *Countries*

Africa

MORGAN O. EVANS, Digest of criminal cases in the superior courts of South Africa (Cape, Transvaal, Natal and O.F.S.). Cape Town &c. 1909. pp.xxxiv.coll.348. [2500.]

VIVIENNE CHRISTINE FOX, Prison & penal reform in south Africa, 1938–1948. Including a section on juvenile delinquency and a number of important english and american publications. University of Cape Town: School of librarianship: Bibliographical series: [Capetown] 1950. ff.iv.25. [176.]*

I[SAAC] ROSEN and F[RANCIS] DE F[ONTAINE] STRATTON, A digest of east african criminal case law 1897–1954, containing decisions of the Court of appeal for eastern Africa and the Judicial committee of the Privy council on appeal from that court. Durban 1957. pp.xxiii.341. [1250.]

J[OSEPH] R[AE] BROKENSHA, A digest of selected south african criminal cases. Durban 1960. pp. xlvii.387. [2500.]

Argentina

EUSEBIO GÓMEZ, Criminología argentina. Reseña bibliográfica. Buenos Aires 1912. pp.lix.287. [1300.]

Brazil

HILDEBRANDO DANTAS DE FREITAS and JOSÉ RANGEL DE ALMEIDA, Repertório de jurisprudência do código de processo penal (1945–1960). São Paulo [1960]. pp.557+[iii].565–1103+[iii].1107–1665. [1838.]

Burma

S. S. HALKAR [SUBBARĀU ṢESHAGIRI HĀLKAR], A digest of criminal rulings of Burma, including cases reported in all official and non-official reports (1872 to 1925). . . . Second edition. Mylapore [printed] 1926. pp.[iii].32.coll.588.v. [3000.]

Canada

GEORGE E. MCCROSSAN, SAMUEL D. SCHULTZ and ANDREW M. HARPER, The digest of canadian criminal case law . . . from the earliest times to the year 1907. Toronto 1908. pp.liii.coll.1152. [3000.]

THE CANADIAN criminal law digest, being a consolidated digest of the cases under the criminal code reported in . . . the 'Canadian criminal cases', 1893–1913, together with the important criminal law decisions prior to the enactment of the criminal code, and decisions under the liquor laws and other quasi-criminal statutes both federal and provincial. Toronto 1913. pp.xxix.coll.1074. [2500.]

R[OBERT] M[ICHAEL] WILLES CHITTY, An abridgment of the canadian criminal case law, 1892–1925. Toronto 1925. pp.xlvi.813. [5000.]

—— Vol.2. Chitty's abridgment . . . 1925–1939. . . . Edited by Melville Pierce. 1939. pp.xlvi. 596. [3000.]

—— Vol.3. . . . 1939–1949. . . . [Edited by] Cecil A. Wright [*and others*]. 1950. pp.xxxviii. 800. [4000.]

LEONARD G. WRINCH, The Canadian abridgment: criminal code (1954) judicially considered. Toronto &c. 1955. pp.xxiv.252. [6500.]

Ceylon

E. P. WIJETUNGE [EDMUND P. VIJĒTUṄGE], A complete digest of case law on the penal code 1820 to 1955, illustrated with references to english and indian cases. [Colombo 1955]. pp.[vi].xxxvii. 616. [1750.]

Cuba

ERASMO REGÜEIFEROS Y BOUDET, Bibliografía penal de Cuba. Habana 1926. pp.65. [1000.]

Criminal Law

France

TABLE analytique des arrêts de la Cour de cassation rendus en matière criminelle.

1798–1856. Par Émile [André] Duchesne. 1857. pp.[iii].672 + [iii].673 + [iii].644 + [iii].688. [20,000.]

— Appendice. 1857. pp.[iii].558. [4000.]

1857–1873. Par É. Duchesne . . . et Albert Duchesne. 1874. pp.lxxx.471 + 550. [10,000.]

1874–1888. Par Louis Lallemand. 1889. pp. cxiv.521+548. [10,000.]

1888–1900. Par Georges Desvaux . . . René Maufroy. 1901–1902. pp.c.409 + 449. [7500.]

Germany

HUGO [HEINRICH ALBRECHT] BOEHLAU, Quellen und literatur des gemeinen deutschen und preussischen strafrechts. Weimar 1859. pp.31. [200.]

WALTER [BERNARD] LEHMANN, Zur reform des reichsstrafgesetzbuches (allgemeiner teil). Berichte über die literatur der jahre 1902–1904. Universität Berlin: Kriminalistisches seminar: Abhandlungen (n.s. iv.3): Berlin 1905. pp.143.

Criminal Law

Great Britain

JOHN MEWS, A digest of cases relating to criminal law from 1756 to 1883 inclusive. 1884. coll.l.854. [5000.]

— — [another edition]. A digest . . . down to the end of 1897. 1898. pp.xl.coll.862. [10,000.]

SELECT list of references on the administration of the criminal code in England, 1800–1845. Library of Congress: Washington 1909. ff.6. [42.]*

EDMUND D. PURCELL, Criminal appeal reports. A digest. Volumes I to XI. 1916. pp.xxxix.113. [300.]

THE ENGLISH and empire digest . . . being a complete digest of every english case reported from early times to the present day, with additional cases from the courts of Scotland, Ireland, the empire of India, and the dominions beyond the seas. Volume XIV[–XV]. Criminal law and procedure. 1924. pp.xxxv.554 + cxxi.601–1076. [12,171.]

M. E. BARBER, Criminal law and its administration in England. National book council: Book list (no.161): 1940. pp.[2]. [50.]

Criminal Law

CRIMINAL justice, to which is annexed an appendix on capital punishment. House of commons: Library: Bibliography (no.38): [1947]. ff.[i]. 30. [153.]*

India

D. E. CRANENBURGH, A digest of criminal cases reported in the Indian law reports from 1876 to 1885. Second edition. Calcutta 1886. pp.[v].coll. 262.pp.ix. [750.]

S. RAGHAVA AIENGAR [SRINIVASA RAGHAVAIYANGAR], A digest or index to the criminal cases decided by the High courts of Calcutta, Madras, Bombay, and Allahabad and by the Privy council . . . 1885–1890. Kumbakonam 1891. pp.[iii].132. [750.]

J. B. WORGAN, Consecutive tables, criminal cases, being an annotation of the criminal cases in the Indian law reports from their commencement to the end of 1897, and of those in the Calcutta law reports that are not reported in the I.l.r. Calcutta 1898. pp.ix.111. [2500.]

D. E. CRANENBURGH, The general digest of criminal rulings, being a compendium of all criminal rulings of the several high courts in India from 1862 to 1899. [Second edition]. Calcutta 1901. pp.xxii.973. [4000.]

NRISIṂHA-DĀSA VASU, A subject-noted index of criminal cases judicially noticed (1809–1913). Calcutta 1914. pp.154. [3500.]

C. H. OERTEL, A digest of the criminal rulings of the Chief court of the Punjab and High court at Lahore . . . 1866 to 1920. Lahore 1922. pp.[iii].2. coll.1000.pp.xxi. [7500.]

DĪWĀN-CHAND OBHRĀI, The Punjab ready referencer, 1866–1923 (June), or the consolidated subject index to the Punjab criminal references. . . . A–criminal portion. Second edition. Madras 1923. pp.vi.438. [7500.]

V. V. CHITALE [VĀMANA VĀSUDEVA CHIṬALE] and R. NARAYANASWAMI IYER [R. NĀRĀYAṆASVĀMI AIYAR], The criminal and revenue digest, 1911–1923. Mylapore 1924. pp.vii.coll.1140+pp.v.–xiv.195.coll.1141–1992. [10,000.]

A FULL digest of the Madras criminal cases, 1924 to 1936. Madras [1937]. pp.[iv].282. [2500.]

MOHAN-LĀL KHARBANDA, The Allahabad criminal digest. Being a digest of criminal cases decided by the Allahabad High court and the Privy council, 1811–1938. Allahabad 1938. pp.viii.coll.840+ pp.[iv].coll.841–1548. [6500.]

B. K. PAL [VASANTA-KUMĀRA PĀLA], 8 Years criminal digest, 1931–1938. Calcutta 1939. pp.[ii]. ii.496.4. [3000.]

S. K. IYER [S. KṚISHNAMŪRTI AIYAR], The all India criminal digest 1904–1940. Lahore 1941. pp.viii. coll.1816 + pp.[iv].coll.1817–3968 + pp.vi.coll. 3969–6104. [100,000.]

Italy

GUIDO GUIDI, La bibliografia del codice penale. Aquila 1907. pp.iv.359.vii. [525.]

Mauritius

W. GREENE, A digest of the reported criminal jurisprudence of the supreme court of Mauritius from 1842 to 1883. Port Louis [printed] 1884. pp.[xvi].coll.178.pp.[142]. [800.]

Mexico

RAMÓN VICARIO, Índice alfabético de los delitos y cosas notables que se contienen en el código penal. México 1872. pp.52. [1000.]

Netherlands

LUCIENNE VAN MEERBEECK, Inventaire des archives des tribunaux criminels du département de la Dyle et de la cour d'assises de Brabant 1794–1822. Archives générales du royaume: Bruxelles 1954. pp.40. [20,000.]

Peru

JOSÉ ANDRES CATERIAUD [*sic*, CATERIANO], Índice analítico de los codigos penal y de enjuiciamientos en materia penal. Lima 1863. pp.39. [800.]

Russia

[FANNI MARKOVNA ASKNAZY and NINA VASILEVNA MARSHALOVA], Советское уголовное право. Библиография 1917–1960. Москва 1961. pp.524. [5000.]

Spain

FERNANDO DÍAZ PALOS, Bibliografía española de derecho penal. Instituto de derecho comparado: Colección (ser. F, no.2): Barcelona 1954. pp.87. [900.]

Switzerland

BIBLIOGRAPHIE pénale et pénitentiaire. Schweizerischer verein für straf- und gefängnisswesen: Lenzbourg &c. 1885. pp.iv.47. [750.]

United States

THOMAS W. WATERMAN, A digest of decisions

in criminal cases, contained in the reports of the federal courts and the courts of the several states from the earliest period to the present time. New York 1877. pp.xli.816. [6500.]

S[OLOMON] B. BOYER, A digest and index, together with a table of cases, to all criminal cases adjudged by the Supreme court of Pennsylvania from . . . 1799, to . . . 1891. Sunbury [1891]. pp. l.240.855. [1800.]

SELECT list of references on reform in criminal law and procedure. Library of Congress: Washington 1912. ff.14. [125.]*

— [supplement]. List of recent references [&c.]. 1921. ff.6. [74.]*

LIST of references on crime and criminals in the United States, with special reference to statistics. Library of Congress: [Washington] 1922. ff.21. [277.]*

HERMAN K. SPECTOR, Professional literature. Books, periodicals . . . on criminals, crime [&c.]. Department of correction, New York city. [New York] 1942. [loose-leaf.]*

R[AMON] FREDERICK ADAMS, Six-guns & saddle leather. A bibliography of books and pamphlets on western outlaws and gunmen. Norman, Okla. [1947]. pp.xiii.426. [1132.]

DOROTHY CAMPBELL TOMPKINS, Sources for the study of the administration of criminal justice. Special crime study commissions and California state board of corrections: Sacramento 1949. pp. 294. [2500.]

OTTO POLLAK, Crime causation. Selected bibliography of studies in the United States, 1939–1949. Philadelphia 1950. pp.53. [708.]

RAMON F[REDERICK] ADAMS, Six-guns & saddle leather. A bibliography of books and pamphlets on western outlaws and gunmen. Norman, Okla. [1954]. pp.xiii.428. [1132.]

DOROTHY CAMPBELL TOMPKINS, Administration of criminal justice, 1949–1956. A selected bibliography. California state board of corrections: California special study commission on correctional facilities and services: [Sacramento] 1956. pp.ix.351. [3000.]*

5. *Special subjects*

SELECT list of references on reform schools. Library of Congress: Washington 1910. ff.10. [55.]*

PENAL farms and farm colonies. Russell Sage foundation: Library: Bulletin (no.6): New York 1914. pp.[4]. [60.]

BRIEF list of references on the relation between vagrancy and crime. Library of Congress: [Washington] 1916. ff.3. [33.]*

LIST of references on women criminals. Library of Congress: [Washington] 1916. ff.7. [120.]*

LIST of references on the identification of criminals. Library of Congress: Washington 1917. ff.6. [70.]*

— [another edition]. 1918. ff.7. [84.]*

BRIEF list of references on the relation between education and crime. Library of Congress: Washington 1918. ff.3. [31.]*

LIST of recent references on the identification of criminals, with special reference to criminal identification bureaus. Library of Congress: Washington 1922. ff.5. [65.]*

M[IKHAIL] N[IKOLAEVICH] GERNET, Указатель русской и иностранной литературы по статистике преступлений, наказаний и самоубийств. Москва 1924. pp.48. [1750.]

INDETERMINATE sentence and parole. Library of Congress: Washington 1933. ff.3. [40.]*

SELECT list of references on indeterminate sentence. Library of Congress: Washington [*c.*1935]. ff.5. [24.]*

HELEN FULLER [*and others*], Bibliography on housing and crime. Attorney general's advisory committee on crime: [Washington] 1936. ff.[i].6. [73.]*

HELEN FULLER [*and others*], Bibliography on recreation and delinquency. Attorney general's advisory committee on crime: [Washington] 1936. ff.[i].7. [88.]*

DENNIS T. BRETT, Crime detection. National book league: Reader's guide (3rd ser., no.6): Cambridge 1959. pp.30. [100.]

Laws by Places

Africa.

C[HARLES] K[INGSLEY] MEEK, Colonial law. A bibliography with special reference to native african systems of law and land tenure. Nuffield college [Oxford]: 1948. pp.xiii.59. [813.]

J[OHN] H[ENRY] VAUGHAN and GEORGE [MUTLOW] PATERSON, Index-digest of the reported cases determined by the Court of appeal for eastern Africa and an appeal therefrom by the Judicial committee of the Privy council, 1900 to 1938. Nairobi [printed] [1939]. pp.[vi].129.xv. [200.]

W. H. SOMERSET BELL, The digest of the Cape law journal . . . containing most of the decisions of the superior courts of South Africa . . . 1884–1900. Grahamstown 1901. pp.lii.coll.1128. [3000.]

THE DIGEST of south african case law, containing the decisions of the supreme [superior] courts. Cape Town, &c.

To the end of 1905. By Murray Bisset and Percival Frere Smith. 1909. pp.xx.coll. 1448+pp. [iii].1449–2972+pp. [v].46.256. [20,000.]

1906–1908. 1910. pp.viii.coll.934.pp.73. [5000.]

1909–1911. 1913. pp.iii–ix.coll.870.pp.xi.72. [3500.]

1912–1914. 1915. pp.viii.coll.908.pp.xv.75. [4000.]

1915–1916. 1918. pp.viii.coll.676.pp.xii.41. [3000.]

1917–1918. 1920. pp.viii.coll.466.pp.x.31. [2000.]

1919–1920. 1922. pp.viii.coll.464.pp.xx.25. [2000.]

1921. 1923. pp.viii.coll.326.pp.xx.17. [1500.]

To the end of 1921. Edited by Thomas Graeme Duncan. 1926–[1929]. pp.xiv.coll. 1230 + pp.ix.coll.1520 + pp.viii.coll.1500 + pp.viii.coll.1534 + pp.vii.coll.1418 + pp.[vii].128.350. [40,000.]

1922. pp.viii.coll.298.pp.xxviii.16. [1000.]

1923. pp.viii.coll.312.pp.xxxiv.15. [1000.]

1924. pp.viii.coll.354.xxvi.16. [1000.]

1925. By T. G. Duncan. pp.viii.coll.338. pp.xxvi.15. [1000.]

1926. pp.viii.coll.316.pp.xix.8. [1000.]
1927. pp.viii.coll.418.xxvii.11. [1200.]
1928. pp.viii.coll.386.xxvii.10. [1200.]
1929. pp.viii.coll.388.pp.xxx.10. [1000.]
1930. pp.viii.coll.370.pp.xxv.9. [1000.]
1931. pp.viii.coll.342.pp.xxxv.9. [1000.]
1932. pp.viii.coll.322.pp.xxvii.9. [1000.]
1933. pp.viii.coll.320.pp.xxxviii.8. [1000.]

1922–1933. Edited by P. F. Smith and G. Duncan. 1936. pp.[vi].coll.1402+pp.[ii]. coll. 1258.pp.70. [12,500.]

1934. By T. G. Duncan. pp.viii.coll.230. pp.xxvi.8. [750.]

1935. pp.viii.coll.266.pp.xvi.8. [750.]
1936. pp.viii.coll.258.pp.xxi.7. [750.]
1937. pp.viii.coll.282.pp.xxii.8. [1000.]
1938. pp.viii.coll.306.pp.xli.9. [1000.]
1939. pp.viii.coll.356.pp.xlviii.10. [1000.]
1940. pp.viii.coll.310.pp.xliii.8. [1000.]
1941. pp.viii.coll.282.pp.xxxii.7. [750.]
1942. pp.iv.coll.278.pp.xxxiv.7. [750.]
1943. pp.viii.coll.342.pp.xxxix.8. [1000.]
1944. pp.vi.coll.282.pp.xxxvi.8. [1000.]
1945. pp.viii.coll.302.pp.xxxix.7. [1000.]
1946. pp.viii.coll.414.pp.lx.10. [1750.]
1947. pp.ix.coll.396.pp.xlix.15.[1500.]
1948. pp.viii.coll.362.14. [1000.]

1949. pp.vi.coll.268.15. [750.]

— Index and digest . . . 1946–1949. 1951. pp. [vii].coll.400.pp.lxxi.

G. A. MULLIGAN and H. J. CLAYDEN, Continuous digest of union statute case law to end of 1921. Cape Twon &c. [1930.] pp.xlix.207. [3295.]

GRAEME DUNCAN, Index to decisions of the Supreme court of South Africa (Appellate division). June, 1910–December, 1932. South African law reports: Capetown &c. 1933. pp.[iii].183. [2500.]

A[LFRED] A[DRIAN] ROBERTS, Index to the statutes of the Union of South Africa (1910–1934). Pretoria 1936. pp.226. [10,000.]

the same volume, reversed and reading back to front, contains Q[*uertus*] *de West,* Inhoud van die wette van die Unie van Suid-Afrika (*1910–1934*).

C. H. BLAINE, New consolidated index to pre-union and union statutes and provincial ordinances, and the regulations etc. thereunder, up to 31st December, 1936. Durban [1937]. pp.[viii]. 640. [25,000.]

pages 585–640 are blank.

A[LFRED] A[DRIAN] ROBERTS, A south african legal bibliography. Being a bio-bibliographical survey and law-finder of the roman and roman-dutch legal literature in southern Africa, with an historical chart. Pretoria 1942. pp.392. [6000.]

interleaved; privately printed.

C. NORMAN SCOBLE, Index of statute law and regulations of the union, 1945. Durban [1946]. pp.[iii].64. [2000.]

[—] — [another edition]. [1950]. pp.110. [3000.]

[L.] PARIS LE CLERC, Tables chronologique et alphabétique des actes métropolitains et locaux promulgués dans la colonie du Sénégal et dépendances, le Soudan français et les établissements français de la côte occidentale d'Afrique. Melun 1903. pp.872.lii. [7000.]

Alabama.

P. PHILLIPS, Digest of cases decided and reported in the Supreme court of the state of Alabama from 1st Alabama reports to 7th Porter inclusive. Mobile 1840. pp.xlviii.9–350. [4500.]

— — from Minor to VII. Alabama reports inclusive. 1846. pp.xii.629. [9000.]

INDEX to claimants before the Court of commissioners of Alabama claims. Washington 1877. pp.[iii].ff.180. [4000.]

— Alphabetical index [&c.] 1844. pp.60. [7500.]

Algeria.

P. DE MÉNERVILLE, Jurisprudence de la cour impériale d'Alger en matière civile et commerciale, 1834–1854. Recueil contenant l'analyse sommaire de tous les jugements et arrêts rendus sur les questions de droit par le tribunal supérieur et la cour. Alger 1855. pp.viii.507. [2000.]

— — Répertoire de jurisprudence algérienne ... 1857 à 1876. ... Par Henri Narbonne. 1877. pp.ix.559. [2600.]

ÉMILE GOIRAN, Recueil alphabétique et analytique des circulaires émanées du parquet général d'Alger (années 1887 à 1893). . . . 2e édition. Batna 1893. pp.96. [500.]

Alsace, Alsace-Lorraine.

[N. F. LANÇON], Table chronologique des édits, déclarations, lettres patentes et arrêts du conseil, registrés au parlement de Metz ... jusqu'en 1740. [Metz] 1740. pp.339.[xliii]. [2250.]

[—] — Suite de la Table [&c.]. [By L. Chenu]. 1769. pp.101. [800.]

America.

JOSÉ MALUQUER Y SALVADOR, El derecho hispano-americano en la bibliografía española. Madrid 1887. pp.45. [150.]

EDWARD SCHUSTER, Guide to law and legal literature of central american republics. American foreign law association: Bibliographies of foreign law series (no.11): New York 1937. pp.[ii].vi. 153. [750.]

[CRAWFORD MORRISON BISHOP, *ed.*], Legal codes of the latin american republics. Library of Congress: Latin american series (no.1): Washington 1942. pp.95. [148.]

CAHIERS de législation et de bibliographie juridique de l'Amérique latine. Université de Paris: Institut de droit comparé and Société de législation comparée.

i. 1948. pp.239+252+267+228. [500.]
ii. 1949. pp.249+142+229. [500.]
iii. 1952. pp.183+114+208. [500.]
iv. 1953. pp.112+192. [500.]
v. 1954. pp.306+99. [500.]
vi. 1955. pp.111+103. [500.]
vii. 1956. pp.138. [500.]

no more published.

INDEX to latin american legislation 1950 through 1960. Compiled in the Library of Congress. Boston 1961. pp.[iv].752+[ii].753–1474. [15,141.]

reproduces the catalogue cards, to which the number in square brackets refers.

Arabia.

CARL FERDINAND HOMMEL, Bibliotheca jvris rabbinica et Saracenorvm arabica. Byrvthi 1762. pp.63. [xvii]. [250.]

MAULAVI ABDUL HAMID [ʿABD UL-ḤAMĪD], Catalogue of the arabic and persian manuscripts in the Oriental public library at Bankipore. Volume XIX. . . . Jurisprudence. Patna 1931–1933. pp.vii.172+vii.169. [473.]

Argentina.

SYLLA J. MONSEGUR, El derecho internacional privado en la república Argentina. Apuntaciones bibliográficas. Buenos Aires 1898. pp.136. [88.]

EDWIN M. BORCHARD, Guide to the law and legal literature of Argentina, Brazil and Chile. Library of Congress: Washington 1917. pp.523. [2000.]

HELEN L[ORD] CLAGETT, A guide to the law and

legal literature of Argentina, 1917–1946. Library of Congress: Latin american series (no.32): Washington 1948. pp.vii.180. [1250.]

DERECHO constitucional y derecho público provincial. Congreso: Biblioteca: Sección proyectos y asesoramiento legislativo: Información bibliográfica: Publicación (no.1): Buenos Aires 1949. pp.150. [3000.]

DIGESTO Ediar de la legislación argentina. Buenos Aires [1953]. pp.3–335. [20,000.]

DERECHO constitucional y derecho publico provincial. Información bibliográfica. Congreso: Biblioteca: Sección referencia general: Publicación (no.17): [Buenos Aires 1957]. pp.viii.114. [3500.]

Australia.

A DIGEST of all the cases reported in the Commonwealth law reports. Commonwealth law reports: Sydney.

1903–1915. By D. Claude Robertson. pp.[iv].xciv.coll.928. [2000.]

1915–1918. By H. Dallas Wiseman. pp.xxxix. coll.404. [1000.]

1915–1924. By H. G. Edwards. pp.xcvi.824. [2000.]

1924–1930. By G. C. Addison. pp.lxiv.594. [1000.]

— Noter up. pp.24. [1000.]

the last part is a list of cases.

THE AUSTRALIAN digest, 1825–1933, being a digest of the reported decisions of the australian courts and of australian appeals to the Privy council. Sydney &c.

i. Abandonment—Book. [Editor-in-Chief: B. Sugerman]. 1934. pp.lxxii.coll.1248. [2500.]

ii. Bankruptcy. 1935. pp.lviii.coll.1058. [3000.]

ii. Borough—Companies. 1935. pp.lvii. coll.1182. [2500.]

iv. Compensations—Costs. 1935. pp.lx.coll. 1304. [2500.]

v. Council—Criminal. 1936. pp.xliii.coll. 1444. [3000.]

vi. Crops—Cycles. 1935. pp.lvii.coll.1208. [2500.]

vii. Dairies—Estate. 1935. pp.liii.coll.1060. [2500.]

viii. Estoppel—Exhibition. 1936. pp.xlix. coll.1102. [2500.]

ix. Exhibits—High court. 1936. pp.lvi. coll. 1092. [2500.]

x. Highways—Inebriates. 1936. pp.lxxiv. coll.1616. [3500.]

xi. Infants—Irrigation. 1936. pp.lvii.coll. 1310. [3000.]

xii. Issue—Lifts. 1937. pp.lxvi.coll.1346. [3000.]

xiii. Light—Master. 1937. pp.lvii.coll.1268. [3000.]

xiv. Matrimonial—Monopolies. 1937. pp.lii. coll.1208. [2500.]

xv. Month—Powers of appointment. 1938. pp.lvi.coll.1170. [2000.]

xvi.

xvii. Presumption—Real estate. 1939. pp. lxiii.coll.1342. [2500.]

xviii. Real property—Shops. 1939. pp.lvi. coll.1014. [2000.]

xix. Signature—Taxation. 1939. pp.lxiii. coll.1208. [2000.]

xx.

xxi. Truck—Wharves. 1940. pp.liv.coll. 1248. [2500.]

xxii. Wheat—Year. 1940. pp.liv.1938. [3000.]

xxiii. Table of cases. [1941]. pp.xiv.714. [22,500.]

xxiv. Table of cases judicially noticed. [1942]. pp.xvi.coll.872. [17,5000.]

— Supplement.

1934–1930. pp.xcix.coll.1356+pp.[vii].coll. 1357–2740. pp.ci–ccxviii. [5000.]

1940. Editor W. J. Dignam. pp.xxviii. coll.638. pp.642[*sic*, 643]–680. [1250.]

1941. pp.xxvi.coll.588. [1750.]

1942. Editor Jean Malor. pp.xxviii.coll.566. [1750.]

1943. pp.xxiv.coll.556. [1500.]

1944. pp.xxiv.coll.532. [1500.]

1945. pp.xxiv.coll.572. [1500.]

1946. pp.xxiv.coll.628. [1500.]

1947. pp.xxiv.coll.604. [1250.]

1948. pp.xxiv.coll.592. [1000.]

A BIBLIOGRAPHY of the laws of Australia, New Zealand, Fiji and the western Pacific from the earliest times. With lists of reports of cases, digests and collections of statutes and rules. Sweet & Maxwell's legal bibliography (vol.vi): 1938. pp.vii.144. [1500.]

INDEX to the minutes of the proceedings of the Legislative council. Adelaide.

1857–1874. pp.101. [7500.]

1875–1884. pp.61. [4000.]

1885–1904. . . . together with a . . . schedule of all bills introduced into either House, 1857–1904. pp.105. [7500.]

1905–1915. pp.25. [2000.]

in progress in the form of leaflets issued for each session.

INDEX to the parliamentary papers of the Legislature of South Australia. Adelaide.

1857–1881. pp.116. [4000.]

1881–1885. pp.25. [1000.]

1886–1894. pp.29. [1000.]

in progress in the form of leaflets issued for each session.

[EDWARD WILSON LANDOR], Index to the ordinances of Western Australia. Fremantle 1862. pp.[ii].32.lii. [369.]

interleaved.

J. C. H. JAMES, Western Australia. Historical table of the statutes and alphabetical index of their contents. Perth 1891. pp.[v].185. [5000.]

CHARLES W. J. VAN DER WALL, A consolidated index to Government gazette, from 1836 to 1890 inclusive. [1903]. pp.viii.192. [10,000.]

GENERAL index to the printed papers presented to the Legislative council, 1870–1889, and to Parliament, 1890, to session 1 of 1908. Perth 1908. pp.111. [1500.]

— General index to the printed papers presented to Parliament . . . 1908–1923. Compiled by H. B. Collett. 1925. pp.47. [750.]

— General index to the printed papers presented to the Legislative council 1870–1889 and to Parliament . . . 1890–1946. Compiled by L. P. Hawley. 1948. pp.200. [3000.]

Austria.

MORITZ VON STUBENRAUCH, Bibliotheca juridica austriaca. Verzeichniss der von den ältesten zeiten bis zum schlusse des jahres 1846 in Oesterreich (ausser Ungarn und Siebenbürgen) erschienenen druckschriften, und in den österreichischen juridischen zeitschriften enthaltenen aufsätze aus allen theilen der rechtsgelehrsamkeit. Wien 1847. pp.iv.463. [4912.]

MARTIN DAMIANITSCH, Die literatur des allgemeinen bürgerlichen gesetzbuches im auszuge verfasst. Wien 1850. pp.xvi.255. [1000.]

FRANZ STARR, Vollständiges sach- und nachschlage-register zu sämmtlichen landesgesetzblättern der im Reichsrathe vertretenen königreiche und länder von deren beginn 1849 bis zum jahre 1863. Wien.

i. Niederösterreich, Oberösterreich und Salzburg. 1873. pp.vi.358. [5000.]

ii. Steiermark, Kärnthen und Krain. 1873. pp.[iii].288. [4000.]

iii. Böhmen, Mähren und Schlesien. 1874. pp.[iii].408. [5000.]

iv. Tirol-Vorarlberg, Küstenland und Dalmatien. 1874. pp.[iii].428. [6000.]

v. Galizien, Krakau und die Bukowina. 1874. pp.[iii].268. [4000.]

— Ergänzungsband. 1875. pp.136. [1500.]

JOSEF KOCHANOWSKI, Repertorium über gesetze und verordnungen seit 1778 bis ende 1877. Mit besonderer rücksichtnahme auf die agenden der politischen verwaltung. Wien 1878. pp.[iii]. 252. [2500.]

RAIMUND RZIHA, Alphabetisches verzeichniss jener gerichtlichen entscheidungen, verfügungen und beschlüsse gegen welche nach den bestimmungen der neuen civil-processordnung, jurisdictionsnorm und executionsordnung kein oder kein abgesondertes rechtsmittel zulässig ist.

[Österreichische gesetze (no.62):] Wien 1898. pp.15. [300.]

RAIMUND RZIHA, Alphabetisches verzeichniss aller in der neuen civilprocess-ordnung, jurisdictionsnorm und executionsordnung, dann im mahnverfahren vorkommenden gesetzlichen fristenbestimmungen. [Österreichische gesetze (no.65):] Wien 1898. pp.14. [250.]

HUGO VON BALTZ-BALZBERG, Vollständiges sach- und nachschlageregister für alle die civilprocess-reform betreffenden gesetze, verordnungen, formularien, etc., etc. [Österreichische gesetze (no.66):] Wien 1898. pp.326.

JOSEPH STAMMHAMMER, Katalog der bibliothek der Niederösterr. advokatenkammer. Wien 1911. pp.vi.82.

— — Nachtrag 1. [? 1913]. ff.11.

INDEX zu den stenographischen protokollen des Nationalrates . . . vom 10. November 1920 bis 20. November 1923. [*s.l.*, n.d.]. pp.[iii].1206. [5000.]*

Baden, Germany.

FR[IEDRICH] KAPPLER, Handbuch der literatur

des badischen rechts. Heidelberg 1847. pp.[ii].v. 680. [6500.]

Basutoland.

CUMULATIVE index to the laws of Basutoland from 1st january, 1949 to 31st December, 1953. Maseru 1954. pp.27. [400.]

Bavaria.

GEORG KARL VON MAYR, General-index über alle landes-verordnungen, welche durch die königlich baierischen regierungs-blätter von Baiern in München, von der Oberpfalz in Amberg, von Franken in Bamberg, und von Schwaben in Ulm, von den jahren 1802, 1803, 1804, und 1805 promulgirt und bekannt gemacht worden sind. München 1806. pp.[viii].428. [2000.]

— — 1806—1809–1810. 1809. pp.[viii].793. [2500.]

G. DÖLLINGER, Register über die in den regierungs- und gesetz-blättern vom jahre 1799 bis 1825 einschlüssig, und in den vormals bestandenen provinzial-regierungsblättern enthaltenen verordnungen. München 1832. pp.[ii].716. [10,000.]

— — Erste fortsetzung . . . 1826, 1827 und 1828. [1829]. pp.[ii].142. [2000.]

— — Zweyte fortsetzung . . . 1829, 1830 und 1831. 1832. pp.[ii].227. [3500.]

— — Dritte fortsetzung . . . 1832, 1833 und 1834. 1835. pp.[ii].144. [2000.]

— — Vierte fortsetzung . . . 1835 bis 1838. 1839. pp.[ii].208. [3000.]

— — Fünfte fortsetzung . . . 1838 bis 1841. 1842. pp.[ii].111. [1500.]

— — Sechste fortsetzung . . . 1841 bis 1843. 1844. pp.[ii].115. [1500.]

LUDWIG HAUFF, Uebersicht der literatur der bayerischen gesetzgebung auf dem gebiete des rechts und der verwaltung. München 1866. pp. viii.76. [1500.]

F. HIMMELSTOSS, General-register zu den zehn bänden der sammlung von entscheidungen des Königl. oberlandesgerichts München in gegenständen des strafrechts und strafprozesses. Erlangen 1904. pp.xxv.442. [2000.]

LEONHARD MEUKEL, Sammlung von entscheidungen des Bayerischen obersten landesgerichts in strafsachen. General-register zu band I mit X. München 1911. pp.[vii].360. [2000.]

— — zu band XI mit XXX. Bearbeitet von Wilhelm von Ammon. 1931. pp.[vii].302. [1500.]

Belgium.

TABLE générale alphabétique de la jurisprudence belge de 1814 à 1833. Bruxelles 1835. pp.[ii].81. 5–515. [5000.]

BULLETIN officiel des lois et arrêtés royaux de la Belgique. . . . Tables chronologique et alphabétique de 1830 à 1840, rédigées par H. Tarlier. Bruxelles [1841]. pp.xix.318. [7500.]

EDMOND PICARD [vols.i–cxvi; vols.i–xcii: and N. D'HOFFSCHMIDT; xxviii–cxii: and JULES [VICTOR] DE LE COURT; cxvii &c.: LÉON HENNEBICQ], Pandectes belges. Répertoire général [*afterwards:* Encyclopédie] de législation, de doctrine et de jurisprudence belges [*afterwards:* Inventaire général du droit belge à la fin du XIXème siècle; *afterwards:* Corpus juris belgici]. Bruxelles 1878–1949.

RÉPERTOIRE général de la jurisprudence belge, contenant l'analyse de toutes les décisions rendues en Belgique. Bruxelles.

1814–1880. By Lucien Jamar. pp.[iii].4.523+ [iii].502 + [iii].559 + [iii].472 + [iii].490 + [iii].448 + [iii].448 + [iii].434 + [iii]. 514+[iii].414+[iii].196. [47,500.]

1880–1890. pp.[iii].iv.497 + [iii].768 + [iii]. 682. [25,000.]

1890–1900. pp.[iii].768+[iii].768+[iii].682. 111. [30,000.]

1900–1910. By L. Jamar, Georges Marcotty and Fernand Waleffe. pp.[iii].vii.744+ [iii].710+[iii].704+[iii].657. [35,000.]

no more published.

EDMOND PICARD and FERDINAND LARCIER, Bibliographie générale et raisonnée du droit belge. Relevé de toutes les publications juridiques parues depuis 1814. Bruxelles 1882–1890. pp.[vii].1354. [9517.]

CHARLES HENRY HUBERICH and ALEXANDER NICOL-SPEYER, German legislation for the occupied territories of Belgium. . . . Index. The Hague.

Series I–V, 5 September 1914–31 December 1915. [By P. R. Blok]. 1917. pp.[iii].79. [4000.]

Series VI–IX, 1 January–31 December 1916. 1918. pp.[ii].70. [3500.]

Series X–XIII, 3 January–28 December 1917. 1918. pp.[iii].63. [3000.]

Series XIV–XVII, 3 January–9 November 1918. [By S.A.E. van Lier]. 1919. pp.3–29. [1000.]

HENRI BOSLY, CHARLEY DEL MARMOL and CHARLES GOOSSENS, Répertoire bibliographique du droit belge (1919–1945). Liége 1947. pp.iii–xxxviii.456. [10,500.]

QUELQUES livres anciens de droit belge. Exposition organisée à la bibliothèque de l'université. Catalogue. Université libre: Bruxelles [1949]. pp. 84. [397.]

RÉPERTOIRE de l'activité législative de la chambre pendant la législature 1946–1949. Bruxelles [1950]. pp.96. [2500.]

HENRI BOSLY [*and others*], Répertoire bibliographique du droit belge (1946–1955). Liège 1957. pp.iii–xxxv.348. [6745.]

Bengal.

[M. H. TURNBULL], Index to the circular ordres, passed by the Sudder dewanny adawlut. [Calcutta *c.*1818]. pp.7. [100.]

D. DALE, Alphabetical index to the regulations of government for the whole of the territories under the presidency of Fort William in Bengal. Calcutta 1830. pp.iv.509. [16,365.]

INDEX to the circular ordres of the courts of Sudder dewanny adawlut, for the lower and western provinces, to the end of 1845. Calcutta 1847. pp.[ii].iii.79.19. [500.]

J. CARRAU, Index to the decisions of the Sudder dewanny adawlut, from 1792 to 1855. Calcutta 1856. pp.10.ccccxxxii.

INDEX excerpta of selected precedents of the Suddur dewanny court, from 1849 to 1858. Calcutta [1859]. pp.[iii].204. [1500.]

J. V. WOODMAN, A digest of the cases reported in the Bengal law reports, vols. I to XV, and in the supplement volume of full bench rulings. Calcutta 1878. pp.liii.coll.658. [3000.]

A. C. MITRA [AVINĀṢACHANDRA MITRA], A digest of the Indian law reports (Calcutta series . . .), being a complete index to cases determined by the High court, Calcutta, and by the Judicial committee of the Privy council, from 1876 to 1883. Monghyr 1884. pp.[iii].324.x. [1000.]

D. E. CRANENBURGH, A digest of civil cases reported in the Indian law reports, 1876 to 1894, and in the Calcutta law reports, 1878 to 1883. [Second edition]. Vol.I. Calcutta 1895. pp.[ii].ii. coll.2420. [5000.]

a–l only; no more published.

THE ALPHABETICAL index to circulars and circular memos. From 1890 to 1897. [Calcutta 1898]. pp.[ii].xxv. [400.]

THE DISTRICT officers' handy reference book, being a general index to acts and regulations and to important rules, notifications and orders in force in Bengal, with a list of useful books of reference. Second edition. General department: Calcutta 1908. pp.[ii].ix.377. [6000.]

this is an adaptation rather than a second edition of W. C. Macpherson, Aid to revenue and magisterial duties in the lower provinces of Bengal (*1891*).

MANIBHŪSHAN MAJIRMDĀR, Index to the imperial and Bengal council acts and the ordinances. [Calcutta] 1933. pp.[iv].156. [4500.]

Berar.

VAMAN VASUDEO CHITALE [VĀMANA VĀSUDEVA CHITALE] and MAHADEO SITARAM MUNDLE [MAHĀDEVA SĪTĀRĀMA MUNḌḶE], Chitale and Mundle's Digest of C. P. & Berar case-law, 1862–1920 March. Triplicane [printed] 1920. pp.[ii].4. coll.1148.118. [4641.]

Bermuda.

REGINALD GRAY, Index to the acts of the Legislature of the island of Bermuda from 1690 to 1896, no.6. 1896. pp.iv.124. [3500.]

Bihar and Orissa.

BIHAR DIGEST. Civil, criminal & revenue. 1934–1940. Bihar reports: [Lahore 1940]. pp.[ii].xxvi. coll.866. [5000.]

Bohemia.

ALPHABETISCHER auszug der gesammten alt und neuen böhmischen gesetze. Prag &c. [1739]. pp. [x].488. [2000.]

KAJETAN NADHERNY, General-register über die in folge eines a. h. befehls sr. k. k. majestät . . . erschienene . . . provinzial-gesetz-sammlung für die jahre 1819 [1816] bis 1838. Prag 1840. pp.vii. 639. [15,000.]

— — Nachtrag . . . für die jahre 1839–1848 . . . Von Josef Wolf. 1873. pp.64. [1250.]

FRANZ STARR, Vollständiges sach- und nachschlage-register zu sämmtlichen landesgesetzblättern der im Reichsrathe vertretenen königreiche und länder von deren beginn 1849 bis zum Jahre 1873. . . . Dritter theil. Böhmen, Mähren und Schlesien. Wien 1874. pp.[iii].408. [5000.]

COUNT LEOPOLD HARTIG, Gesetz- und normalien-register für die politische verwaltung im königreiche Böhmen. Prag 1897. pp.591. [5750.]

Bolivia.

M[ELQUIADES] LOIZA, Indice alfabético de los casos de jurisprudencia que rejistra la 'Gaceta judicial'. Secunda edición. La Paz 1878. pp.[ii]. lxiii.

BOLIVIA, American foreign law association: Bibliographies of foreign law series (no.3): [New York] 1926. pp.33–47. [75.]

HELEN L. CLAGETT, A guide to the law and legal literature of Bolivia. Library of Congress: Latin american series (no.12): Washington 1947. pp. viii.110. [1000.]

Bombay.

REGINALD M. A. BRANSON, Digest of the printed but unreported judgements of the High court of

Bombay, from 1869 to 1884. Bombay 1886. pp. xxxiii.coll.412. [1250.]

CALENDAR of land revenue settlements for the disctricts comprised in the Bombay presidency, including Sind. [Bombay 1899–1906]. pp.83+iii. 95. [3000.]

RATANLAL RANCHHODDAS [RATANLĀLA RAÑCHHODDĀSA] and DHIRAJLAL KESHAVLAL THAKORE [DHĪRAJLĀLA KEṢAVLĀLA ṬHĀKURA], The twenty years' digest of the Bombay law reporter . . . 1899–1918. Bombay 1921. pp.[iii].lxxxvi.coll.1952.pp. 1953–1957. [5000.]

Bordeaux.

ABRAHAM LAPEIRÈRE, Décisions sommaires du palais, mises par ordre alphabétique, illustrées de . . . plusieurs arrests de la cour de parlement de Bourdeaux. Bourdeaux 1675. pp.[iii].312. [1850.]

Bouillon.

LISTE chronologique des édits et ordonnances de l'ancien duché de Bouillon, de 1240 à 1795. Commission royale pour la publication des anciennes lois et ordonnances de la Belgique: Bruxelles 1895. pp.xv.79. [400.]

Brabant.

GEORGES BARBIAUX, Table alphabétique indicative des affaires dont s'est occupé le Conseil provincial du Brabant... de 1836 à 1885. Bruxelles 1886. pp.193.

J[OSEPH] P[ETER] W[ILLEM] A[NTOON] SMIT, Summiere lijst der noord-brabantsche rechterlijke archieven, vóór de invoering der fransche rechtspraak in het jaar 1811. 's-Gravenhage 1922. pp.19. [very large number.]

Brandenburg.

ACTA brandenburgica. Brandenburgische regierungsakten seit der begründung des Geheimen rates. Veröffentlichungen der Historischen kommission für die provinz Brandenburg (section III): Berlin.

i. 1604–1605. Herausgegeben von Melle Klinkenborg. 1927. pp.ix.632. [690.]
ii. 1606–1607. 1928. pp.[v].647. [853.]
iii. 1607–1608. 1930. pp[v].668. [784.]
iv. I. 1608. 1930. pp.[vi].320. [181.]

Brazil.

REPERTORIO constitucional ou indice alphabetico

e systematico de todas as disposições contenidas na constituição politica do imperio e no acto addicional. Rio de Janeiro 1863. pp.106. [400.]

DEODATO C[ESINA] VILELLA DOS SANTOS, Catálogo da exposição de trabalhos juridicos realizada pelo Instituto da ordem dos avogados brazileiros. Rio de Janeiro 1894. pp.viii.223. [970.]

INDICE da colleção de ordens régias, 1719–1807. Archivo publico nacional: Publicações (vol.v): Rio de Janeiro 1906. pp.[v].212. [5000.]

EDWIN M. BORCHARD, Guide to the law and legal literature of Argentina, Brazil and Chile. Library of Congress: Washington 1917. pp.523. [2000.]

JOSÉ TAVARES BASTOS, Repertorio das decisões do Supremo tribunal federal 1896–1910. Rio-de-Janeiro [1918]. pp.469+469. [3300.]

INDEX alfabetico das leys, alvarás, cartas régias, decretos, e mais órdens que há no archivo da Provedoria da fazenda real. Archivo nacional: Publicações (vol.xxi): Rio de Janeiro 1923. pp.354. [2000.]

[JEAN LOUIS MARIE] EGGEN VAN TERLAN, Eine brasilianische juristische bibliothek. [Berlin *c.*1928]. ff.4. [150.]

JOÃO ALVES DE MOURA, Indice alfabetico de legislação e jurisprudencia administrativas. Rio de Janeiro.

1939. pp.264. [5000.]
1945. pp.[iv].829. [12,000.]
there were probably other issues.

BIBLIOGRAFIA das obras jurídicas publicadas no Brasil. Rio de Janeiro.

i. 1951. pp.107. [1500.]
in progress.

BIBLIOGRAFIA brasileira de direito constitucional. Primeiras pesquisas. Coleção de estudos juridicos: [Rio de Janeiro] 1956. pp.xv.137. [943.]

British Columbia.

J. EDWARD BIRD, The digest of British Columbia case law, 1849–1904. Toronto 1906. pp.xlvi. coll.848.pp.849–971. [2500.]

Brittany.

[L. P. ABEILLE], Table raisonnée des ordonnances, édits, déclarations et lettres patentes du roi enregistrés au parlement de Bretagne. Rennes 1757. pp.xxxiii.187.70.4. [large number.]

Bulgaria.

IVAN SIPKOV, Legal sources and bibliography of Bulgaria. Praeger publications in russian history and world communism (no.18): New York [1956]. pp.[xv].199. [1000.]

ABSTRACTS of bulgarian scientific literature. 3. Economics and law. Sofia 1958 &c.*

details of this work are entered under Economics, below.

Burma.

THE BURMA laws list: a list of unrepealed statutes, acts, and regulations and rules and notifications thereunder in force in Burma. Fourth edition. Rangoon 1892. pp.[ii].vii.503.xxix.7. [2500.]

— Fifth edition. 1897. pp.viii.336.64.xxiv. [2500.]

many pages are blank.

N. C. DATTA [NAGENDRA-CHANDRA DATTA], Index of Burma cases judicially noticed. Rangoon 1909. pp.[xi].151.23. [1500.]

T. Z. OUNG [AUNG], A digest of Burma rulings of the courts of the Judicial commissioners, upper and lower Burma, and the Chief court, lower

Burma, from 1872–1908. Rangoon 1912. ff.viii. pp.ix–xxxiv.coll.662. [2000.]

S. S. HALKAR [SUBBARĀU ṢESHAGIRI HĀLKAR], A digest of civil rulings of Burma, including cases reported in . . . reports . . . 1872 . . . to 1917 . . . Second edition. Rangoon [printed] 1918.

S. S. HALKAR [SUBBARĀU ṢESHAGIRI HĀLKAR], A digest of criminal rulings of Burma, including cases reported in all official and non-official reports (1872 to 1925). . . . Second edition. Mylapore [printed] 1926. pp.[iii].32.coll.588.v. [3000.]

California.

E. B. CROCKER, California digest; being a digest of the decisions of the Supreme court of the state of California. Sacramento 1856. pp.[iii].243. [3500.]

CHARLES H. PARKER, Digest of California reports and statutes, from the organization of the state to the present time. San Francisco 1869. pp.[ii]. xxvi.669+675. [15,000.]

INDEX of opinions of the attorney general of the state of California. Sacramento 1940 &c.

CALIFORNIA special legislative committees and their reports, a survey and index 1937–1947. California legislature: [Sacramento] 1949. pp.48. [326.]

— [another edition]. Chronological list of California legislative interim committees and their reports, 1937–1953. 1953. pp.88. [552.]

— — [supplement]. California interim legislative committees and reports, 1953–1955. [1955]. pp.37. [144.]

Canada.

i. *Statute law*

a. *General*

LISTE des lois expirantes. Assemblée législative: Quebec 1854. pp.24. [150.]

LAWS and ordinances.—Canada. [Colonial office (no.2 of a series of lists of works in the library): 1860]. pp.5. [50.]

JOHN WEBSTER HANCOCK, A synoptical index of the consolidated statutes of Canada and Upper Canada. Toronto 1865. pp.479. [20,000.]

JOHN S. EWART, Ewart's Index of the statutes; being an alphabetical index of all the public statutes passed by the legislatures of the late province of Canada, the dominion of Canada, and the province of Ontario, subsequent to the consolidation, and down to, and inclusive of, the year 1871. Toronto 1872. pp.[ii].158. [4500.]

— — Second edition. 1874. pp.[ii].191. [6000.]

— — — [supplement]. 1878. pp.[iii].99. [3000.]

J[OSEPH] F[ÉRÉOL] DUBREUIL, The reference book. Being a detailed index of all public and private statutes and orders in council contained therein passed by the canadian parliament and by the legislatures of the several canadian provinces ... down to ... 1887. Second edition. Montreal 1888. pp.viii.409. [8000.]

HARRIS H[ARDING] BLIGH and WALTER TODD, The dominion law index, embracing all the legislation of the Dominion parliament; and such unrepealed provincial enactments, and imperial statutes, treaties and orders as bear a special relation to Canada down to and including the year 1890. Toronto 1891. pp.176. [5000.]

—— Third edition . . . [1867–1914]. By H. H. Bligh. 1915. pp.439. [12,500.]

CHECK list of the statutes of the dominion of Canada, the provinces, the earlier legislatures and Newfoundland. [Toronto 1909]. pp.52. [1500.]

A. MCNAUGHTON STEWART, Index to dominion and provincial statutes from the earliest period down to 1st July, 1909. Montreal 1910. pp.[ii].4.745. [15,000.]

—— down to 1916. 1918. pp.3–1013. [50,000.]

MAURICE OLLIVIER, Index, local and private acts, dominion of Canada, 1867–1941. Followed by a table of public statutes 1907 to 1942, showing all the chapters of the revised statutes, 1927, with amendments thereto, and certain public acts and amendments thereto from 1907 to 1942. Ottawa 1942. pp.146. [9000.]

C. R. BROWN, P. A. MAXWELL and L. F. MAXWELL, A legal bibliography of the British Commonwealth of nations. Second edition. Volume 3. Canadian and british-american colonial law from the earliest times. 1957. pp.x.220. [3000.]

b. *Parts of Canada*

New France

PIERRE GEORGES ROY, Inventaire des ordonnances des intendants de la Nouvelle-France. Archives de la province de Québec: Beauceville 1919. pp.[iii]. vii.296+[v].304+[v].296+[v].242. [5000.]

Lower Canada

A COMPLETE index to the ordinances and statutes of Lower-Canada, to the 57th year of George the Third. Quebec 1817. pp.[193]. [2500.]

— A continuation . . . from 7th Geo. IV. to 2d Will. IV. 1832. pp.[164]. [2500.]

G[USTAVUS] W[ILLIAM] WICKSTEED, Index to the statutes in force in Lower Canada, at the end of the session of 1856. Toronto 1857. pp.xv.506. [12,500.]

G. W. WICKSTEED, Table of the provincial statutes and ordinances in force or which have been in force in Lower Canada . . . with a continuation of the index to the statutes in force. Toronto 1857. pp.iv.184. [2500.]

— — [another edition]. Table des statuts provinciaux [&c.]. 1857. pp.iv.200. [2500.]

North-West Territory

C. C. MCCAUL and HORACE HARVEY, Ready reference guide to the ordinances of the North-West Territories. Toronto 1896. pp.[v].54. [1000.]

Upper Canada

G. W. WICKSTEAD, Index to the statutes in force in Upper Canada, at the end of the session of 1854–5. Toronto 1856. pp.vii.419. [10,000.]

G. W. WICKSTEED, Table of the provincial statutes in force or which have been in force in upper Canada . . . with a continuation of the index to the statutes in force. Toronto 1856. pp.iv.147. [2000.]

ii. *Case law*

C. W. COOPER, Digest of reports of cases decided in the Court of chancery, in the Court of error & appeal, on appeal from the Court of chancery, and in chancery chambers, from the establishment of the court in Upper Canada to the present time. Toronto 1868. pp.748. [3500.]

—— Supplement. 1873. pp.xxxiv.415. [2000.]

[JEAN BAPTISTE] ALPHONSE LUSIGNAN, Jurisprudence canadienne. Index analytique des décisions judiciaires rapportées de 1864 à 1871. Montréal 1872. pp.[ii].307. [1608.]

THE CANADIAN law times. Notes of cases and index-digest. Toronto.

xiii. 1893. Edited by E. Douglas Armour and E[dward] B. Brown. pp.xi.561. [700.]
xiv. 1894. pp.xii.634. [800.]
xv. 1895. pp.xi.530. [700.]
xvi. 1896. pp.x.517. [700.]
xvii. 1897. pp.x.536. [700.]
xviii. 1898. pp.xii.556. 800.]
xix. 1899. pp.x.510. [700.]

[*continued as:*]

The Canadian law times annual digest of canadian cases reported and noted during the year.

1900. Edited by E. B. Brown. pp.[iii].coll. xlviii.500. [1000.]
1901. pp.[iii].coll.lxiv.640. [1000.]
1902. pp.[iii].coll.xlviii.514. [1250.]
1903. pp.[iv].coll.xliv.472. [1250.]
1904. pp.[iv].coll.lviii.520. [1250.]
1905. pp.[iii].coll.lii.538. [1500.]
1906. pp.[iii].coll.lv.606. [2000.]
1907. pp.[iii].coll.lxxviii.708. [2500.]
1908. pp.[iii].coll.lxxii.652. [2000.]

earlier issues formed part of the main work.

ROBERT CASSELS, A digest of cases determined by the Sypreme court of Canada from the organization of the court, in 1875, to the 1st day of May, 1893. Toronto 1893. pp.[iv].949. [1500.]

—— 1893–1898. By Louis William Coutlée. 1899. pp.[ii].viii.317. [1000.]

—— 1875–1903. 1904. pp.[ii].xiv.coll.1568. pp.1569–1670. [3000.]

THE CANADIAN annual digest. Toronto.

1896. By Charles H. Masters and Charles Morse. pp.xxxix.coll.372. [1250.]
1897. pp.xxxvi.coll.398. [1250.]
1898. pp.xxxvi.coll.476. [1500.]
1899. pp.xxvi.coll.468. [1500.]
1900. pp.xix.coll.406. [1250.]
1901. pp.xxvi.coll.498. [1500.]
1902. pp.xx.coll.484. [1500.]
1903. pp.xix.coll.402. [1250.]
1904. pp.xx.coll.376. [1250.]
1905. pp.xxi.coll.432. [1250.]
1906. pp.xx.coll.406. [1250.]
1907. pp.xx.coll.360. [1250.]
1908. pp.xxii.coll.432. [1250.]
1909. pp.xxii.coll.426. [1250.]
1910. pp.xxvi.coll.644. [1500.]
1911. pp.xliii.coll.1052. [2000.]
1912. pp.lxii.coll.1228. [2250.]
1913. pp.xlii.coll.980. [2500.]
1914. pp.xl.coll.824.pp.iv. [2500.]

1915. pp.liv.coll.740. [2250.]
1916. pp.xlviii.coll.632. [2000.]
1917. pp.lix.coll.654. [2000.]
1918. pp.liii.coll.618. [2000.]
1919. pp.l.coll.626. [2000.]
1920. pp.l.coll.690. [2000.]
1921. pp.lvi.coll.746. [2000.]

GEORGE SMITH HOLMESTED, Index of cases relating to the British North America act, the Revised statutes of Canada, (1886) and all subsequent public acts of Canada and . . . of Ontario. Toronto 1903. pp.xlii.318. [6000.]

W. J. TREMEEAR, The canadian ten-year digest, 1901 to 1910 . . . Vol.1 . . . a to l. Toronto &c. 1911. pp.[v].coll.2302. [6000.]
no more published.

EDWARD ROBERT CAMERON, Index of canadian cases judicially noticed . . . in the . . . provincial courts and the Supreme and Exchequer courts of Canada, as well as of the Judicial committee of the Privy council, from the earliest times down to . . . 1910. Toronto 1912. pp.[viii].979. [35,000.]

DIGEST. Canadian case law. Toronto.
1900–1911. By Walter E. Lear. pp.[iii].coll.

2020 + pp.[iii].coll.2021–3804 + pp.[iii]. coll.3805–5300. [20,000.]

1911–1914. pp.lviii.coll.2596. [7500.]

1914–1915. pp.xv.coll.684. [2500.]

1915–1916. pp.xxiv.coll.656. [3500.]

1916–1917. By Esten K. Williams. With which is incorporated The Quebec annual digest, by E. Fabre Surveyer. pp.xx.coll. 564. [2500.]

1918–1919. pp.xxvi.coll.804. [2373.]

1919–1920. pp.xxiv.coll.658. [1944.]

1920–1921. pp.xxiv.coll.640. [1893.]

no more published.

CANADIAN encyclopedic digest (western edition), being a complete digest . . . of all reported decisions in Alberta-British Columbia-Manitoba and Saskatchewan from the earliest time down to date, together with the decisions on appeal therefrom and with certain further references to leading cases in the Privy council and in the Supreme court of Canada. Calgary.

i. Abduction-conditional. General editors: W. J. Tremeear, W. Kent Power. 1919. pp.cxxxi.758. [5000.]

ii. Conflict-crown. 1920. pp.cxxvii.707. [5000.]

iii. Damages-executors. 1920. pp.cxl.725. [5000.]

— First supplement . . . covering vols. 1, 2 and 3. By W. J. Tremeear. 1921. pp.xix. 250. [1500.]

iv. Exemptions-injunctions. 1921. pp.cxxxii. 750. [5000.]

v. Insolvency-mechanics. 1922. pp.cl.824. [6000.]

— Permanent supplement, vols. 1 to 5. By W. J. Tremeear. 1923. pp.xli.524. [4000.]

vi. Medicine-prize. 1923. pp.clii.816. [6000.]

vii. Professions-wounding. 1925. pp. ccxxxix.1004. [7500.]

— Second permanent supplement, vols. 1 to 7. By W. J. Tremeear. 1926. pp.li.462. [5000.]

1927. pp.xv.224. [2500.]

1928. pp.xviii.266. [3000.]

1929. pp.xvii.238. [2500.]

1930. pp.xix.246. [2500.]

1926–1931. By W. K. Power and I. K. Stevens. pp.lxxxii.631. [10,000.]

1932. pp.xvi.189. [2000.]

1933. pp.xvi.200. [2000.]

1934. pp.xiv.184. [2000.]

1935. pp.xiii.172. [2000.]
1936. pp.xiii.164. [1750.]
1937. pp.xv.180. [1800.]
1938. pp.xv.174. [1750.]
1939. pp.xv.176. [1750.]
1940. pp.xiv.164. [1750.]
1941. By Stuart J. Shaw. pp.xlv[*sic* xiv].158. [1500.]
1942. By W. K. Power. pp.xiv.152. [1500.]
1943. pp.xiv.172. [1750.]
1944. pp.xiii.160. [1750.]
1945. pp.xiii.149. [1750.]
1946. pp.xv.168. [1750.]
1947. pp.xvi.196. [2000.]
1948. pp.xvii.188. [2000.]
1949. pp.xvi.200. [2000.]
1950. pp.xvi.207. [2000.]
1951. pp.xv.216. [2000.]
1952. pp.xvii.204. [2000.]
1953. pp.xix.226. [2300.]
1954. pp.xxi.239. [2400.]
1955. pp.xix.236. [2400.]
1956. pp.xxi.240. [2500.]
1957. pp.xxiii.247. [2600.]
1958. pp.xxx.287. [3000.]
1959. pp.xli.315. [3200.]
1960. pp.xlvii.333. [3500.]

1961. pp.lv.364. [3800.]
1962. pp.lxi.432. [4500.]
in progress.

W. KENT POWER, An index-digest of western practice cases in civil actions. Calgary 1921. pp.xxxix.369. [5000.]

PIERRE GEORGES ROY, Inventaire des procès-verbaux des grands voyers. Archives de la province de Québec: Beauceville.

i. [1667–1803]. 1923. pp.3–304. [1250.]
ii. [1803–1841; ville de Québec 1667–1767]. 1923. pp.3–251. [1250.]
iii. [Montréal 1764–1841; Trois-Rivières 1708–1841; miscellaneous]. 1930. pp.[v]. 297. [1500.]
iv. [miscellaneous]. 1930. pp.[iii].293. [1250.]
v. [miscellaneous]. 1931. pp.312. [1250.]
vi. [index]. 1932. pp.[iii].303.

THE CANADIAN abridgment. A digest of decisions of the provincial and dominion courts, including appeals therefrom to the Privy council, but excluding decisions based on the Quebec civil code. From the earliest time to date [*afterwards:* to the end of 1935]. [Edited by Frederick Clyde Auld]. Toronto &c.

i. Absentee to agency. 1935. pp.xxxviii.coll. 1238. [2500.]

ii. Aliens to auditors. 1935. pp.xxxi.coll.1218. [2500.]

iii. Bailment to bankruptcy. 1935. pp.xxxv. coll.1392. [3000.]

iv. Banks and banking to barristers and solicitors. 1936. pp.xxvii.coll.1176. [2500.]

v. Bastards to boundaries. 1936. pp.xxxi.coll. 1308. [2500.]

vi. Building contracts to cemeteries. 1936. pp.xxiv.coll.1120. [2000.]

vii. Certiorari to chattel mortgages and bills of sale. 1936. pp.xxiv.coll.1108. [2000.]

viii–ix. Choses in action to companies and corporations. 1937. pp.xv.coll.1320+pp. xlii.coll.1036. [5000.]

x. Compensation to conspiracy. 1937. pp. xxix.coll.1170. [2000.]

xi. Constitutional law to contracts. 1937. pp. xxxviii.coll.1614. [3000.]

xii. Conversion to costs. 1938. pp.xxxiv.coll. 1194. [2000.]

xiii. Criminal law. 1938. pp.lx.coll.1760. [4500.]

xiv. Courts to crown. 1938. pp.xxxi.coll.988. [2000.]

xv. Damages to devolution of estates. 1938. pp.xxx.coll.1024. [2000.]

xvi. Discovery to drainage. 1939. pp.xxix. coll.1256 [2500.]

xvii. Easement to estoppel. 1939. pp.xxxiii. coll.1030. [2000.]

xviii. Evidence. 1939. pp.xliii.coll.1476. [3000.]

xix. Executions to executors and administrators. 1940. pp.xlvi.coll.1306. [2500.]

xx. Extradition to gaming. 1940. pp.xxxiii. coll.1186. [2000.]

xxi. Garnishment to highways. 1940. pp. xxxviii.coll.1308. [2500.]

xxii. Homesteads to injunctions. 1940. pp. xxxv.coll.1022. [2000.]

xxiii. Insurance. 1941. pp.lv.coll.1440. [3000.]

xxiv.

xxv. Judicial sales to limitation of actions. 1941. pp.xxxvii.coll.1206. [2500.]

xxvi. Lis pendens to military and naval law. 1941. pp.xxxii.coll.1014. [2000.]

xxvii. Mines and minerals to mortgages. 1942. pp.xxxvi.coll.1412. [3000.]

xxviii. Motor vehicles to nuisance. 1942. pp. xxxv.coll.1104. [2000.]

xxix. Negligence to patents of inventions.

1942. pp.xxxvi.coll.1118. [2500.]

xxx. Penalties and forfeitures to radio. 1942. pp.xlii.coll.1182. [2500.]

xxxi. Railways to revenue. 1943. pp.xxxviii. coll.992. [2000.]

xxxii. Sale of goods to sheriffs and bailiffs. 1943. pp.xl.coll.1298. [3000.]

xxxiii. Shipping to taxation (dominion and provincial). 1944. pp.xliii.coll.1210. [2500.]

xxxiv. Taxation (municipal) to trials. 1945. pp.xliv.coll.1284. [3000.]

xxv. Trusts and trustees to workmen's compensation. 1946. pp.xlvi.coll.1216. [2500.]

— The canadian abridgment annual. . . . A digest of all decisions reported in Canada . . . and appeals to the Privy council.

1936. pp.xxii.coll.1210.pp.1213–1248. [2500.]

1937. pp.xxiv.coll.988.pp.989–1025.coll. 1027–1148. [2000.]

1938. pp.xxvi.coll.1128.pp.1129–1164.coll. 1165–1284. [2250.]

1939. pp.xxvii.coll.1350.pp.1353–1396.coll. 1397–1534. [2750.]

1940. pp.xxvii.coll.854.pp.857–893.coll.895–986. [1750.]

1941. pp.xxvi.coll.926.pp.927–963.coll.965–1066. [2000.]

1942. pp.xxvii.coll.980.pp.981–1017.coll. 1019–1116. [2000.]

1943. pp.xxvi.coll.1002.pp.1003–1035.coll. 1037–1134. [2000.]

1944. pp.xxvi.coll.944.pp.945–982.coll.983–1080. [2000.]

1945. pp.xxvi.coll.948.pp.949–994.coll.995–1090. [2000.]

1946. pp.xxvii.coll.792.pp.793–826.coll.827–874. [1750.]

— The Canadian abridgment table of cases, including the abridgment consolidation (1936–1945). 1949. pp.544+[iii].545–1024. [75,000.]

1947. pp.xxix.coll.906. [1750.]

1948. pp.xxviii.coll.750. [1500.]

1949. pp.xxv.coll.816. [1500.]

1950. pp.xxvii.coll.888. [1500.]

1951. pp.xxviii.coll.928. [1750.]

1952. pp.26.coll.932. [1750.]

1953. pp.xxvii.coll.976. [1750.]

1954. pp.xxv.coll.1050. [2000.]

1955. pp.xxxi.coll.1046. [2000.]

1956. pp.xxx.coll.1010. [2000.]

1957. pp.xxx.coll.1006. [2000.]

1958. pp.xxxii.coll.1038. [2000.]

1959. pp.xxxii.coll.876. [2000.]

1960. pp.xxx.pp.[379]. [1780.]
1961. pp.xxx.pp.[341].96. [1644.]
1962. pp.xxxi.[363].106. [1710.]
1963. pp.xxx.[327].114. [1563.]

in progress; the volumes from 1961 contain cumulative indexes from 1956 inclusive.

Canary islands.

LUCIEN WOLF, Jews in the Canary islands. Being a calendar of jewish cases extracted from the records of the canariote inquisition in the collection of the marquess of Bute. Jewish historical society of England: 1926. pp.xliii.274. [750.]

Cape of Good Hope.

JAMES BUCHANAN [vols.ii–iii: EBEN J. BUCHANAN], Index and digest of cases decided in the Supreme court of the Cape of Good Hope, as reported by the late hon. William Menzies [vol. ii–iii: and revised . . . by James Buchanan]. Cape Town 1877. pp.88+82+79. [3000.]

apparently covers the period 1828–1850.

M[ALCOLM] W[ILLIAM] SEARLE, Digest of reported cases in the Courts of the Cape of Good Hope, from 1850. Cape Town 1885. pp.xxviii.94. [2750.]

— — Consolidated digest of reported cases in the courts of the Cape colony to the end of 1895. . . . Compiled by M. W. Searle . . . and Howel Jones. 1902. pp.lxxxi.276. [5000.]

ERNEST EDWARD WEBB, A digest of decisions and dicta in civil cases heard in the Supreme court, Cape Colony, from 1850 to 1900 inclusive. East London 1907[–1909]. pp.x.coll.1388.coll.lvi. [4000.]

Carinthia.

FRANZ STARR, Vollständiges sach- und nachschlage-register zu sämmtlichen landesgesetzblättern der im Reichrathe vertretenen königreiche und länder von deren beginn 1849 bis zum jahre 1873. . . . Zweiter theil. Steiermark, Kärnthen und Krain. Wien 1873. pp.[iii].288. [4000.]

Carniola.

FRANZ STARR, Vollständiges sach- und nachschlage-register zu sämmtlichen landesgesetzblättern der im Reichsrathe vertretenen königreiche und länder von deren beginn 1849 bis zum jahre 1873. . . . Zweiter theil. Steiermark, Kärnthen und Krain. 1873. pp.[iii].288. [4000.]

Carolina, North.

THOMAS B[ROWN] WOMACK, Womack's North Carolina digest. A complete civil digest of the reports of the Supreme court of North Carolina from 1866 to 1891 [to 1905], inclusive, and a digest of cited cases prior to that time. Raleigh 1891–1906.

—— Analytical index to volumes I and II . . . by T. B. Womack [or rather, by Thomas Henry Calvert]. 1902. pp.323.

Carolina, South.

WILLIAM RICE, A digest index of the statute law of South-Carolina, from the earliest period to the year 1836, inclusive. Charleston 1838. pp.xix.396. [8000.]

WILLIAM RICE, A digest of the cases decided in the superior courts of law in the state of South-Carolina, from the earliest period to the present time. Charleston 1838–1839. pp.xx.404+xi.425+xvii.396. [15,000.]

SARAH E. LEVERETTE and CHARLES E. LEE, A check-list of S. C. session laws. Columbia 1963. ff.[i].35. [250.]*

Catalonia.

G. M. DE BROCÁ, Taula de les stampaçions de les constituçions y altres drets de Cathalunya y de les costumes y ordinaçions de sos diverses paratges. Barcelona 1907. pp.145. [243.]

JOAQUÍN DE CAMPS Y ARBOIX, Bibliografía del derecho catalán moderno. Barcelona [1956]. pp. 119. [900.]

Central Provinces.

VAMAN VASUDEO CHITALE [VĀMANA VĀSUDEVA CHIṬALE] and MAHADEO SITARAM MUNDLE [MAHĀDEVA SĪTĀRĀMA MUNḌḶE], Chitale and Mundle's digest of C. P. & Berar case-law, 1862–1920 March. Triplicane [printed] 1920. pp.[ii].4.coll. 1148.118. [4641.]

N. B. CHANDURKAR [CHANDRA-KARA], The Triennial digest of Central Provinces & Berar case law & Privy council & federal court cases 1936. 1937 & 1938. Nagpur 1939. pp.xxvii.coll.622. [2000.]

Ceylon.

JOSEPH MARTINUS PERERA, A collection of select decisions of the Supreme court on points of kandyan law. . . . Vol.II [of Perera's edition of J. Armour's translation of Nīti-nighaṇḍuva]. Colombo 1892. pp.xviii.338. [1500.]

B. P. DE S. BASNAYEKE SAMARASINHA, A numerical and an alphabetical list of the legislative enactments of Ceylon. Colombo 1893. pp.[iii].v.111. [1000.]

interleaved.

[EDWARD BEAUMONT FRASER SUETER], Index and epitome of government minutes and circulars issued from 1896 to 1905. Colombo 1907. pp.[ii]. 58. [1500.]

E. B. F. SUETER, Index to proclamations and notifications under ordinances, published in the "Ceylon government gazette" from 1860 to 1908. Colombo 1909. pp.[iii].76. [3500.]

A DIGEST of Ceylan cases reported. Jaffna [Colombo].

1820–1914. By S. Rajaratnam. [1919]. pp. [vi].1901. [12,500.]

1914–1936.

1936–1940. By V. S. Sivagurunathan. pp.[ii]. coll.2417–2624. [1000.]

S. GUNAWARDANA, Index to papers and sessional papers laid before the Legislative council of Ceylon from 1855 to July 1931, and before the State council of Ceylon from July 1931, to end of 1933. Colombo 1934. pp.53. [2500.]

K. BALASINGHAM, Corpus juris. A digest of statute law, common law and case law of Ceylon. Colombo [printed] [1947]. pp.iii.coll.320. [500.]

Channel islands.

THE DU PARCQ library of Channel islands law. University of London: Institute of advanced legal studies: 1950 &c.*
an accessions list; in progress.

Chile.

JOSÉ SANTOS LIRA SMITH, Índice de decretos i leyes del Ministerio de relaciones esteriores, culto i colonización, 1897 a 1903. Santiago de Chile 1905. pp.731. [1000.]

EDWIN M. BORCHARD, Guide to the law and legal literature of Argentina, Brazil and Chile. Library of Congress: Washington 1917. pp.523. [2000.]

HELEN L[ORD] CLAGETT, A guide to the law and legal literature of Chile, 1917–1946. Library of

Congress: Latin american series (no.28): Washington 1947. pp.viii.103. [750.]

Colombia.

COLOMBIA. American foreign law association: Bibliographies of foreign laws series (no.1): [New York] 1926. pp.18. [150.]

RICHARD C[ECIL] BACKUS and PHANOR J[AMES] EDER, A guide to the law and legal literature of Colombia. Library of Congress: Latin american series (no.4): Washington 1943. pp.vii. 222. [500.]
a supplement by R. C. Backus appears in the Tulane law review *(New Orleans 1946), xx.392–410.*

Congo.

TH[ÉODORE] HEYSE, Bibliographie juridique du Congo belge et du Ruanda-Urundi, "droit et administration". Tableau d'assemblage. Bruxelles 1953. pp.12. [150.]

Connecticut.

HENRY DUTTON, The Connecticut digest, comprising all the decisions in Kirby's . . . Root's . . . Day's . . . and the . . . Connecticut reports. New Haven 1833. pp.viii.553. [3000.]

Laws by Places

THOMAS DAY, A digest of the reported cases, decided by the Supreme court of errors of the state of Connecticut, from 1786 to 1838. Hartford 1840. pp.xi 507. [4000.]

THOMAS W. WATERMAN, A digest of the reported decisions of the Superior court, and of the Supreme court of errors, of the state of Connecticut. New York 1858. pp.xc.884. [5000.]

SIMEON E. BALDWIN, A digest of all the reported cases decided in the Supreme court of errors and the Superior court of the state of Connecticut, and in the United States courts for the district of Connecticut. Boston 1871. pp.lxxxiii.694. [7500.]

ALBERT CARLOS BATES, Connecticut statute laws. A bibliographical list . . . from the earliest issues to 1836. Acorn club, Connecticut (publication no.3): Hartford 1900. pp.[ix].120. [494.]

SELECT list of references on the "blue laws" of Connecticut. Library of Congress: Washington 1908. ff.4. [14.]*

FREDERICK L. PERRY, A general index to the private laws and special acts of the state of Connecticut. Rockville, Conn. [printed] 1922. pp.266. [15,000.]

RICHARD H. PHILLIPS, Index-digest of the Connecticut reports, volumes 107, 108, 109 and 110. Washington 1930. pp.vii.127. [4500.]

[JOHN HAMILTON KING], Index to the general statutes of Connecticut, revision of 1930. Orange, Conn. [printed] [1932]. pp.iii.2041–2515.lx. [50,000.]

Costa Rica.

LUIS DOBLES SEGREDA, Índice bibliográfico de Costa Rica. San José.

vii. Política y derecho desde 1831 hasta 1921. 1935. pp.xxiv.444. [306.]

viii. Política y derecho 1921 hasta 1935. Catálogo de abogados. Milicia. 1936. pp.[vii]. 525. [201.]

FABIO SOLÓRZANO CALVO, Índice alfabético de leyes y acuerdos del poder legislativo. Congreso constitucional: San José de Costa Rica 1947. pp. 215. [3000.]

Côte d'Or.

L. GREY and J. CHAPUSOT, Répertoire à l'usage des maires, adjoints, conseillers municipaux et secrétaires de mairies du département de la Côte-d'Or, ou table alphabétique et raisonné des matières contenues dans le Recueil des actes administratifs ... de 1819 à 1885. Dijon 1885. pp.iv.107. [1000.]

Cracow.

FRANZ STARR, Vollständiges sach- und nachschlage-register zu sämmtlichen landesgesetzblättern der im Reichsrathe vertretenen königreiche und länder von deren beginn 1849 bis zum jahre 1873. . . . Fünfter theil. Galizien, Krakau und die Bukowina. Wien 1874. pp.[iii].268. [4000.]

Cuba.

CRAWFORD M[ORRISON] BISHOP and ANYDA MARCHANT, A guide to the law and legal literature of Cuba, the Dominican republic and Haiti. Library of Congress: Latin american series (no.3): Washington 1944. pp.ix.276. [Cuba: 750.]

Curaçao.

[THOMAS W. PALMER and S. G. C. VAN DER VEEN ZEPPENFELDT], The law and legal literature of Curaçao. American foreign law association: Bibliographies of foreign law series (no.10): New York 1934. pp.42. [100.]

Cyprus.

INDEX to the statute law of Cyprus since the english occupation, including all ordinances and laws and orders of the queen or king in council passed or made since the 12th of July, 1878, which were in force on the 1st of January, 1903. 1903. pp.40. [2000.]

BENJAMIN DICKINSON, A list of the orders of his majesty in council, and the subsidiary legislation thereunder, the local orders of his excellency the Governor in council, the orders of his excellency the Governor made under powers conferred by local legislation, and notifications made with the authority of the government of Cyprus, which are of a non-recurring character. Nicosia 1929. pp.[ii]. 32. [1000.]

— — [another edition], A list of laws enacted between 1st January 1924, and 31st December 1932, and a list of the orders [&c.]. Compiled by M. Shemri. 1933. pp.[iii].46. [2500.]

— — — 1924–1936. 1937. pp.[iii].74. [4000.]

Czechoslovakia.

ALPHABETISCHER index der normen die der verlag Gebrüder Stiepel . . . in den sammlungen Stiepels Gesetzsammlung des tschechoslowakischen staates and Stiepels textausgaben tsechoslowakischer gesetze herausgegeben hat. Reichenberg 1929. pp.87. [2000.]

[ZDENĚK MADAR and JAROSLAV MORÁVEK] Bibliography of czechoslovak legal literature 1945–1958, Czechoslovak academy of sciences: Institut of law: Prague 1959. pp.263. [1500.]

Dalmatia.

FRANZ STARR, Vollständiges sach- und nachschlage-register zu sämmtlichen landesgesetzblättern der im Reichsrathe vertretenen königreiche und länder von deren beginn 1849 bis zum jahre 1873. . . . Vierter theil. Tirol-Vorarlberg, Küstenland und Dalmatien. Wien 1874. pp.[iii]. 428. [6000.]

Denmark.

JACOB HENRIC SCHOU, Chronologisk register over de kongelige forordninger og aabne breve, som fra aar 1670 til 1775 [–1813] aars udgang ere udkomme, tilligemed et nøiagtigt udtog af de endnu gieldende, for saavidt samme i almindelighed angaae undersaatterne i Danmark og Norge. Kiøbenhavn.

i. Som indeholder Kong Christian v. Forordninger. 1777. pp.xxiv.452. [1000.]
ii. Friderich iv. 1777. pp.[ii].472. [1000.]
iii. Christian vi. 1777. pp.[ii].544. [1000.]
iv. Friderich v. 1777. pp.[ii].560. [1000.]
v. Christian vii. 1777. pp.[ii].400. [1000.]
vi. 1776–1777. 1778. pp.[ii].284. [500.]
— Alphabetisk register . . . 1670 til 1777. 1778. pp.[ii].251.
vii. 1778–1779. 1780. pp.[iv].403. [200.]
viii. 1780–1783. 1784. pp.[ii].577. [400.]
ix. 1784–1787. 1783. pp.[ii].518. [400.]
x. 1788–1792. 1793. pp.[ii].761. [500.]
— Anhang . . . 1–x deel. 1795. pp.xvii.282 + [iii].72 + [iii].70 + [iii].120 + [iii].212. [2500.]

contains additions and extracts.

xi. 1793–1796. 1797. pp.[ii].492. [300.]
xii. 1797–1799. 1800. pp.801. [400.]
xiii. 1800–1803. 1804. pp.760. [500.]
xiv. 1804–1808. 1808. pp.914. [600.]
xv. 1808–1811. 1812. pp.866. [600.]
xvi. 1812–1813. 1813–1814. pp.231+233–526. [500.]

C. P. N. PETERSEN, Lovlexicon, eller alphabetisk repertorium over den danske lovgivning og de dertil henhørende offentlige actstykker. Kjøbenhavn 1837–1842. pp.xv.v.648+[ii].vi.438+[ii].x. 754 + [ii].xiii.670 + [ii].xvi.926 + [iii].xii.205. [40,000.]

— — Syvende bind [1842–1850]. 1851. pp.xx. 453. [5000.]

— — Ottende bynd. 1851–1860. 1860. pp.[vii]. 568.xvi. [6000.]

— — Niende bind. 1860–1863. 1864. pp.xxi. 398. [4000.]

— — Tiende bind. 1863–1867. 1867. pp.xix. 277. [3000.]

— — Ellevte bind. 1867–1870. 1870. pp.xvii. 281. [3000.]

A[NDREAS] AAGESEN, Fortegnelse over retssamlinger, retsliteratur m.m. i Danmark, Norge, Sverig og til dels Finland. Kjøbenhavn 1876. pp.[vii].167. [3000.]

REALREGISTER over love og reskripter m.m. Kjøbenhavn.

[i–ii]. 1660–1892. Udgivet af Oskar Damkier og Fr. Kretz. [1893–]1894–1895. pp.[ii]. iii.882+[ii].842. [17,500.]

iii. 1893–1896. 1898. pp.xx.230. [2500.]
iv. 1897–1903. 1904. pp.[iii].vii.374. [4000.]
[*continued as:*]

Hovedregister til love ob anordninger, offentlige kundgøreleser, ministerielle cirkulærer og skrivelser m.m.

v. 1904–1911. Ved O. Damkier, F. Kretz og W. Oxholm. 1912. pp.xii.524. [6000.]
vi. 1911–1919. Udgiven efter Indenrigsministeriets foranstaltning. 1931. pp.[ii].xiii.860. [10,000.]
vii. 1920–1930. 1934. pp.xvi.861+xiv.863–1644. [20,000.]

in progress?

DANSK lovregister. København 1935 &c.
in progress?

TORBEN LUND, Den danske retslitteratur 1950–1955. København 1956. pp.94. [1000.]

East Indies.

W. N. VERLEGH, Algemeen alphabetisch register op de verzameling der algemeene orders voor het leger in nederlandsch Indie . . . 1830–1868. Zaltbommel 1869. pp.[iv].107. [2000.]
interleaved.

REALIA. Register op de generale resolutiën van het kasteel Batavia, 1632–1805. Bataviaasch genootschap van kunsten en wetenschappen: Leiden [vols.ii–iii: 's-Hage] 1882–1886. pp.[iii].ii.504+[iii].285+[iii].406. [50,000.]

JOHAN DUPARC, Verzameling van nederlandsch-indische rechtspraak en rechtsliteratuur, 1898–1907. 's-Gravenhage 1909. pp.779.

— — [supplements.]

i. 1908–1909. pp.169.

ii. 1909–1919. Door A. S. Hirsch.

iii. 1920–1924. Door Joh. Paulus.

iv. 1925–1929. pp.176.

Ecuador.

HELEN L[ORD] CLAGETT, A guide to the law and legal literature of Ecuador. Library of Congress: Latin american series (no.18): Washington 1947. pp.viii.100. [500.]

ÍNDICE de la legislación ecuatoriana desde 1898 hasta 1918. [Academia de abogados de Quito: Quito 1918–1921]. pp.iii.vi.112. [2000.]

Ferrara.

FRANCESCO BERLAN, Bibliografia degli statuti

municipali editi ed inediti di Ferrara. Roma 1878. pp.94. [500.]

Fiji.

A BIBLIOGRAPHY of the laws of Australia, New Zealand, Fiji and the western Pacific from the earliest times. With lists of reports of cases, digests and collections of statutes and rules. Sweet & Maxwell: legal bibliography (vol.vi): 1938. pp. vii.144. [1500.]

Florida.

JOHN B. GALBRAITH, Index to the decisions of the Supreme court of Florida, reported in Florida reports. Tallahassee 1866. pp.xxiv.252. [2000.]

HUGH E. MILLER, A complete table of Florida cases cited, approved, modified, distinguished, denied, doubted, or overruled by the Supreme court of the state of Florida. Charleston, S.C. 1892. pp.89. [750.]

France.

Laws by Places

i. *Manuscripts*

MICHEL PRÉVOST, Inventaire sommaire des pièces manuscrites contenues dans la collection Morel de Thoisy au Département des imprimés de la Bibliothèque nationale. 1924. pp.[ii].xxiii. 584. [4000.]

ii. *History*

[ANDRÉ MARIE JEAN JACQUES] DUPIN, Notices historiques, critiques et bibliographiques, sur plusieurs livres de jurisprudence française, remarquables par leur antiquité ou leur originalité. 1820. pp.[iii].iv.88. [25.]

— — [another edition]. [1832]. pp.73. [25.]

LOUIS J[EAN] KOENIGSWARTER, Sources et monuments du droit français antérieurs au quinzième siècle, ou bibliothèque de l'histoire du droit civil français depuis les premières origines jusqu'à la rédaction officielle des Coutumes. 1853. pp.xi.132. [500.]

G[ASTON] GAVET, Sources de l'histoire des institutions et du droit français. Manuel de bibliographie historique. 1899. pp.iii–xi.783. [2000.]

LOUIS MORIN, Recherches sur l'impression des *coutumes* au XVIe siècle, à Troyes et en Bourgogne. 1927. pp.35. [100.]

iii. *General*

[PIERRE] ARMAND DALLOZ, Dictionnaire général et raisonné de législation, de doctrine et de jurisprudence. 1835–1837. pp.xi.804+[iii].721+[iii].735+[iii].740+[iii].192.24. [100,000.]

reprinted in 1844 as a 'nouvelle édition . . . première partie . . . 1790 à 1835', the supplement forming the [second part] and fifth volume.

— — Partie supplémentaire. Période de 1834 à 1842. Tome cinquième. 1841. pp.[iii].4.1096.88. [30,000.]

[*continued as:*]

Jurisprudence générale. Table . . . du recueil périodique de législation et de doctrine.

1841–1856. Par [Victor Alexis Désiré] Dalloz . . . et [Pierre] Armand Dalloz. 1857. pp.viii.

1845–1867. Par D. Dalloz. 1867. pp.16.856+[iii].880.92. [50,000.]

1867–1877. Par Édouard Dalloz . . . Charles Vergé. 1877. pp.8.1039. [30,000.]

1877–1887. Par C. Vergé . . . Jules Jannet. 1887. pp.8.1069. [30,000.]

1887–1897. Par Gaston Griolet . . . C. Vergé. 1897. pp.8.1424. [40,000.]

1897–1907. 1907. pp.8.1694.5. [50,000.]

1907–1911. 1912. pp.8.747. [30,000.]

the subtitle varies.

[F. W. HALFPENNY], Catalogue of books on foreign law, founded on the collection presented by Charles Purton Cooper, esq. to the Society of Lincoln's inn. Laws and jurisprudence of France. 1849. pp.xv.436. [700.]

RÉPERTOIRE des ouvrages de législation, de droit et de jurisprudence en matière civile, administrative, commerciale et criminelle publiés spécialement en France depuis 1789 jusqu'à la fin de décembre 1856. 1857. pp.[iii].122. [3000.]

COSSE & MARCHAL, Bibliographie ou catalogue général et complet des livres de droit et de jurisprudence publiés jusqu'au 31 décembre 1856. 1857. pp.xi.53. [1500.]

[COUNT A. C. T.] DE FONTAINE DE RESBECQ, Répertoire des ouvrages de législation, de droit et de jurisprudence en matière civile, administrative, commerciale et criminelle publiés, spécialement en France, depuis 1789. 1859. pp.[vi].57.12. 131. [4000.]

—— Nouvelle édition. Par B[arnabé] Warée. 1870. pp.[iii].iv.387. [6000.]

[A. F. R.] TEICHMANN, Bibliographische uebersicht des römischen, deutschen, französischen und englischen rechts. Basel 1876. pp.118. [5000.]

E[UGÈNE] DRAMARD, Bibliographie raisonnée du droit civil. 1879.[v].xv.371. [4038.]

RÉPERTOIRE général alphabétique du droit françois. Tome I. 1886. pp.xxxviii.645. [11,000.]

[CHARLES HENRI JADART], Catalogue de la bibliothèque du tribunal de première instance de Reims. Reims 1887. pp.39. [400.]
150 copies printed.

CATALOGUE de la bibliothèque de la Chambre des avoués de 1re instance de Lyon. Lyon 1897. [100.]

BIBLIOGRAPHIA juridica gallica. Fascicule n° 1[–7]. Office international de bibliographie: Bibliographia universalis (no.24): Bruxelles 1899–1901. ff.156. [2500.]
no more published.

BIBLIOGRAPHIE Dalloz. Droit privé, droit public, économie politique, histoire du droit, droit international.

i. 1925. pp.160. [1000.]
ii. 1926. pp.144. [1000.]
iii. 1927. pp.184. [1500.]
iv. 1928. pp.136. [1500.]
v. 1929. pp.136. [1500.]
vi. 1930. pp.144. [1500.]

vii. 1931. pp.120. [1000.]
viii. 1932. pp.107. [1000.]
ix. 1933. pp.140. [1000.]
x. 1934. pp.132. [1000.]
xi. 1935. pp.115. [1000.]
xii. 1936. pp.87. [1000.]
xiii. 1937. pp.88. [1000.]

EDWIN M[ONTEFIORE] BORCHARD and GEORGE WILFRED STUMBERG, Guide to the law and legal literature of France. Library of Congress: Washington 1931. pp.v.242. [750.]

MICHEL ANTOINE [*and others*], Guide des recherches dans les fonds judiciaires de l'ancien régime. Direction des archives de France: 1958. pp.xiii.417. [very large number.]

iv. *Statute law*

HIERÔME NARDEAU DE LA GRANGE [*and others*], Recueil des lettres patentes, édits, déclarations, arrests, sentences et réglemens concernant l'exercise et fonction des sergens à verge du roy au Chastelet. 1669. pp.xiv.194. [97.]

LAURENT JOUET, La bibliothèque des arrests de tous les parlemens de France, enrichie de plusieurs belles dispositions et raisons de droit tant civil que canonique, des conciles, des ordonnances et des coutumes. 1669. pp.[xiv].507+340. [6000.]

GUILLAUME BLANCHARD, Table chronologique contenant un recueil en abrégé des ordonnances, édits, déclarations et lettres patentes des rois de France, qui concernent la justice, la police, & les finances, avec la datte de leur enregistrement dans les greffes des compagnies supérieures, depuis l'année 1115 jusqu'à présent. 1687. pp.viii.657. [6340.]

a copy in the Bibliothèque nationale contains ms. notes.

— — [another edition]. Compilation chronologique . . . depuis l'année 987. jusqu'à présent. 1715. pp.[viii].coll.1219+pp.[ii].coll.1220–2938. lxxxii. [27,500.]

[ANTOINE BRUNEAU], Table chronologique de la rédaction ou de la reformation de toutes les coutumes de France. 1699. pp.15. [420.]

[EUSÈBE JACQUES DE LAURIÈRE, CLAUDE BERROYER and CLAUDE ALEXANDRE LOGER], Table chronologique des ordonnances faites par les rois de France de la troisième race, depuis Hugues Capet jusqu'en 1400. 1706. pp.318. [1580.]

[F. D. GIRAUD], Table alphabétique des décrets

rendus depuis le 6 mai 1789. jusqu'au 30 septembre 1791. . . . Première partie. [1794]. pp.[ii].vi.45.29. [750.]

YVES CLAUDE JOURDAIN, Extrait alphabétique de tous les décrets de l'Assemblée nationale, servant de table générale. 1791–1792. pp.iv.556+[iii].554. [10,000.]

— — [continuation]. Table générale alphabétique des matières contenues dans les Décrets rendus par les Assemblées nationales de France depuis 1789 jusqu'au 18 brumaire an 8. [1801]. pp.658. [6000.]

[ ] CHAMBON, Table des lois, arrêtés et circulaires depuis le régime constitutionnel jusqu'au 1er vendémiaire an VIII]. [1799]. pp.viii.235. [2100.]

J[EAN] B[APTISTE] SIREY, Notices décennales de législation et de jurisprudence depuis l'avènement de Napoléon (1800–1810). 1811. pp.viii.843. [6000.] *also issued under the title of* Table alphabétique et raisonnée.

— — 1800–1820. Jurisprudence du XIXe siècle. Par J.-B. Sirey, J.-B. Duvergier et L.-M. de Villeneuve. 1821. pp.[iv].iv.812. [15,000.]

— — 1800–1825. 1826.
a–acc only; no more published.

— — 1800–1830. 1834. pp.viii.1111.54. [20,000.]

— — 1830–1840. 1841. pp.viii.1059. [20,000.]

— — 1800–1850. Par L.-M. Devilleneuve et P.Gilbert. 1851–1852. pp.[viii].608+679. [50,000.]

— — 1850–1860. 1862. pp.viii.680. [20,000.]

— — 1860–1870. Par J. Ruben de Couder. 1872. pp.viii.728. [25,000.]

— — 1871–1880. Par Éd. Fuzier-Herman. 1822. pp.iv.761. [25,000.]

— — 1881–1890. Par É. Fuzier-Herman [and] Th. Griffond. 1894. pp.iv.1209. [40,000.]

— — 1891–1900. Par Olivier de Gourmont. 1902. pp.vii.1623. [50,000.]

— — 1921–1925. Recueil général des lois et des arrêts. 1927.

— — 1926–1930. 1932.

[LOUIS RONDONNEAU], Table générale, par ordre alphabétique de matières, des lois, sénatus-consultes, décrets, arrêtés, avis du Conseil d'état, &c. publiés dans le Bulletin des lois et les collections officielles, depuis l'ouverture des États généraux, au 5 mai 1789, jusqu'à la restauration de la Monarchie française au 1er avril 1814. 1816. pp.[iii].574+[iii].547+[iii].548+[iii].504. [30,000.]

— — Table . . . des lois . . . publiés dans les ve, vie, et viie séries du Bulletin des lois, depuis le

1er avril 1814, jusqu'au 1er janvier 1819. 1819. pp.161. [3000.]

—— Table décennale du Bulletin des lois, depuis le 1er avril 1814 jusqu'au 31 décembre 1823, . . . par E. Longchamps. 1827. pp.iii–viii.682. [15,000.]

—— Table décennale . . . depuis le 1er janvier 1824 jusqu'au 31 décembre 1833. 1835. pp.vii.838. [20,000.]

—— Table décennale . . . depuis le 1er janvier 1834 jusqu'au 31 décembre 1843. 1844. pp.[iii]. ii.650. [15,000.]

—— Table décennale . . . depuis le 1er janvier 1844 jusqu'au 31 décembre 1853. 1856. pp.iii–viii.1037. [25,000.]

—— Table décennale . . . depuis le 1er janvier 1854 jusqu'au 31 décembre 1863, . . . par Ch. de Picamilh. 1865–1866. pp.[iv].760 + [iv].573. [50,000.]

—— Table décennale . . . depuis le 1er janvier 1864 jusqu'au 31 décembre 1883.

—— Table décennale. . . . Rédacteur Franz Caze de Caumont. Du 1er janvier 1884 au 31 décembre 1893. 1899–1900. pp.xviii.1622+ xiii.2029. [500,000.]

[CLAUDE JOSEPH] LALOUETTE, Classification des

lois administratives depuis 1789 jusqu'au 1er avril 1814. pp.xxviii.764. [8250.]

incomplete; no more published.

[JEAN] B[APTISTE] DUVERGIER, Table générale, analytique et raisonnée des lois, décrets, ordonnances, règlements, etc., depuis 1788 jusques et y compris 1830. 1834–1838. pp.23.600+764. [6500.]

— — depuis 1831 jusques et y compris 1889 . . . par J. Duvergier . . . Ed. Goujon. 1890. pp.[iii]. iv.311+[iii].230+[iii].217+[iii].202. [40,000.]

— — Table décennale . . . depuis 1890 jusques et y compris 1899 . . . par Ed. Goujon . . . Marcel Demonts. 1900. pp.[iii].504. [20,000.]

[NICOLAS ANTOINE PASCAL MODESTE] GILLET, Analyse chronologique des circulaires, instructions et décisions, émanées du Ministère de la justice, depuis le 12 janvier 1791 jusqu'au 1er janvier 1840. 1840. pp.[iii].vii.452. [1500.]

— — Troisième édition. 1876. pp.viii.545+519. [4482.]

[— LA PEYRIE], Bibliographie administrative ou nomenclature . . . des recueils de lois et d'arrêts, des instructions et règlements ministériels. . . . Par un employé du Ministère de l'intérieur. 1848. pp.xii.208.

J[EAN] M[ARIE] SAINT-LANNE-PESSALIER, Indicateur chronologique de toutes les lois ou décisions souveraines françaises . . . rendues et publiées depuis l'an 420 jusqu'en 987. Auch 1851. pp.103. [158.]

A[UGUSTE] F[RANÇOIS] TEULET, Bulletin analytique et raisonné de tous les décrets, lois et arrêtés rendus par les divers pouvoirs qui ont gouverné la France . . . depuis le 4 septembre 1870 . . . jusqu'au 4 septembre 1871. 1872. pp.36.23.5. [700.]

ÉMILE SCHAFFHAUSER, Table générale des "Lois nouvelles" 1882–1900. 1901. pp.184. [4000.]

ÉMILE SCHAFFHAUSER and HENRI CHEVRESSON, Table générale des textes législatifs, contenant dans un ordre alphabétique et chronologique, la nomenclature des principaux textes . . . en vigueur de 1789 au 1er janvier 1880. 1904. pp.[iv].556. [18,000.]

ALEXANDRE THARASSE, Inventaire des arrêts du Conseil du roi, novembre–décembre 1760. Vincennes [printed] 1938. pp.xx.184. [512.]

v. *Case law*

[JEAN SIMON] LOISEAU, Dictionnaire des arrêts modernes ou répertoire analytique, sommaire et critique de la nouvelle jurisprudence française civile et commerciale. 1809. pp.viii.446+655. [6500.]

JOURNAL du Palais. Répertoire général contenant la jurisprudence de 1791 à 1845, l'histoire du droit et la doctrine des auteurs.

i. a–as. Par [Alexandre Auguste] Ledru-Rollin. . . . Publié par F.-F. Patris. 1845. pp.[vi].vii.xxxvi.879. [20,000.]
ii. as–car. 1845. pp.[iv].850. [20,000.]
iii. cas–com. 1846. pp.[iv].956. [22,500.]
iv. com–cuv. 1846. pp.[iii].1052. [25,000.]
v. d. 1846. pp.[iii].934. [22,500.]
vi. e–ev. 1846. pp.[iii].960. [22,500.]
vii. ex–f. 1847. pp.[iii].1045. [25,000.]
viii. g–j. Par Ledru-Rollin. Publié par [Ev.] d'Auvilliers et Giraudeau. 1848. pp.[iii]. 954. [22,500.]
ix. k–o. Publié par d'Auvilliers . . . et Giraudeau. 1850. pp.[iii].949. [22,500.]
x. p–q. Publié par d'Auvilliers. 1850. pp.[iii]. 926. [22,500.]
xi. r–s. 1850. pp.[iii].1094. [25,000.]
xii. t–z. 1850. pp.[iii].1022. [22,500.]
xiii. Table chronologique des arrêts et décisions. 1854. pp.[iv].751. [75,000.]

—Journal . . . de 1791 à 1857. Supplément.

1957. pp.viii.1278+[iii].1219. [45,000.]

— Table complémentaire [alphabétique et chronologique].

[i]. 1857–1870. Par J. Ruben de Couder. 1872–1873.pp.viii.872+[iii].1025.[30,000.]

ii. 1871–1880. Par Éd[ouard] Fuzier-Herman. 1883. pp.viii.1286. [20,000.]

iii. 1881–1890. Par Éd. Fuzier-Herman . . . Th. Griffond. 1894.

iv. 1891–1900. Par Olivier de Gourmont. 1902. pp.viii.1623. [25,000.]

P. PERRUCHE DE VELNA, Répertoire des arrêts de la cour d'appel de Besançon de l'an VIII à 1871. Besançon 1874. pp.vi.355. [3750.]

FERNAND [GUSTAVE GASTON] LABORI, Gazette du Palais. Table alphabétique de cinq années et répertoire universel de la jurisprudence française (1882 à 1887). 1888. pp.xii.1027. [22,500.]

PANDECTES françaises. Pandectes chronologiques ou collection nouvelle résumant la jurisprudence. &c.

i. 1789–1829. Par Ruben de Couder. 1893. pp.iv.511.303.144. [15,500.]

ii. 1830–1844. 1891. pp.400.240.112. [2500.]

iii. 1845–1859. 1890. pp.404.211.103. [2000.]

iv. 1860–1869. 1889. pp.368.244.118. [2000.]
v. 1870–1877. 1888. pp.360.304.94. [2250.]
vi. 1878–1886. 1887. pp.384.216.88.28. [2000.]
[vii]. 1886–1896. Par André Weiss, P. Louis Lucas. 1897. pp.iv.1029. [22,500.]
[viii]. 1896–1906. 1908. pp.iv.1335. [23,000.]

M. PLATY-STAMATY [*and others*], Répertoire alphabétique de la jurisprudence civile de Marseille, contenant les sommaires et les rubriques des décisions importantes rendues . . . de 1877 à 1884. Marseille 1889. pp.357. [2750.]

FERNAND [GUSTAVE GASTON] LABORI [and ÉMILE SCHAFFHAUSER], Gazette du Palais. Répertoire encyclopédique du droit français.
i. [a–aubergistes]. 1889. pp.xii.812. [25,000.]
ii. [audiences–chose]. 1889. pp.752. [25,000.]
iii. [cigares–conseil]. 1890. pp.798. [25,000.]
iv. [conseil–domicile]. 1890. pp.803. [25,000.]
v. [domicile–enquête]. 1891. pp.761. [25,000.]
vi. [enquête–établissements]. 1892. pp.813. [25,000.]
vii. [établissements–f]. 1893. pp.761. [25,000.]
viii. [g–j]. 1893. pp.755. [25,000.]
ix. [l–paiement]. 1894. pp.847. [25,000.]
x. [papiers–remise]. 1894. pp.929. [30,000.]

xi. [remise–subvention]. 1895. pp.661. [20,000.]

xii. [succession–w]. 1896. pp.771. [25,000.]

— — Supplément. 1909–1910. pp.[iii].806+[iii].1021. [60,000.]

ÉMILE MUZARD, Répertoire alphabétique de jurisprudence commerciale . . . comprenant la table générale du Journal des tribunaux de commerce. 1891–1894. pp.vii.691+[iii].879. [25,000.]

AMBROISE RENDU and PAUL BENARD, Répertoire alphabétique du droit usuel. Recueil de décisions pratiques. 1895–1896. pp.xvi.520. [300.]

JOSEPH JOUGLAR, Table générale des références de jurisprudence aux recueils Sirey, Dalloz, Gazette du Palais, Gazette des tribunaux et des Pandectes françaises, classée par ordre chronologique . . . 1845 à 1880 [–1910]. 1912–1914. pp.[iv].380+[iv].944. [150,000.]

vi. *Miscellaneous*

S[IGISMOND] ROPARTZ, Études sur quelques ouvrages . . . par des Bretons. . . . Suivis d'une bibliothèque de jurisprudence bretonne, par m. le comte [Jacques Joseph Guillaume Pierre] de

Corbière. Nantes 1879. pp.[iii].288. [250.]
300 copies printed.

ALBERT AMIAUD, Recherches bibliographiques sur le notariat français. 1881. pp.xvi.233. [1500.]
330 copies printed.

ANDRÉ JOUBERT, Un recueil de plaidoyers inédits des avocats angevins aux XVIIe et XVIIIe siècles (1680–1730). Angers 1888. pp.16. [45.]

CATALOGUE des factums et d'autres documents judiciaires antérieurs à 1790. Bibliothèque nationale.

i. Abadie–Cyvadat. Par A[ugustin] Corda. 1890. pp.xi.567. [9000.]
ii. D–Kuntz. 1892. pp.[iii].592. [9000.]
iii. La Bachellerie–Mython. 1894. pp.[iii].723. [10,000.]
iv. Nacquart-Quoinat. 1896. pp.[iii].623. [9000.]
v. Rabaça–Syrot. 1900. pp.[iii].699. [10,000.]
vi. Taaff–Zutter. Continué par A[médée Louis Alexandre] Trudon des Ormes. 1902. pp.[iii].399. [6000.]
vii. Supplément. 1905. pp.[iii].639. [10,000.]
viii–x. Table alphabétique 1921–1936. pp. [iii].602+[iii].474+[iii].584.

LÉON LOSSEAU, Bibliographie des discours de rentrée prononcés aux audiences solennelles des cours de justice de Belgique, de France, de Luxembourg et de Monaco, 1851–1899. Bruxelles 1900. pp.[iii].coll.158. [3699.]

LUCIEN MUNSCH, Répertoire général des circulaires et instructions du Ministère de la justice . . . 1790– . . . 1899. 1900. pp.viii.464+[iii].465–915. [1918.]

ÉMILE SCHAFFHAUSER and HENRI CHEVRESSON, Table générale des textes législatifs, contenant . . . la nomenclature des principaux textes . . . en vigueur de 1789 au 1er janvier 1880. 1904. pp.544. [5750.]

ARTHUR DAGUIN, Les greffiers et leurs œuvres. Contribution à la bibliographie des volumes et plaquettes dus à des greffiers et des commis-greffiers, plus particulièrement depuis 1870. Marmande [printed] 1905. pp.24. [200.]

ARTHUR DAGUIN, Les juges de paix et leurs œuvres. Contribution à la bibliographie des volumes et plaquettes dus aux juges de paix depuis . . . 1790. Lille 1907. pp.46. [250.]

[FRÉDÉRIC ALEXANDRE] HENRI STEIN, Inventaire

analytique des ordonnances enregistrées au parlement de Paris jusqu'à la mort de Louis XII. Archives nationales: 1908. pp.xii.132.

FRANCE. American foreign law association: Bibliographies of foreign law series (no.4): [New York] 1927. pp.[ii].8. [60.]

TABLES alphabétique, analytique et chronologique des instructions et circulaires . . . publiées par les ordres du Garde des sceaux. Ministère de la justice: 1898. pp.[iv].185.

Franconia.

GEORG KARL VON MAYR, General-index über alle landes-verordnungen, welche durch die Königlich baierische regierungs-blätter von Baiern in München, von der Oberpfalz in Amberg, von Franken in Bamberg, und von Schwaben in Ulm, von den jahren 1802, 1803, 1804, und 1805. promulgiert und bekannt gemacht worden sind. München 1806. pp.[viii].428. [2000.]

— — 1806 — 1809–1810. 1809. pp.[viii].793. [2500.]

Galicia, Poland.

FRANZ STARR, Vollständiges sach- und nachschlage-register zu sämmtlichen landesgesetzblättern der im Reichsrathe vertretenen königreiche und länder von deren beginn 1849 bis zum jahre 1873. . . . Fünfter theil. Galizien, Krakau und die Bukowina. Wien 1874. pp.[iii].268. [4000.]

Gambia.

DONALD KINGDOM, A chronological table and index of the ordinances of the colony of the Gambia . . . and of the rules, regulations and orders passed and made by the Governor-in-council and of the proclamations, acts of parliament, orders of the King-in-council, treaties, etc., published in the Gambia government gazettes, 1901–1908 (inclusive). 1909. pp.103. [3000.]

Genoa.

L[UIGI] T[OMMASO] BELGRANO, Saggio bibliografico degli statuti di Genova. Genova 1878. pp.[ii].67–123. [250.]

Georgia, U.S.A.

HOWARD VAN EPPS and JOHN W. AKIN, Analytical index-digest of Georgia reports, embracing . . . the Supreme court reports . . . , T. U. P. Charlton's Reports, R. M. Charlton's Reports, Dudley's

Reports, and Georgia reports. Nashville, Tenn. 1899. pp.xvi.1180 + 1181–2428 + 2429–3718. [100,000.]

Germany.

i. *History*

CHRISTIAN HECHT, Schediasma historicum ad juris publici germanici de obsidione . . . Francofurti ac Aquisgrani in dissidiosa duorum imperatorum electione, ab altero eorum olim . . . instituta. Francofurti ad Moenum 1724. pp.16. [50.]

GUSTAV ADOLF STENZEL, Grundriss und litteratur zu vorlesungen über deutsche staats- und rechtsgeschichte. Breslau 1832. pp.[ii].158. [1500.]

JOHANN FRIEDRICH BÖHMER, Die reichsgesetze von 900 bis 1400. Frankfurt a. M. 1832. pp.15. [200.]

C[ARL] G[USTAV] HOMEYER, Verzeichniss deutscher rechtsbücher des mittelalters und ihre handschriften. Berlin 1836. pp.iv.64. [527.]

— — [another edition]. Die deutschen rechtsbücher [&c.]. 1856. pp.viii.176. [741.]

ETHBIN HEINRICH COSTA, Bibliographie der deutschen rechtsgeschichte. Braunschweig 1858. pp.[viii].342. [3911.]

O. A. WALTHER, Die literatur des gemeinen, ordentlichen civil-processes und seine bearbeiter bis auf die zeiten des jüngsten reichsabschieds. Ein beitrag zur culturgeschichte des gemeinen deutschen civil-processes überhaupt. Nordhausen 1865. pp.xiv.82. [500.]

HANS PLANITZ and THEA BUYKEN, Bibliographie zur deutschen rechtsgeschichte. Frankfurt a. M. [1950–]1952. pp.xx.1044. [17,500.]

ii. *General*

[JOHANN CHRISTIAN LÜNIG], Bibliotheca juris feudalis, in welcher die vornehmsten und wichtigsten schrifften . . . angeführet werden. [Frankfurt a. M. 1727]. coll.88.[xvi]. [1250.]

also issued as part of the author's Corpus juris feudalis germanici, *1727, vol.iii.*

JOHANN JACOB MOSER, Bibliotheca juris publici S. r. german. imperii, enthaltende eine genugsame nachricht von denen autoribus, innhalt, einrichtung, auflagen, fatis, recensionen, davon gefällten urtheilen, und anderem zu wissen nöthig- und nützlichem. Stuttgardt 1729–1734. pp.[xvi].342. [x] + 367–777.[viii] + [xvii].791–1272.[lxviii]. [500.]

REPERTORIVM reale pragmaticvm ivris pvblici et fevdalis imperii romano-germanici. . . . Nebst anführung der neuesten und besten von jedem titul herausgekommenen abhandlungen: so, dass dieses werk zugleich als eine hinlängliche bibliotheca ivris pvblici et fevdalis dienen wird. Jena 1751. pp.[xxiv].536+537–1276. [6000.]

[JOHANN STEPHAN] PÜTTER, Litteratur des teutschen staatsrechts. Göttingen 1776–1783. pp. [xx].480.[xvi] + [xx].496.[xviii] + 12.870.[li]. [10,000.]

— — Vierter theil. Fortgesetzt . . . von Johann Ludwig Klüber. Erlangen 1791. pp.[ii].734.[xxix]. [5000.]

FRIEDRICH CHRISTOPH JONATHAN FISCHER, Litteratur des germanischen rechts. Leipzig 1782. pp. xxii.311. [750.]

JOHANN THEODOR ROTH, Beiträge zum deutschen staatsrecht und zur litteratur desselben. Nürnberg 1794–1798. pp.[viii].175+[iv].177–352 +[viii].343+[viii].296. [1000.]

EBERHARD JULIUS WILHELM ERNST VON MASSOW Handbuch der litteratur, angehenden justizbedienten . . . gewidmet. Berlin &c. 1794. pp.lxxii.928. [xxxvi]. [1000.]

E[DUARD] HERMSDORF, Jahresberichte über die deutsche gesetzgebung. Leipzig.

i. 1844. pp.xii.264. [750.]
ii. 1845. pp.xxii.554. [1000.]
iii. 1846. pp.xxii.517. [1000.]
no more published.

BIBLIOTHECA juridica, oder geordnete uebersicht der . . . in Deutschland neu erschienenen bücher. Edited by C. J. F. W. Ruprecht. Göttingen.

i. 1848. pp.[iv].38. [450.]
ii. 1849. pp.[ii].59. [750.]
no more published.

WILH[ELM] NIC[OLAS] SCHULZE, Die reichsrechtliche literatur seit entstehung des norddeutschen bundes — 1867 bis ende 1874. Leipzig 1875. pp. [iv].92. [1500.]

— Nachtrag . . . bis ende 1876. [1877]. pp.93–135. [500.]

also bound up together in a cover bearing the date 1875 and issued as a 'Zweite . . . auflage'.

[A. F. R.] TEICHMANN, Bibliographische uebersicht des römischen, deutschen, französischen und englischen rechts. Basel 1876. pp.118. [5000.]

KARL BIRKMEYER, Zusammenstellung der gesammten bis jetzt zur reichs-civilprozessordnung erschienenen literatur. Berlin [1884]. pp.vii.59.

[WILHELM CONSTANT HELMRICH], Katalog der Bibliothek des gemeinschaftlichen Thüringischen oberlandsgerichts zu Jena. 1885. pp.x.494. [4500.]

— — Nachtrag. 1895. pp.ix–ivx [*sic*, xiv].431–673. [2000.]

— — Zweiter nachtrag. 1905. pp.xv–xx.603–924. [2500.]

includes an index to the whole.

SYSTEMATISCHE uebersicht über die gesetzgebung des deutschen reichs von 1867 bis 1888. München 1888. pp.x.154. [1500.]

FRIEDRICH PFAFF, Vereinigtes sachregister zu dem Bundes- bezw. Reichs-gesetzblatt, sowie zu dem Centralblatt für das Deutsche reich, von 1867 bis 1890. Mainz 1891. pp.[viii].268. [15,000.]

OTTO MÜHLBRECHT, Die litteratur des entwurfs eines bürgerlichen gesetzbuches für das Deutsche reich ausgearbeitet durch die von dem Bundesrathe berufene kommission. 1e lesung. Berlin 1892. pp.58. [800.]

C. F. REATZ, Die litteratur über den entwurf eines bürgerlichen gesetzbuches für das Deutsche reich. Juristischer litteraturbericht, 1884–1894 (part 3): Leipzig 1895. pp.[iii].60. [300.]

CARL GAREIS, Die litteratur des privat- und handelsrechts, 1884 bis 1894. Centralblatt für rechtswissenschaft (ergänzungsband iv): Leipzig 1896. pp.44. [450.]

GEORG KLEINFELLER, Die litteratur des deutschen prozessrechts, 1884 bis 1894. Juristischer litteraturbericht (part 5): Leipzig 1896. pp.52. [250.]

GEORG MAAS, Bibliographie der amtlichen materialien zum bürgerlichen gesetzbuche für das Deutsche reich und zu seinem einführungsgesetze. Berlin 1897. pp.36. [304.]

OTTO MÜHLBRECHT, Bibliographie des bürgerlichen gesetzbuches für das Deutsche reich. Berlin 1898–1901. pp.44+75+28. [2000.]

GEORG MAAS, Bibliographie des bürgerlichen rechts. Verzeichnis von einzelschriften und aufsätzen über das im bürgerlichen gesetzbuche für das Deutsche reich vereinigte recht, sachlich geordnet . . . 1888–1898. Berlin 1899. pp.xl.388. [3500.]

—— 1899. 1900. pp.68. [750.]

—— 1900. 1901. pp.84. [1000.]

—— 1901. 1902. pp.84. [1000.]

—— 1902. 1903. pp.84. [1000.]

—— 1903. 1904. pp.94. [1000.]

—— 1904. 1905. pp.94. [1000.]

GEORG MAAS, Jurisprudentia Germaniae 1905. Berlin 1906. pp.xvi.224. [3500.]

GEORG MAAS, Bibliographie der deutschen gesetzgebung und rechtswissenschaft. Berlin 1907. pp.xxii.268.

EDWIN M[ONTEFIORE] BORCHARD, Guide to the law and legal literature of Germany. Library of Congress: Washington 1912. pp.226. [500.]
reissued at The Hague in the same year.

KATALOG der Dernburgs bibliothek in der Kaiserlichen universitäts-bibliothek zu Tokyo. Tokyo 1916. pp.[iii].x.293. [3750.]

ALFRED DEHLINGER, Deutsches recht seit 1867.... Systematische übersicht. 1917.
— — 32. auflage. [1959]. pp.102. [7500.]

[ ] DIEPGEN, General-register zu Grotefend-Cretschmar gesetzsammlung, enthaltend die preussischen und deutschen gesetze und verordnungen usw. von 1806 bis 1926. Düsseldorf [1927]. pp.[iii].789. [75,000.]

CLÄRE KORTUM and WILLY MEERWALD, Schrifttum des geltenden verfassungsrechts des reichs und der länder einschliesslich der freien stadt Danzig. Berlin 1929. pp.vii.116. [2000.]

PAUL GÜNTZEL, Verzeichnis der zeitschriften, entscheidungssammlungen und jahrbücher. Reichsgericht: Bibliothek: Leipzig 1929. pp.viii. 95. [1250.]

GEORG VOLKHARDT, Deutscher gesetzesanzeiger. Sammlung von fundstellen des geltenden reichsrechts in systematischer und alphabetischer ordnung. Stuttgart 1935. pp.xii.421.96. [8330.]

QUELLENVERZEICHNIS der justizverwaltungsvorschriften. Berlin [1942]. pp.170. [2684.]

CATALOGUE de la bibliothèque juridique. Régie autonome des publications officielles: Baden-Baden [*c.*1947]. pp.34. [300.]

HANS SCHNEIDER, Bibliographie zum öffentlichen recht in der Bundesrepublik Deutschland. München &c. 1960. pp.112. [750.]

HANS GRÖPPER, Verzeichnis aller zeitschriften, amtsblätter und rechtsprechungssammlungen der bücherei des Hanseatischen oberlandesgerichts. Hamburg 1962. pp.xix.262.*

Gold Coast.

SMALMAN SMITH, Analytical index to the ordinances regulating the civil and criminal procedure of the Gold Coast colony and of the colony of Lagos. 1888. pp.119. [3000.]

STANLEY W. MORGAN, A chronological table and an alphabetical index of the ordinances of the Gold Coast colony. 1895. pp.[ii].xxiv. [300.]

Great Britain.

i. *Bibliographies and periodicals*

A COMPLETE check list of current legal periodicals and law reports (british & colonial). Compiled by Sweet & Maxwell ltd. 1909. pp.11. [178.]

JOHN D[UNCAN] COWLEY, A bibliography of abridgments, digests, dictionaries and indexes of english law to the year 1800. Selden society: 1932. pp.xcv.187. [330.]

WILLIAM L[AWRENCE] FRIEND, Anglo-american legal bibliographies. An annotated guide. Library of Congress: Washington 1944. pp.xii.166. [298.]

ii. *History*

[SIR] ERNEST CLARKE, Law books written by or attributed to sir Anthony Fitzherbert. 1894. ff.[i].28. [18.]
privately reproduced from typewriting.

CHARLES C[ARROLL] SOULE, Year-book bibliography. [Cambridge, Mass. 1900]. pp.31. [500.]

CLARENCE C. CRAWFORD, A guide to the study of the history of English law and procedure. Toronto 1923. pp.xi.83. [750.]

CATALOGUE of the exhibits of the Hampton L. Carson collection of books, documents . . . illustrative of the growth of english-american law. Historical society of Pennsylvania: Philadelphia 1924. pp.54. [110.]

PERCY H[ENRY] WINFIELD, The chief sources of English legal history. Cambridge [Mass.] 1925. pp.xviii.374.

SIR W[ILLIAM] S[EARLE] HOLDSWORTH, Sources and literature of english law. Oxford 1925. pp. xi.247. [500.]

JOSEPH HENRY BEALE, A bibliography of early english law books. [Harvard university]: Ames foundation (vol.ii): Cambridge [Mass.] 1926. pp. viii.304. [1300.]

— — A supplement . . . by Robert Bowie Anderson. Ames foundation: Cambridge, Mass. 1943. pp.xii.50. [120.]

H. A. C. STURGESS, A catalogue of lord chancellor Eldon's law books from the library at Encombe placed on loan in the library of the Honourable society of the Middle temple. Glasgow [printed] 1934. pp.38. [400.]

LEGAL manuscripts and printed books: a sequence illustrating the development of english and american law, for the visit of the American bar association. Henry E. Huntington library: San Marino [1935]. pp.31. [60.]

iii. *Manuscripts*

A CATALOGUE of manuscripts, formerly in the possession of Francis Hargrave . . . now deposited in the British museum. 1818. pp.[iii].188. [1000.]

[S. R. SCARGILL BIRD], List of plea rolls of various courts. Public record office: Lists and indexes (no.iv): 1894. pp.[iv].203. [20,000.]

—— New . . . edition. [Revised by E. Salisbury]. 1910. pp.[iv].209. [25,000.]

[J. E. E. S. SHARP], List and index of court rolls. . . . Part I. Public record office: Lists and indexes (no.vi): 1896. pp.vi.462. [20,000.]

no more published.

LIST of Exchequer K. R. memoranda rolls and Exchequer L.T.R. chancellor's rolls, memoranda rolls, originalia rolls and pipe rolls. Public record office: 1926. ff.[ii].117. [1102.]*

JENNIFER NICHOLSON, Register of manuscripts of year books extant. Preliminary edition. Historical manuscripts commission: 1956. ff.[iv].31. [500.]*

iv. *General*

THO[MAS] BASSETT, A catalogue of the common and statute law-books of this realm. 1671. pp. [x].120. [350.]

— — [second edition]. 1682. pp.[viii].144. [500.]

this edition is found in two states, in one of which the author's name appears as Bassett, in the other as Basset.

— — The third edition. 1694. pp.[xii].142. [500.]

[—] — [another edition]. 1714. pp.[iv].132. [750.]

[—] — [another edition]. 1716. pp.[iv].116. [750.]

[—] — [another edition]. 1720. pp.[iv].99. [750.]

[—] — [another edition]. 1722. pp.[iv].94. [750.]

[—] — [another edition]. 1726. pp.[iv].92. [750.]

[—] — [another edition]. 1732. pp.[iv].96. [800.]

the editions of 1714–1732 are given the appearance of being by John Walthoe.

THOMAS BASSETT, An exact catalogue of the common & statute law books of this realm. 1673. single leaf. [350.]

— — [another edition]. 1684. single leaf. [500.]

[GILES JACOB], Catalogue of all the writs and processes, that issue out of the several courts at Westminster &c. 1717. pp.[viii].120.[xii]. [600.]

JOHN WORRALL, Bibliotheca legum: or, a new and compleat list of the common and statute law books of this realm. 1732. pp.[ii].78.xvii. [1000.]

— — The second edition. 1734.

— — The third edition. 1736. pp.82. [1000.]

— — The fourth edition. 1738. pp.[iv].88.[xiv]. [1000.]

page 82 is followed by a leaf numbered lxxxii.

— — The fifth edition. 1740. pp.v.110. [1250.]

— — The sixth edition. 1746. pp.[vi].177. [1500.]

— — The seventh edition. 1749. pp.[ix].192. [1750.]

— — A new edition. 1753. pp.[xii].192. [1750.]

— — A new edition. 1756. pp.[viii].196. [1750.]

— — A new edition . . . to which is added, a list of the principal scotch law books, and some relating to Ireland. 1768. pp.[xiv].144. [2000.]

— — A new edition. [By Edward Brooke]. 1776. pp.[xvi].150. [2000.]

— — A new edition. 1763. pp.[x].168.[xxii]. [2000.]

— — A new edition. 1765. pp.[x].133. [2000.]

— — A new edition. 1768. pp.[xii].144. [2250.]

— — A new edition. 1776. pp.[xiv].150. [2250.]

— — A new edition. 1777. pp.[xvi].162[*sic*, 172]. [2250.]

— — A new edition. 1782. pp.[xvi].204. [2500.]

— — A new edition. Bibliotheca legum Angliæ. 1788. pp.[xvi].272.[xxvi]+viii.256. [4000.]

— — — Supplement . . . 1788 to . . . 1794. 1794. pp.[iv].32. [200.]

— — — Supplement . . . 1788 to . . . 1800. 1800. pp.[iv].46. [300.]

— — — Supplement . . . 1788 to . . . 1801. 1801.

— — — Supplement. A catalogue of modern law books . . . 1788, to . . . 1805. [By Clarke W.]. 1806. pp.[iii].14[*sic*, 114].[x]. [750.]

— — Supplement . . . 1788, to . . . 1807. 1808.

— — [another edition]. Clarke's bibliotheca legum. . . . Originally compiled by J. Worrall; now further improved . . . by John Clarke. [Edited by Thomas Hartwell Horne]. [1810]. pp.[ii].xii. 418.[xlii].461–462. [4000.]

— — — Supplement . . . 1810, to . . . 1812. pp.3–18. [136.]

— — New edition. [Edited by Thomas Hartwell Horne]. 1819. pp.xx.426.[xlviii]. [5000.]

J[OSEPH] BUTTERWORTH, A general catalogue of law-books. 1801. pp.[vi].102. [900.]

— — Seventh edition. By Joseph Butterworth and son. 1824. pp.xx.208. [2000.]

RICHARD WHALLEY BRIDGMAN, A short view of legal bibliography. 1807. pp.xviii.430. [500.]

one of the British museum copies (now destroyed by enemy action) contained voluminous ms. additions made by the author in preparation for a second edition; and a copy in the Bodleian library contains a few ms. notes.

WILLIAM REED, A catalogue of modern law books, arranged in a perspicuous method. 1808. pp.[v].156. [1000.]

— — Bibliotheca nova legum Angliæ: or a complete catalogue of law books. 1809. pp.390. [5500.]

— — — Supplement . . . to Hilary term 1812. [1812]. pp.16. [125.]

HENRY BUTTERWORTH, A catalogue of law books. . . . Second edition. 1820. pp.[vii].130. [1100.]

— — Fifth edition. 1836. pp.[ix].268. [2500.]

JOSEPH BUTTERWORTH & SON, A catalogue of modern law books, and also of the old reports. 1826. pp.viii.96. [1000.]

[S. GREENLEAF], Catalogue of a select law library. [Cambridge, Mass. 1836]. pp.16. [750.]

S. SWEET, A catalogue of modern law books, including the irish and scotch, and all the reporters from the earliest period. 1843. pp.xi–xx.272. [3500.]

—— Second edition. 1883. pp.[vii].502. [5500.]

J[OHN] G[AGE] MARVIN, Legal bibliography, or a thesaurus of american, english, irish, and scotch law books. Philadelphia 1847. pp.iii–vii.800. [5000.]

WILLIAM BENNING & CO., A catalogue of modern law books, including all the old reporters. 1850. pp.xii.233. [3000.]

—— [another edition]. By V. & R. Stevens, sons, & Haynes. 1864. pp.vi.104. [2000.]

—— [another edition]. By Stevens and sons. 1865. pp.[viii].68. [1000.]

—— [another edition]. Stevens & sons' catalogue of modern law works. [1932]. pp.xii.106. [1500.]

there are numerous intermediate editions; the subtitle varies.

MESSRS BUTTERWORTH, Catalogue of law works ... with a chronological list of all the reports. 1864. pp.84. [2000.]

A CATALOGUE of the books in the law library of the Leeds corporation. Leeds 1864.

— [third edition]. Catalogue of the law library. 1960. pp.71. [750.]*

H[ENRY] G. STEVENS and R[OBERT] W. HAYNES, A catalogue of modern law books, including all the reports in England, Scotland, and Ireland. 1865. pp.lii.177. [2000.]

— — — Supplement. A catalogue of modern law works published during the years 1865–1914. 1914. pp.viii.298. [3500.]

there are numerous intermediate editions; the subtitle varies.

[A. F. R.] TEICHMANN, Bibliographische uebersicht des römischen, deutschen, französischen und englischen rechts. Basel 1876. pp.118. [5000.]

ROBERT CLARKE & CO.'s digest of law publications: being a catalogue of american and british law books. Cincinnati 1877. pp.vii.246. [2000.]

HERBERT G. SWEET, A complete catalogue of modern law books, british, american and colonial;

with a selection of such old works as are still of value. The very full index of subjects by John Nicholson. 1882. pp.[vii].472. [6000.]

— — Second edition. 1883. pp.[v].502. [7500.]

J. HOLMES CONVERSE, A complete subject index of the text books and books of leading cases. Library company of the Baltimore bar: Baltimore 1882. pp.[iii].175. [2000.]

printed on one side of the leaf.

CHARLES C[ARROLL] SOULE, The lawyer's reference manual of law books and citations. Boston 1883. pp.x.497. [6000.]

reprinted in 1884.

AN INDEX to legal periodical literature. [American, english, canadian, british colonial]. Boston [vol.v: Indianapolis; vol.vi: Los Angeles].

[i. 1770–1886]. By Leonard A[ugustus] Jones. 1888. pp.xix.635. [40,000.]
ii. 1887–1899. 1899. pp.xvii.607. [30,000.]
iii. 1898–1908. By Frank E. Chipman. 1919. pp.vi.549. [15,000.]
iv. 1908–1922. 1924. pp.vii.975. [25,000.]
v. 1923–1932. 1933. pp.vii.1335. [30,000.]
vi. 1932–1937. [1939]. pp.vii.817. [20,000.]

a preliminary vol.v, covering 1923–1927, was pub-

lished at New York in 1928; vol.ii has a wider scope than the rest in subject-matter; no more published.

WILLIAM CLOWES & SONS, A catalogue of modern law books: including a chronological list of the english and irish reports. 1883. pp.89. [1000.]

G. J. JOHNSON, Books on law and jurisprudence. Birmingham reference library: Lectures (no.1): [1885]. pp.28. [50.]

G. J. JOHNSON, Books on legal and constitutional history. Birmingham reference library: Lectures (no.3): [1886]. pp.30.viii. [50.]

THE LAW library, A monthly record of legal literature. No.1[–10]. January, 1892 [–March, 1893]. pp.112+32. [250.]
no more published.

W. HAROLD MAXWELL, A catalogue of modern law books, british and colonial. 1895. pp.[vii]. 468. [4500.]

ERNEST ARTHUR JELF, Where to find your law. Being a discursive bibliographical essay upon the various divisions and sub-divisions of the law of England and the statutes, reports of cases, and text-books containing such law. 1897. pp.xxxvi.508. [2500.]

— — Third edition. 1907. pp.xliii.574. [7500.]

CATALOGUE of all the more important british and colonial law books published during the last ten years. 1899. pp.[vi].114. [1250.]

— [another edition]. 1911. pp.[viii].viii.132. [1500.]

there are numerous intermediate editions.

MATTHIAS LEVY, Catalogue of the books in the library of the Institute of shorthand writers, practising in the Supreme court of judicature. 1900. pp.93. [1000.]

— — Addenda. 1901. pp.11. [150.]

— — — 1903. pp.39. [650.]

— — — [1904]. ff.6. [75.]

CATALOGUE of the library of the lord chief justice's court and courts 1 to 9 king's bench. 1904. ff.110. pp.111–130. [2500.]

J. SCOTT DUCKERS, A guide to students' law books. 1906. pp.viii.178. [200.]

WHERE to look for your law. 1908.

— — Thirteenth edition. By C[harles] W[illiam] Ringrose. 1960. pp.viii.228. [6000.]

W[ILLIAM] HAROLD MAXWELL, A complete list of british & colonial law reports & legal periodicals

. . . and current editions of british & colonial statute law & digest. 1913. pp.vi.88. [2000.]

—— Supplement, 1913–1920. [1920]. pp.16. [300.]

—— Supplement. Check list of british and colonial law reports, legal periodicals, digests and statutes, 1920–24. [1924]. ff.11. [150.]

—— Third edition. 1937. pp.viii.142. [2250.]

the canadian edition, Toronto 1937, has two additional leaves containing a list of canadian statutes.

JAMES J. THOMAS, Catalogue . . . of the Bristol incorporated law society. [Bristol] 1914. pp.[ii]. 238. [2500.]

CATALOGUE of the Home office library. 1915. pp.306. [6000.]

JOHN J. DALEY, A subject index to the books in the library of the Law society of Upper Canada. Toronto 1923. pp.[vi].480. [12,500.]

CATALOGUE of the books in the Court-house library of the Faculty of procurators in Glasgow. Glasgow 1924. pp.xiv.50. [600.]

SWEET & MAXWELL's complete law book catalogue [legal bibliography].

i. A bibliography of english law to 1650 . . .

by W[illiam] Harold Maxwell. 1925. pp. xvi.444. [4000.]

ii. — from 1651 to 1800 . . . by Leslie F. Maxwell. 1931. pp.viii.270. [2000.]

iii. — from 1801 to June, 1932 . . . by L. F. Maxwell. 1933. pp.iv.334. [5000.]

— — First cumulative supplement. 1936. pp. iii.64. [500.]

— — Second cumulative supplement. 1939. pp.iv.92. [1000.]

— — Third cumulative supplement. 1946. pp.iv.144. [1500.]

— — Fourth cumulative supplement. 1950. pp.iv.168. [2000.]

— — Second edition. A legal bibliography of the British Commonwealth of nations.

i. English law to 1800, including Wales, the Channel islands and the Isle of Man. Compiled by W. H. Maxwell and L. F. Maxwell. 1955. pp.xvi.687. [6000.]

ii. English law from 1801 to 1954. . . . Compiled by John S. James and L. F. Maxwell. 1957. pp.vii.520. [7500.]

iii. Canadian and british-american colonial law from the earliest times to December, 1956. Compiled by C. R. Brown, P. A.

Maxwell and L. F. Maxwell. 1957. pp.x. 220. [3000.]

volume iv is entered below under Ireland: Law, vol.v under Scotland: Law, vol.vi under Australia, vol.vii under Great Britain: Commonwealth: Law.

ANNUAL survey of english law. London school of economics and political science (university of London), Department of law.

1928. pp.xv.302. [2000.]
1929. pp.xxx.278. [2000.]
1930. pp.xl.328. [2000.]
1931. pp.lvi.381. [2000.]
1932. pp.lv.402. [2500.]
1933. pp.xxxii.396. [2500.]
1934. pp.xxviii.308. [2000.]
1935. pp.xxxiii.355. [2000.]
1936. pp.xl.431. [2500.]
1937. pp.xxxix.419. [2500.]
1938. pp.xxxvi.434. [2500.]
1939. pp.xxxvi.439. [2500.]
1940. 1943. pp.xxvii.296. [1500.]

SWEET & MAXWELL's guide to law reports and statutes. 1929. pp.70. [750.]

—— Fourth edition. 1962 [1963]. pp.143. [1500.]

SWEET & MAXWELL's law finder. A guide to the contents of current law books. 1930. pp.72. [1500.]

— Fourth edition. The law finder. A guide to current law books and statutes. 1937. pp.164. [3000.]

RODOLFO BLEDEL, Fuentes bibliográficas para el estudio del derecho angloamericano. Buenos Aires 1940. pp.89. [100.]

CATALOGUE of the Darlington law library. Public library: Darlington 1942. pp.[ii].34. [350.]*

A BIBLIOGRAPHICAL guide to the law of the United Kingdom, the Channel islands and the Isle of Man. University of London: Institute of advanced legal studies: 1956. pp.xi.219. [2000.]

THE CATALOG of the Carson law collection, Free library of Philadelphia. Boston 1962. pp.[vi].896 +[ii].897–1842. [38,661.]

this is a reproduction of the catalogue cards; the number in square brackets refers to these cards.

v. *Statute law*

a. *Public*

A TABLE to all the statutes made in the tyme of

the most victorious reigne of kynge Edward the sixte. Londini 1553. pp.[8]. [600.]

A TABLE to al the statutes made from the beginning of the raigne of kyng Edwarde the .vi. vnto this present .xii. yeare of the reigne of oure moste gratious and soueraigne ladye queene Elizabeth. [1570]. pp.[12]. [400.]

[GILES JACOB], A general table of all the statutes, from Magna charta, down to the year 1715 . . . shewing in the reigns of what kings, and the years of the reigns, the said statutes have been . . . passed into laws. 1716. pp.[ii].40. [3000.]

WILLIAM SHEPPARD, An epitome of all the common & statute laws of this nation, now in force. 1656. pp.[xxiv].1132. [15,000.]

— — A grand abridgment of the common and statute law of England. 1675. pp.[xii].468.461–580 +[ii].512+[ii].344+[ii].144.149–250. [20,000.]

OWEN RUFFHEAD, A complete index to the statutes at large, from Magna charta to the tenth year of George III. inclusive. 1772. pp.[520]. [10,000.] *reissued as vol.x of the* Statutes at large, *1786.*

JOHN RAITHBY, An index to the statutes at large, from Magna carta, to the forty-ninth year of

George III. inclusive. 1814. pp.xx.[639]+[659]+[624]. [50,000.]

B. SPILLER, Index to the public general statutes of the United Kingdom, from January 1801 to July 1828. 1829. pp.xxi.ff.306. [9961.]

RICHARD LOWNDES, A chronological index to the statutes at large, from Magna charta to July 23, 1830. 1831. pp.[iv].180. [14,000.]

GEORGE CRABB, A digest and index, with a chronological table, of all the statutes; from Magna charta to the end of this last session. 1841. pp.[iii].xliv.988. [45,000.]

HENRY RIDDELL and JOHN WARRINGTON ROGERS, An index to the public statutes from 9 Hen. III. to 10 & 11 Vict. inclusive, (excepting those relating exclusively to Scotland, Ireland, the colonies and dependencies). . . . Part the first. 1848. pp.xv.406. [3000.]

no more published.

GEORGE STAMP, An index to the statute law of England, to the close of the session 10 & 11 Vict. (1847). 1848. pp.lxx.311. [4500.]

— — Third edition, brought down to the close of the session 24 & 25 Vict. (1861), by James Edward Davis. 1862. pp.xcv.468. [7000.]

JOHN BIDDLE, A table of reference to 3,000 unrepealed public general acts. 1864. pp.[iii].68. [3000.]

—— Second edition . . . to the end of the session 32 & 33 Vict. 1869. pp.viii.218. [12,500.]

——— Supplement . . . session 33 & 34 Vict. 1870. pp.[ii].219–260. [2000.]

AN INDEX to the statutes, public and private, passed in the several years from the union with Ireland to the termination of the eighteenth parliament of the United Kingdom: 41 Geo. 3. (1801) to 28 & 29 Vict. (1865). 1867.

i. The public general acts; with a chronological list of acts repealed. pp.vii.704. clxxi. [30,000.]

the remaining volumes of this work are entered in section b, next below.

CHRONOLOGICAL table of and index to the statutes to the end of the session of 1869 [&c.].

1869. pp.ix.666. [10,000.]
1878. Fifth edition. pp.xii.1031. [30,000.]
1886. Tenth edition. pp.xi.369.1278. [50,000.]
1899. Fifteenth edition. pp.x.499+iv.1270. [60,000.]
1904. Twentieth edition. pp.x.517+iv.1285. [60,000.]

1909. Twenty-fifth. edition. pp.x.560+iv. 1515. [75,000.]
1914. Thirtieth edition. pp.x.570+iv.1536. [75,000.]
1919. Thirty-fifth edition. pp.xi.689+iv. 1768. [85,000.]
1924. Fortieth edition. pp.xi.710+iv.1741. [85,000.]
1929. 45th edition. pp.x.709 + iv.1915. [100,000.]
1934. 50th edition. pp.x.746 + iv.2025. [100,000.]
1935. 51st edition. pp.x.750 + iv.2057. [100,000.]
1936. 52nd edition. pp.x.756 + iv.2096. [100,000.]
1939. 55th edition. pp.x.797 + iv.2191. [100,000.]
1945. 58th edition. pp.x.841 + iv.2299. [100,000.]

[*continued in two parts:*]

Chronological table of the statutes.
1947. 59th edition. pp.x.1112. [50,000.]
1950. pp.xi.998. [50,000.]
1951. pp.xiii.1010. [50,000.]
1952. pp.xiii.1006. [50,000.]
1953. pp.xiii.1028. [50,000.]

[*and:*]

Index to the statutes in force.

1948. pp.[x].cxl.1092 + [iii].1093–2251. [50,000.]

1950. pp.[xii].cxxxvii.1052+[iii].1053–2093. [50,000.]

1952. pp.[x].clxxvi.1050 + [iii].1051–2181. [50,000.]

only the first and latest editions, and every fifth between them, are set out.

EDWARD HENSLOWE BEDFORD, A table of leading statutes. 1876. single leaf. [150.]

ALPHABETICAL Index to principal public general acts, from 1 William IV. to 47 & 48 Vict. (1884). [1884]. pp.[ii].50. [2500.]

ALEXANDER PULLING, Index to the orders in council, proclamations, royal commissions of inquiry, orders and notices of government departments, and all other matter published in the London gazette, from January 1st, 1830 to December 31st, 1883. 1885. pp.xlii.2010. [40,000.]

INDEX to the statutory rules and orders in force on 1st January 1891 [&c.].

1891. [By Alexander Pulling]. pp.vii.356. [7500.]
1893. Second edition. pp.vii.525. [10,000.]
1899. Third edition. pp.x.732. [15,000.]
1903. Fourth edition. pp.x.720. [15,000.]
1906. Fifth edition. pp.x.759. [17,500.]
1909. Sixth edition. pp.x.833. [20,000.]
1912. Seventh edition. pp.x.754. [17,500.]
1915. Eighth edition. pp.x.852. [20,000.]
1919. Ninth edition. [By A. Pulling and Cecil T. Parr (*sic*, Carr)]. pp.xii.1032. [22,500.]
1924. Tenth edition. [By C. T. Carr]. pp.vi.942. [17,500.]
1927. Eleventh edition. pp.vi.921. [20,000.]
1930. Twelfth edition. pp.vi.967. [20,000.]
1933. Thirteenth edition. pp.vi.1009. [20,000.]
1936. Fourteenth edition. pp.vi.vi.1053. [20,000.]
1939. Fifteenth edition. pp.vi.1131. [22,500.]
1946. Sixteenth edition. pp.vi.1310. [25,000.]
1949. Seventeenth edition. pp.xv.1190. [22,500.]

[*continued as:*]

Guide to government orders.

1951. Eighteenth edition. pp.ccvii.1263. [25,000.]

1952. pp.ccviii.1247. [25,000.]

LIST of statutory rules and orders issued by H.M. Stationery office from 1st to 8th May, 1917 [–1st to 7th December, 1921]. [283 weekly issues ranging from 2 to 5 pp. each]. [5000.]

no more published.

INDEX to statutory definitions. Prepared in the office of the Parliamentary counsel. 1936. pp.[iv]. 301. [8000.]

LIST of emergency [acts and] statutory rules and orders. Revised to September 27, 1939. 1939. pp.28. [300.]

BUTTERWORTH'S emergency legislation service annotated. Sept. 3rd, 1939 to March 1st, 1941. Descriptive-word index. 1941. pp.[v].158. [12,500.]

J[OSEPH] BRAY FREEMAN, Butterworth's emergency legislation service (annotated). . . . A complete master index (September 3, 1939–April 30, 1942). 1942. pp.x.230. [25,000.]

—— Second edition. September 3, 1939–September 3, 1943. 1944. pp.xi.339. [35,000.]

——— 1st cumulative supplement. September 3, 1943–January 31, 1944. 1944. pp.[ii].68. [7500.]

b. *Private and local*

GEORGE BRAMWELL, An analytical table of the private statutes, passed between the 1st Geo. II. A.D. 1727, and 52d Geo. III. A.D. 1812, both inclusive. 1813. pp.12.[454]. [12,500.]

—— Vol.II. 1813–1834. 1835. pp.26.[160]. [5000.]

THOMAS VARDON, Index to the local and personal and private acts. 1798–1839. 1840. pp.[iii]. 485. [20,000.]

INDEX to parliamentary notices published in the London, Edinburgh, [Belfast] and Dublin Gazettes . . . for the ensuing Session.

[i]. 1862–1863. pp.
[ii]. 1863–1864. pp.
[iii]. 1864–1865. pp.32. [600.]
[iv]. 1865–1866. pp.
[v]. 1866–1867. pp.19. [350.]
[vi]. 1867–1868. pp.14. [250.]
[vii]. 1868–1869. pp.13. [250.]
[viii]. 1869–1870. pp.15. [300.]
[ix]. 1870–1871. pp.19. [350.]

[x]. 1871–1872. pp.21. [400.]
[xi]. 1872–1873. pp.23. [450.]
[xii]. 1873–1874. pp.20. [400.]
[xiii]. 1874–1875. pp.17. [350.]
[xiv]. 1875–1876. pp.19. [350.]
[xv]. 1876–1877. pp.18. [350.]
[xvi]. 1877–1878. pp.20. [400.]
[xvii]. 1878–1879. pp.18. [350.]
[xviii]. 1879–1880. pp.16. [300.]
[xix]. 1880–1881. pp.18. [350.]
[xx]. 1881–1882. pp.21. [400.]
[xxi]. 1882–1883. pp.27. [500.]
[xxii]. 1883–1884. pp.21. [400.]
[xxiii]. 1884–1885. pp.18. [350.]
[xxiv]. 1885–1886. pp.16. [300.]
[xxv]. 1886–1887. pp.15. [300.]
— 1868–1887. pp.[iii].108. [8000.]
[xxvi]. 1887–1888. pp.16. [300.]
[xxvii]. 1888–1889. pp.17. [300.]
[xxviii]. 1889–1890. pp.26. [500.]
[xxix]. 1890–1891. pp.21. [400.]
[xxx]. 1891–1892. pp.19. [350.]
[xxxi]. 1892–1893. pp.16. [300.]
[xxxii]. 1893–1894. pp.15. [300.]
[xxxiii]. 1894–1895. pp.15. [300.]
[xxxiv]. 1895–1896. pp.17. [300.]
[xxxv]. 1896–1897. pp.21. [400.]

[xxxvi]. 1897–1898. pp.21. [400.]
[xxxvii]. 1898–1899. pp.26. [500.]
[xxxviii]. 1899–1900. pp.26. [500.]
[xxxix]. 1900–1901. pp.23. [450.]
[xl]. 1901–1902. pp.22. [400.]
[xli]. 1902–1903. pp.21. [400.]
[xlii]. 1903–1904. pp.19. [350.]
[xliii]. 1904–1905. pp.17. [300.]
[xliv]. 1905–1906. pp.18. [350.]
[xlv]. 1906–1907. pp.13. [250.]
[xlvi]. 1907–1908. pp.13. [250.]
[xlvii]. 1908–1909. pp.12. [200.]
xlviii. 1909–1910. pp.12. [200.]
xlix. 1910–1911. pp.13. [250.]
l. 1911–1912. pp.12. [200.]
li. 1912–1913. pp.12. [200.]
lii. 1913–1914. pp.13. [250.]
liii. 1914–1915. pp.9. [150.]
liv. 1915–1916. pp.4. [60.]
lv. 1916–1917. pp.4. [60.]
lvi. 1917–1918. pp.6. [100.]
lvii. 1918–1919. pp.5. [75.]
lviii. 1919–1920. pp.9. [150.]
lix. 1920–1921. pp.7. [125.]
lx. 1921–1922. pp.7. [125.]
lxi. 1922–1923. pp.6. [100.]
lxii. 1923–1924. pp.7. [125.]

lxiii. 1924–1925. pp.8. [150.]
lxiv. 1925–1926. pp.7. [125.]
lxv. 1926–1927. pp.7. [125.]
lxvi. 1927–1928. pp.7. [125.]
lxvii. 1928–1929. pp.8. [150.]
lxviii. 1929–1930. pp.8. [150.]
lxix. 1930–1931. pp.7. [125.]
lxx. 1931–1932. pp.5. [75.]
lxxi. 1932–1933. pp.5. [75.]
lxxii. 1933–1934. pp.5. [75.]
lxxiii. 1934–1935. pp.6. [100.]
lxxiv. 1935–1936. pp.7. [75.]
lxxv. 1936–1937. pp.8. [100.]
lxxvi. 1937–1938. pp.7. [75.]
lxxvii. 1938–1939. pp.6. [100.]
lxxviii. 1939–1940. pp.[3]. [44.]

no more published.

AN INDEX to the statutes, public and private, passed in the several years from the union with Ireland to the termination of the eighteenth parliament of the United Kingdom: 41 Geo. 3. (1801) to 28 & 29 Vict. (1865). 1867.

i. [see section a, next above].
ii. The local and personal acts, local acts, and private acts. pp.vi.1033. [40 000.]

— An index to the local and private acts.

1866–1877. 1878. pp.vi.326. [10,000.]
1878–1887. 1890. pp.iv.386. [12,500.]

INDEX to local acts, consisting of classified lists of the local and personal and private acts from 41 Geo. VI. (1801) to 62–3 Vict. (1899) (both inclusive). 1900. pp.viii.807. [30,000.]

INDEX to local and personal acts, consisting of classified lists of the local and personal and private acts and special orders and special procedure orders, 1801–1947. 1949. pp.viii.1140. [45,000.]

vi. *Case law*

a. *General*

α. *Lists of reports*

JOHN WILLIAM WALLACE, The reporters chronologically arranged. Philadelphia 1844. pp.77. [600.]

— — Fourth edition. Published under the superintendence of Franklin Fiske Heard. Boston 1882. pp.vii.654. [800.]

INDEX of contemporaneous reports, from the year 1847 to the year 1862, both inclusive. [1863]. single sheet. [1750.]

— 1847–1865. [1866]. single sheet. [750.]

HENRY G[EORGE] STEVENS and ROBERT W[ILLIAM]

HAYNES, A Chronological catalogue of law reports in the various courts of England, Scotland and Ireland. 1873. pp.5–32. [500.]

AN ALPHABETICAL catalogue of the reports of cases in the various courts of the United Kingdom. [1875]. pp.5.32. [500.]

SYNOPSIS of contemporary reports in equity. 1832–1868 [at common law, 1832–1868 . . . in all the courts, 1866–83]. Law journal: [1883]. single sheet. [750.]

— 1832–1868 [at common law, 1832–1868 . . . in all the courts, 1866–89] . . . [1890]. single sheet. [750.]

— 1832–1895. ff.3. [1000.]

ARTHUR CANE, Tables, alphabetical and chronological, of all reports of cases decided in the superior courts of England, Scotland and Ireland, prior to the . . . law. reports. Council of law reporting: 1895. pp.46. [500.]

CHA[RLE]S COWLES TUCKER, A chronological list of english and american reports from the earliest times. National university: Law department: Washington 1907. pp.57. [500.]

[SIR J[OHN] C[HARLES] FOX, A handbook of english law reports from the last quarter of the eighteenth century to the year 1865. Part I. House of lords, Privy council, and Chancery reports. 1913. pp.ix.107. [75.]

no more published.

β. *Digests and indexes*

[NICHOLAS STATHAM?], [*begins:*] Accompte./ Aiel+ / Addiciōn / [&c.]. [?1488]. ff.[190.]

[—] — [another edition]. Abridgment of the law. Translated by Margaret Center Klingelsmith. Boston 1915.

[SIR ANTHONY FITZHERBERT] [*begins:*] Prima pars huius libri. [London 1516]. ff.[i].287[*sic,* 289] +[i].274[*sic,* 273]+231[*sic,* 230]. [7500.]

a copy containing contemporary ms. notes is in the British museum.

— — [index by John Rastell]. Tabula prime partis magni abbreuiamēti librorū legū anglorū. 1517. ff.[108]+[130]+[94].

— — La graunde abridgement collect par . . . Anthony Fitzherbert . . . et par ceo correct. 1565. ff.[i].379+[i].128.207. [15,000.]

— — — [second edition of the index]. La table cōteynant en sommarie les choses notables en la graunde Abridgment. 1565. ff.[ii].210. [25,000.]

— — La graunde abridgment [&c.]. 1577.

ff[i].342[*sic,* 341]+[i].265.[i].67. [25,000.]
the last pagination comprises Rastell's index.

SIR ROBERT BROOKE, La graunde abridgement. London 1573. ff.[iv].360+338. [35,000.]
a copy containing ms. notes is in the British museum.

—— [second edition]. 1576. ff.[iv].352+328.
reprinted in 1586.

—— Ascuns nouell cases de les ans et temps le roy, H. 8. Ed. 6. et la roygne Mary, escrie [by Richard Bellewe] ex la graund Abridgement, compose per sir Robert Brooke. 1578. ff.[i].116. [iii]. [533.]
reprinted in 1587, 1597, 1604, 1625 and perhaps in 1585; the colophon of the 1604 impression is dated 1904; a copy of this impression in the British museum contains ms. notes.

——— Some new cases of the years and time [&c.]. 1651. pp.[xxxii].295. [1000.]
the pagination is irregular; a copy containing ms. notes is in the British museum.

—— [reprint of the 1578 edition and 1651 translation]. Ascuns novell cases. 1873.
the translation only was reprinted in vol.lxxiii of the English reports, *Edinburgh 1907.*

—— The grand abridgment of the law continued. . . . By William Hughes. 1660–1663. pp.[xlviii].344.353–758.[lviii]. + [lvi].759–1576.

[xc] + [xxxiv].1577–2055.2054–2132.[lxvi] + [xxxvi].2133–2418.[lxviii]. [12,500.]

GUILHELMUS FLETEWOODUS [WILLIAM FLEETWOOD], Annalium tam regum Edwardi quinti, Richardi tertii, & Henrici septimi, quàm Henrici octavi titulorum ordine alphabetico digestorum, elenchus. London 1579. pp.[400]. [6000.]

— — multo iam melius, quam ante, digestorum. 1597. pp.[408]. [6000.]

— — [another edition]. 1679. pp.[60]. [6000.]

[? ARTHUR GREGORIE], De legibus Angliae municipalibus liber ordine locorum communium dispositus. 1583. ff.[i].371.

a copy in the Inner temple library contains ms. notes [? by William Petyt].

[—] — L'abridgment des cases concernants les titles plus materiall [&c.]. 1599. ff.[xxvi].370.36.

another edition forms the first part of William Hughes's Nomotomia, *1657; this part alone was reprinted as* Gregories moot-book *in 1663.*

RICHARD BELLEWE, Les ans dv roy Richard le second collect ensembl' hors de les abridgments de Statham, Fitzherbert et Brooke. London 1585. pp.[351]. [2000.]

the pagination is erratic.

T[HOMAS] A[SHE], La table al lieur des reports del tresreuerend iudge sir Iames Dyer . . . per quel facilment cy troueront toutes choses conteinus in icel. London 1588. ff.[viii].167. [6000.]

a copy containing numerous contemporary ms. notes is in the British museum.

— — [another edition]. 1600. ff.[vii].167.

— — Ore nouelment imprimee & corrigee. 1622. ff.[viii].167.

[RICHARD CARY], Le necessarie vse & fruit de les pleadings, conteine en le liuer de . . . Edward Coke. Londini 1601. ff.[v].98.[i]. [1250.]

[ROBERT BARNEWAL], Syntomotaxia del second part del roy Henrie le sixt, per quel facilment cy troueront soubs apt titles, touts choses conteinus en le dit liuer. London 1601. pp.[118].

[—] — [another edition]. 1679. pp.[107].

VN ABRIDGMENT de touts les cases, reportes per mounsieur Iasqves [sir James] Dyer. Londini 1602. ff.99. [1250.]

THOMAS ASHE, Vn perfect table a tovts les severall livers del reportes de sir Edvvard Coke. London 1606. ff.[xvi].148. [2000.]

— — Vn general table, a touts les seueral liures

des les reports de . . . sir Edward Coke. 1618. ff.[278]. [4000.]

— — A generall table to all the severall books of the reports of . . . sir Edvvard Coke. 1652. pp.[xxiv].468. [9000.]

reissued in 1653.

— — Vn general table [&c.]. 1672. ff.[86]. [9000.]

reissued in 1680.

THOMAS ASHE, 'Επιεικεια: et table generall a les annales del ley, per quel facilment troueres touts les cases contenus in yceux; queux concerne le exposition des statutes per equitie. Societie of the stationers: London 1609. ff.[xv].215.[xliv]. [10,000.]

THO[MAS] ASHE, Le primier [second] volvme del promptuarie, ou repertory generall de les annales, et plvsors avters livres del common ley Dengleterre. Companie of Stationers: London 1614. ff.[vii].286.215+[iii].261.194. [150,000.]

[SIR THOMAS IRELAND], An exact abridgment in english, of the eleven books of reports . . . of sir Edward Coke. 1650. pp.[xxii].427[*sic*, 443].[li]. [600.]

WILLIAM STYLE, Regestum practicale: or, the

practical register, . . . concerning the common-laws. London 1657. pp.[xxxvi].359. [1750.]

— — The second edition. The Practical register. 1670. pp.[520].

the pagination is erratic.

— — The third edition. Style's practical register. 1694. pp.[xx].588. [2000.]

— — The fourth edition [by John Lilly]. 1707. pp.[xvi].688.

— — [another edition]. A continuation of the Practical register. . . . By John Lilly. 1710. pp.viii. 496.[viii]+[ii].459.[xviii]. [5000.]

— — [another edition]. The practical register: or, a general abridgment of the law. . . . By John Lilly. 1719. pp.[xvi].662+[ii].728. [15,000.]

— — — The second edition. 1735. pp.[xx]. 144.155–882+[ii].886. [17,500.]

— — — The second edition. To whic his added, a supplement. 1745. pp.[xx].144.155–882.[vi].56 +[ii].880.[viii].58. [17,500.]

the earlier editions are of a miscellaneous nature.

EDWARD TROTMAN, Un exact alphabetical table de tout l'principal matteires, maximes, et axiomes, conteynus en le abridgment de le siegneur Cokes reportes. London 1664. pp.[35]. [500.]

the British museum copy contains voluminous additions in ms.

HENRY ROLLE, Un abridgment des plusieurs cases et resolutions del common ley. [Edited by sir Matthew Hale]. London 1668. pp.[xvi].688. 725–940+524.545–844. [20,000.]

probably compiled before 1640.

— — A general abridgment of the common law, . . . by [or rather, translated and edited by] Knightley d'Anvers. 1705–1727. pp.[xxxiv].810. [lxii]+[xxxii].794.[lviii]+[vi].112.[xvi]. [25,000.]

— — — The second edition. 1725–1737. pp. [xxviii].810.lxiv] + [xxiv].794.[lvi] + [xxx].430. [xlviii]. [30,000.]

incomplete; no more published.

TABLES of all the cases printed in the books of reports, digested under proper heads. [London] 1719. pp.[xiv].392. [30,000.]

reissued in 1726 as A general index to the common law *&c.*

[KENNETT FREEMAN], Repertorium juridicum: an index to all the cases in the year-books, entries, reports and abridgments in law and equity. 1742. pp.[504]+[434]. [40,000.]

[—] — [another edition]. Part the first. By [or rather, edited by] [sir] T[homas] E[dlyne] Tomlins. 1786–1787. pp.[ii].viii.[660]. [65,000.]

[—] — [another edition]. Dublin 1788. pp.[ii].

x.[490]+[574]. [65,000.]

the second part, containing the index, was not published in these two editions.

[MATTHEW BACON, JOSEPH SAYER and OWEN RUFFHEAD], A new abridgment of the law. By a gentleman of the Middle temple. 1736–1766. pp.[xxii].694 + [xx].688 + [xxii].824 + [xviii]. 698+[xiii].544.[xii].

the first three volumes were reprinted in 1762 as a so-called 'second edition'; the whole was reprinted in 1768–1770, (?Dublin 1770), and 1778 as successive 'editions'; reprinted Dublin 1793 with the addition of the supplement.

— — The fifth edition . . . by Henry Gwillim. 1798 pp.viii.759+[iii].741+[iii].803+[iii].768+[iii].867+[iii].776+[iii].711. [30,000.]

— — The sixth edition. 1807. pp.viii.759+[ii].741 + [ii].803 + [ii].768 + [ii].867 + [ii].776 +[ii].711. [30,000.]

— — [another edition]. To which are added notes and references to american law and decisions, by John Bouvier. Philadelphia 1846. pp. xvi.831 + [iii].848 + 752 + 734 + 722 + 876 + 710+737+696+736. [50,000.]

— — A supplement to Bacon's Abridgment . . . by T[imothy] Cunningham. 1786. pp.[112].

the pagination is erratic; reprinted Dublin 1787 and reissued as part of the 1793 edition of the main work.

CHARLES VINER, A general abridgment of law and equity. Aldershot 1742 [–? 1756]. 23 vols. [25,000.]

planned originally as a supplement to D'Anvers's edition of Rolle; published out of sequence and somewhat erratically; for details see Strickland Gibson, Proceedings and papers of the Oxford bibliographical society *(1930), ii.227–326.*

— — Indexes to mr. Viner's General abridgment of law and equity. [*c.*1760]. pp.xv.482. [25,000.]

— — The second edition. 1791–1795. 24 vols. [50,000.]

— — An abridgment of the modern determinations in the courts of law and equity: being a supplement to Viner's Abridgment. By several gentlemen in the respective branches of the law. 1799–1806. pp.xv.606 + xii.583 + xvi.563 + xix.452+xx.568+xvi.302.[clxvi]. [25,000.]

[S. H. PONT], An alphabetical index to all the abridgments of law equity, and to several books of the crown law, conveyancing, and practice. . . . Chiefly calculated to facilitate the references to the General abridgment . . . by Charles Viner. . . . By a gentleman of Lincoln's inn. 1758. pp.[275]. [15,000.]

also attributed to Robert Kelham; reissued in 1795 as vol.xxiv of Charles Viner's A general abridgment of law and equity.

SIR JOHN COMYNS, A digest of the laws of England. 1762–1767. pp.xii.672+vii.595+viii.591+viii.558+viii.720. [35,000.]

— — A digest of the laws of England. Being a continuation . . . by a gentleman of the Inner-temple. 1776. pp.[iii].623. [6000.]

— — [second edition]. Continued down to the present time, by a gentleman of the Inner temple. 1780. pp.xii.670[*sic*, 660]+vii.699+viii.572+viii.583+viii.752. [40,000.]

reprinted in 1785.

— — The third edition . . . by Stewart Kyd. 1792. pp.xvi.749 + [ii].754 + [ii].735 + [ii].775 +[ii].880+[ii].594. [75,000.]

— — Fourth edition . . . by Samuel Rose. 1800.

— — The fifth edition . . . by Anthony Hammond. 1822. pp.iii.xxx[*sic*, xxxi].788+[ii].826+[ii].638 + [ii].442.315–876 + [ii].640 + [ii].574 + [ii].813+[ii].1044. [60,000.]

— — First American edition by Thomas Day. Philadelphia &c. 1824–1826.

THOMAS WALTER WILLIAMS, An abridgment of cases argued and determined in the courts of law during the reign of . . . George the third. 1798–1803. pp.xx.930 + xii.920 + xiv.921 + xii.911 + [xv].1004. [35,000.]

AN ANALYTICAL digest of the reports of cases decided in the courts of common law, and equity of appeal, and nisi prius [*afterwards:* and in the ecclesiastical courts].

1817. By a barrister [Henry Jeremy], pp.xii. 107. [750.]
1817–1823. pp.xxiii.689. [7500.]
1824. pp.xvi.179. [1250.]
— A general index . . . 1817 to 1824. By H. Jeremy. 1824. pp.[iii].166.
1825. pp.xiv.178. [1250.]
1826. pp.xii.136. [750.]
1827. pp.x.150. [1250.]
1828. pp.xi.184. [1250.]
1829. pp.xii.173. [1250.]
1830. pp.xii.195. [1500.]
1831. pp.xii.148. [1000.]
1832. pp.xii.196. [1250.]
1833. pp.xii.196. [1250.]
1834. pp.xii.234. [1500.]
1835. pp.xiv.260. [1750.]

1836. pp.xii.232. [1500.]
1837. pp.xii.268. [1750.]
1838. pp.xii.188. [1250.]
1839. pp.xii.214. [1500.]
1840. pp.xii.228. [1750.]
1841. pp.xii.236. [1750.]
1842. pp.xii.248. [1750.]
1843. pp.xii.252. [1750.]
1844. pp.xii.293. [2000.]
1845. pp.xii.224. [1750.]
1846. pp.xii.206. [1500.]
1847. pp.xii.221. [1750.]
1848. pp.xii.194. [1500.]
1849. By W. Tidd Pratt. pp.xii.164. [1000.]
1850. pp.xii.174. [1250.]
1851. pp.xi.159. [1000.]
1852. pp.xi.188. [1250.]
1853. pp.xi.164. [1000.]
1854. pp.xi.180. [1250.]

THOMAS COVENTRY and SAMUEL HUGHES, An analytical digested index to the common law reports from the time of Henry III. to the commencement of the reign of George III. 1827. pp.lxxix.820+[iii].821–1666. [30,000.]

S. B. HARRISON, An analytical digest of all the reported cases determined in the House of lords and the several courts of common law . . . from Mich. term 1756. 1828. pp.[iv].xxxii.768+[iii]. 844. [20,000.]

— — Second edition. 1835. pp.lxxi.876 [*sic*, 877] + [ii].877–1748[*sic*, 1749] + [ii].1749–2389. [30,000.]

— — — Addenda. 1837. pp.[iv].2275–2938. [6000.]

incorporates the addenda which form pp.2275–2387 of the main work.

— — Third edition, by R. Tarrant Harrison. 1844. pp.[v].lxxi.coll.2282 + pp.[iv].coll.2285–5432 + pp.[iv].coll.5433–7490 + pp.[689]. [75,000.]

— — — Continued . . . to . . . 1855, by R. A. Fisher. 1856. pp.vii.coll.viii–cxlviii.2084+pp.[ii]. coll.2081–4342. [30,000.]

— — [fourth edition]. A digest of the reported cases determined in the House of lords & Privy council, and in the courts of common law, divorce, probate, admiralty & bankruptcy from Michaelmas term, 1756, to Hilary term, 1870. . . . By R. A. Fisher. 1870. pp.xlviii.coll.2208+pp. xxxiv.coll.2209–4352+pp.xxxviii.coll.4353–6624 + pp.xl.coll.6625–8772 + pp.xxvi.coll.8773–9746. pp.9749–10,054. [70,000.]

[—] — [fifth edition]. A digest of the reported decisions of the courts of common law, bankruptcy, probate, admiralty, and divorce . . . from 1856 to 1883 . . . by John Mews. 1884. pp.xiii. coll.2120 + pp.xi.coll.2440 + pp.xi.coll.2188 + pp.xi.coll.2072 + pp.xi.coll.2048 + pp.xi.coll.2104 + pp.xi.coll.1104. pp.400. [80,000.]

the successive editions incorporate the series of annual supplements and cumulations, which are not set out separately; for the continuation of this work see section k. Superior courts, below.

AN ANALYTICAL digest of the cases published in the Law journal, and in all reports.

1822–1828. 1831. pp.[vii].572.xxxvii. [5000.]

1828–1831. By Montagu Chambers. 1835. pp.[vii].331. [3000.]

1831–1835. By John Greenwood. 1838. pp. [ix].608. [6000.]

1835–1840. By Francis Towers Streeten and Ewen Henry Cameron. 1843. pp.[vii].694. [7000.]

1840–1845. By F. T. Streeten and Thomas Dickson Archibald. 1847. pp.[viii].xvii. 871. [9000.]

1845–1850. By F. T. Streeten and Henry John Hodgson. 1852. pp.[ii].xxiv.774. [8000.]

1850–1855. By F. T. Streeten and George

Stevens Allnutt. 1857. pp.xxiii.796. [8000.]
1855–1860. 1863. pp.xxiii.716. [7000.]
1860–1865. By F. T. Streeten and Edward Alfred Hadley. 1868. pp.xiii.686. [6000.]
1865–1870. By Edmund Story-Maskelyne. 1872. pp.xxxiii.732. [6000.]
1870–1875. By E. Story-Maskelyne and Cecil C. M. Dale. 1877. pp.xxxix.683. [6000.]
1875–1880. By C. C. M. Dale. 1881. pp.xxiv. 765. [6000.]
1880–1885. 1886. pp.xxviii.724. [6000.]
1885–1890. By George A. Streeten. 1892. pp.xxxix.658. [5000.]
1890–1895. pp.xxxvi.672. [5000.]
1896–1900. By James S. Henderson. 1901. pp.lix.coll.964.pp.965–992. [4000.]
1901–1905. 1906. pp.lxi.coll.944.pp.945–969. [4000.]

[*continued as:*]

A digest of all the cases reported in the Law journal reports.

1921–1925. pp.xx.coll.840. [2000.]

no more published; the issues for 1906–1920 and since 1925 are merely Mews's Digest, *with a different wrapper; also issued quarterly in 1895–1896.*

AN ANALYTICAL digest of all the cases reported in the house of lords, in the courts of law and equity, in the Privy council, and in the Ecclesiastical and Admiralty courts.

1833–1834. pp.viii.156. [1500.]
1834–1835.
1835–1836.
1836–1837.
1837–1838.
1838–1839. pp.viii.149. [1250.]
1839–1840. pp.viii.150. [1250.]
1840–1841. pp.[viii].180. [1500.]
1841–1842. pp.[viii].222. [1750.]
1842–1843. pp.[viii].202. [1500.]
1843–1844. pp.[viii].206. [1750.]
1844–1845. pp.[viii].212. [1750.]

HENRY ROSCOE, A general digest of the law for the year 1834, containing all the reported decisions in all the courts. 1835. pp.v.742. [2500.]
— — 1835. 1836. pp.xxxviii.420. [2500.]

R. T[ARRANT] HARRISON, A digested index to all the reported decisions in the several courts of law and equity published during the year . . . to which is added, A digested index to the statutes at large for the year.

1838. pp.[iv].148. [2500.]
1839. pp.[iii].184. [3500.]
1840. pp.[ii].200. [4000.]

1841. pp.[ii].229. [4500.]
1842. pp.[ii].376. [7000.]

GEORGE FARREN, The common law and equity digest. 1841. pp.iii–xx.146+[x].62. [4000.]
the title of vol.ii reads The equity digest.

THE MONTHLY digest and analytical index of the cases reported in the Law journal reports [&c.]. Part I. 1843. pp.xii.31. [250.]
no more published.

THE LAW digest: a general index to the reports [and statutes]: Law times.
[i]. 1845–1846. pp.xii.viii.172. [5000.]
ii. 1846–1848. By Edward Wise and Daniel Thomas Evans. pp.[lxxviii]. coll.1376. [7500.]
iii. 1848–1850. pp.[lxxiv].coll.1365[*sic*, 1366]. [7500.]
iv. 1850–1852. pp.[v].lx.coll.1424. [7500.]
v. 1852–1854. pp.[v].lx.coll.1318. [7500.]
vi. 1854–1856. pp.[v].xlviii.coll.1348. [7500.]
[*new series.*]
i. 1856–1858. By D. T. Evans. pp.[viii].liv. coll.1366. [7500.]
ii. 1858–1860. pp.[viii].liii.coll.1348. [7500.]
iii. 1860–1862. pp.[ix].xlv.coll.1322. [7500.]
iv. 1862–1864. pp.[viii].lv.coll.1396. [7500.]

v. 1864–1866. pp.[viii].xxxvi.1138. [6000.]
vi. 1866–1868. pp.[viii].xlvii.1092. [6000.]
vii. 1868–1870. pp.[viii].xxxix.1220. [6000.]
viii. 1870–1872. pp.[viii].xxxvi.1102. [6000.]
ix (no.1). 1872. pp.[vi].viii.coll.296. [1500.]
no more published.

RICHARD MORRIS, An analytical digest of selected practice cases, decided in the common law courts, to Trinity term, 1847. 1847. pp.lxxxiv.381. [2000.]

THE MONTHLY digest. . . . An analytical digest of equity, common law bankruptcy (appeal), ecclesiastical and criminal cases. Edited by Edward Bourne Lovell.

1850. pp.xxx.coll.528. pp.529–568. [2000.]
1850–1851. pp.xliv.coll.588. [2250.]
1851–1852. pp.lvi.coll.656. [2500.]
1852–1853. coll.464. [2000.]
1853–1854. coll.532. [2000.]

CHAUNCEY SMITH, A digest of the decisions of the courts of England contained in the english law and equity reports. Boston 1857. pp.xxi.910. [7500.]

DIGEST of cases reported in the New reports. . . . Editors . . . George Osborne Morgan [*and others*].

i. 1862–1863. pp.[ii].74. [1000.]
ii. 1863. pp.v.67. [500.]

iii. 1863–1864. pp.v.50. [500.]
iv. 1864. pp.v.66. [500.]
v. 1864–1865. pp.v.37. [250.]
vi. 1865. pp.iv.48. [250.]
no more published.

DIGEST of cases. Council of law reporting for England and Wales: Law reports.
1865–1868. pp.lxxv.coll.872. [2000.]
1868–1871. Compiled by Martin Ware. pp.lxxxiii.coll.1012. [2000.]
1865–1875. pp.ccxlii.coll.3028. [6000.]
1875–1878. Compiled by Martin Ware and John Edward Hall. pp.lxxxviii.coll.920. [2000.]
1865–1880. Compiled by Martin Ware, John Edward Hall and H. Lacy Fraser. pp.dxxii. coll.1832 + pp.[iv]. coll.1833–4620. [10,000.]
1880–1883. Compiled by M. Ware, J. E. Hall and H. L. Fraser. pp.cxxxi.coll.1104. [2000.]
1881–1885. Compiled by M. Ware, Peter Burrowes Hutchins and Sir G. Sherston Baker. pp.cciv.1724. [3500.]
1886–1888. The consolidated current index. . . . Compiled by Alexander Pulling. pp. clxxxvi.coll.680. [4000.]

1865–1890. Editor Arthur Paul Stone. pp. dccccii + [iv].coll.3524 + pp.[iv].coll.3525–7376. [15,000.]

1891–1895. Five years' digest.... By A. Pulling. pp.cclxv.coll.1016. [5000.]

1891–1900. Ten years' digest.... Compiled by Meryon White. pp.cclxvii.coll.2396. [10,000.]

1901–1905. Five years' digest.... Compiled by M. White. pp.ccxcv.coll.1614. [3000.]

1901–1910. Ten years' digest.... Compiled by M. White-Winton. pp.dcxxix.coll. 3046. [12 500.]

1911–1920. Ten years' digest.... Compiled by James Robert Vernam Marchant. pp. dcccxliii+[v].coll.4438. [10,000.]

1921–1930. Ten years' digest.... Compiled by James S. Henderson. pp.cdxcvii+[vii]. coll.3362. [7500.]

1931–1950. Twenty years' digest. Edited by Peter Bristow. pp.716+coll.3392+3393–6478. [15,000.]

in progress; also published in quarterly and annual cumulative issues entitled The [complete] current index; *only the cumulations for periods of three years and upwards are set out above, together with the current annual issues.*

A DIGEST of all the cases in all the reports decided by all the courts relating to magistrates', parochial, ecclesiastical, election, municipal, and criminal law, from 1856 to 1869. 1870. pp.iv.399. [4000.]

JAMES SIMMONS, Digest of Moak's English reports, volumes 1 to 15, inclusive. Albany, N.Y. 1878. pp.xlii.728. [3000.]

ALFRED EMDEN, A digest of all reported cases not contained in the 'Law reports'.

1881. pp.xl.coll.164. [500.]
1882. pp.xli.coll.170. [500.]
1883. pp.lxviii.coll.180. [500.]

THE REVISED REPORTS. Table of cases in volumes I–X. . . . 1785–1809. 1893. pp.x.51. [2250.]

— An index of all reported cases decided in the english courts during the period covered by the revised reports. Vols.I to XV . . . 1785–1816. 1894. pp.xiv.313. [12,500.]

— — Vols.I to XL. . . . 1785–1836. 1900. pp. xxiv.786. [32,000.]

PETER V. ROSS, Index to the notes in Annotated cases, american and english, volumes 1912 A to 1916 B. San Francisco 1916. pp.xxxv.358. [10,000.]

— 1916 C to 1918 B. 1918. pp.[ii].119. [3000.]

DIGEST of the cases reported in Annotated cases cases (american and english), 1912 A to 1916 B. San Francisco &c. 1916. pp.[ii].1708. [10,000.]
— 1916 C to 1918 B. 1918. pp.liii.905. [5000.]
— 1918 C to 1918 E. 1919. pp.275. [2000.]

THE ENGLISH and empire digest . . . being a complete digest of every english case reported from early times to the present day, with additional cases from the courts of Scotland, Ireland, the empire of India, and the dominions beyond the seas.
i. Action-agency. 1919. pp.xcii.700. [6000.]
ii. Agriculture–arbitration. 1919. pp.lxxi.640. [5000.]
iii. Auction–bastardy. 1920. pp.lxx.408. [3500.]
iv–v. Bankruptcy. 1920. pp.xxxv.598+ cl.601–1194. [9638.]
vi. Bills of exchange. 1921. pp.lxxiii.515. [3286.]
vii. Bills of sale–burial. 1921. pp.lxxxii.568. [4000.]
viii. Carriers–clubs. 1922. pp.lxxxviii.531. [3500.]
ix–x. Companies. 1924. pp.xxxv.684 + cxlviii.713–1221. [8636.]

xi. Commons–constitutional law. 1922. pp. xciii.592. [4000.]

xii. Contract. 1923. pp.lxxxi.632. [5168.]

xiii. Copyholds–county courts. 1923. pp. lxxviii.559. [4000.]

xiv–xv. Criminal law and procedure. 1924. pp.xxxv.554+cxxi.601–1076. [12,171.]

xvi. Contempt of court–crown practice. 1923. pp.xciii.494. [6000.]

xvii. Custom and usage–dependencies. 1924. pp.lxxxix.510. [6000.]

xviii. Descent–distress. 1924. pp.lxxvi.456. [4000.]

xix. Easements–education. 1924. pp.lxxvi. 613. [5000.]

xx. Elections–equity. 1925. pp.lxxxvii.552. [4500.]

xxi. Estate . . . duties–execution. 1925. pp. xcii.678. [6000.]

xxii. Evidence. 1925. pp.ciii.636. [6969.]

xxiii. Executors and administrators. 1925. pp. xxxv.530. [5970.]

xxiv. Executors–ferries. 1925. pp.cxx.531–986. [5000.]

xxv. Fisheries–gifts. 1925. pp.lxxxi.558. [5000.]

xxvi. Guarantee–highways. 1926. pp.lxxix. 592. [5000.]

xxvii. Husband and wife. 1926. pp.lxxvii. 574. [6309.]

xxviii. Income tax-injunction. 1926. pp. lxxxiv.552. [5000.]

xxix. Inns–interpleader. 1926. pp.lxxxiii.514. [5000.]

xxx–xxxi. Intoxication liquors–landlord. 1926. pp.lxxxviii.522+lxxix.587. [10,000.]

xxxii. Libel–loan societies. 1927. pp.xc.560. [5000.]

xxxiii. Local government–markets. 1927. pp.xci.569. [5000.]

xxxiv. Master and servant–mines. 1927. pp.xcvii.758. [6000.]

xxxv. Misrepresentation–name. 1927. pp. xcvi.713. [6000.]

xxxvi. Negligence–patents. 1927. pp.cxiv. 859. [8000.]

xxxvii. Pawns–prize law. 1928. pp.xciv.690. [6000.]

— [Out of series]. Pleading, practice. 1932. pp.lxxii.999. [7000.]

xxxviii. Public authorities–real property. 1928. pp.cxxxiii.791. [8000.]

xxxix. Receivers–sale of goods. 1928. pp. ciii.695. [7000.]

xl. Sale of land–settlements. 1928. pp.cvi.799. [8000.]

xli. Sewers–shipping. 1928. pp.cxvii.998. [10,000.]

xlii. Small holdings–tort. 1929. pp.cxlvii. 998. [10,000.]

xliii. Trade–water supply. 1929. pp.cxlii.1105. [12,500.]

xliv. Waters–work. 1929. pp.cliii.1318. [15,000.]

xlv–xlvi. Consolidated table of cases. 1930. pp.xv.1292+xi.1293–2458. [225,000.]

xlvii–xlviii. Comprehensive index. 1930. pp. x.995+[viii].995–1969.

— Cumulative supplement bringing the work up to 1941. Edited by Philip F. Skottowe. 1941. pp.ccclxxxii+44 parts. [60,000.]

— Second cumulative supplement. 1952. pp. ccvii+44 parts. [50,000.]

there are intermediate annual cumulations.

AUBREY J. SPENCER, Mews' digest of english case law. Quarterly issue, July 1925. pp.xiv.coll.232. [600.]

no more published.

γ. *Cases overruled*

CHARLES WILLIAM MITCALFE DALE and RUDOLF CHAMBERS LEHMANN, A digest of cases overruled, not followed, disapproved, approved, distinguished, commented on and specially considered in the english courts from the year 1756 to 1886 inclusive. 1887. pp.[458].coll.1600. [6000.]

— — A digest of cases, overruled, approved, or otherwise dealt with in the english and other courts. . . . By William Andrew George Woods . . . and John Ritchie. . . . Founded on Dale and Lehmann's 'Digest . . .'. 1907. pp.ccxxxii.coll.1430 + pp.[iv].coll.1431–3532 + pp.[iv].coll.3533–5592. [40,000.]

b. *Court of admiralty*

JOSHUA GREENE, A digested index of the cases determined in the High court of admiralty, before . . . sir William Scott. 1818. pp.viii.136. [1000.]

WILLIAM TARN PRITCHARD, An analytical digest of all the reported cases determined by the High court of admiralty of England . . . also of the analogous cases. 1847. pp.lxxxviii.707. [5000.]

— — Second edition. A digest of the law and practice of the High court of admiralty. . . . By Robert A. Pritchard and W. T. Pritchard. 1865. pp.xxiii.494+[ii].495–1996.cclxxxvi. [7500.]

— — Third edition. Pritchard's digest of admiralty and maritime law. By James C. Hannen and W. T. Pritchard. 1887. pp.lxxxviii.1128+[iv].1129–2548. [12,500.]

HUBERT HULL, Digest of cases decided in british prize courts, August, 1914–November, 1927. 1927. pp.xxxviii.126. [1250.]

c. *Court of chancery*

1200–1500

[H. RODNEY], Index of ancient petitions of the Chancery and the Exchequer. Public record office: Lists and indexes (no.1): 1892. pp.vi.127. [15,000.]

1219–1349

CALENDAR of inquisitions, miscellaneous (chancery) preserved in the Public record office. 1916. pp.xvi.902+ix.790. [5000.]

1244–1326

[R. C. FOWLER], Calendar of chancery warrants preserved in the Public record office. . . . A.D. 1244–1326. 1927. pp.xi.753. [5000.]

1377–1603

[JOHN BAYLEY], Calendars of the proceedings in Chancery in the reign of queen Elizabeth, to which are prefixed examples of earlier proceedings in that court, namely, from the reign of Richard the second to that of queen Elizabeth, inclusive. From the originals in the Tower. [Record commission:] 1827–1832. pp.[xxviii]. cxlvii.565+[ix].lxxvi.527+[vii].398. [15,000.]

see 1558–1603 below.

1385–1467

CLAUDE A. WALMISLEY, An index of persons named in early chancery proceedings, Richard II (1385) to Edward IV (1467), preserved in the Public record office, London. Publications of the Harleian society (vols.lxxviii–lxxix): 1927–1928. pp.vii.117+xxxix.111. [45,000.]

1387–1558

[J. B. W. CHAPMAN *and others*], List of early chancery proceedings. Public record office: Lists and indexes (nos.xii, xvi, xx, xxix, xxxviii, xlviii, l, li, liv, lv): 1901–1936. pp.vii.392+7.566+5.519 + 5.459 + [iv].612 + [ii].364 + [ii].364 + [iii]. 270+[iii].372+[iv].322. [100,000.]

1558–1603

RICHARD HOLWORTHY, Calendar of chancery

proceedings, Elizabeth, being those suits omitted from the printed calendar published in 1827/30 [*sic*] by the Record commissioners. Society of genealogists: 1913. pp.24. [400.]

bundles A1–B10 only; no more published; see 1377–1603, above.

1558–1660

[A. J. GREGORY], Index of chancery proceedings (series II.) — A.D. 1558–1579[–1660]. Public record office: Lists and indexes (nos.vii, xxiv, xxx): 1896–1909. pp.[iv].456+[iii].328+[iii].395. [50,000.]

1548–1800

GEORGE KEKEWICH, A digested index to the earlier chancery reports. 1804. pp.xii.460. [6000.]

1603–1625

[J. V. LYLE], Index of chancery proceedings (series I.) . . . James I. Vol.I. A–K. Public record office: Lists and indexes (no.xlvii): 1922. pp.[iii].490. [15,000.]

no more published.

1613–1714

[A. J. GREGORY], Index of chancery proceedings, Bridges' division, 1613–1714. Public record office:

Lists and indexes (nos.xxxix, xlii, xliv, xlv): 1913–1917. pp.[iii].433 + [iii].348 + [iii].370 + [iii].390. [60,000.]

1625–1649

W[ILLIAM] P[HILLIMORE] W[ATTS] PHILLIMORE [vol.iv: EDWARD ALEXANDER FRY], A calendar of chancery proceedings. Bills and answers filed in the reign of king Charles the first. British record society: Index library (vols.ii, v, vi, xiv): 1889–1896. pp.vi.265 + [iv].264 + [iv].190 + vi.240. [100,000.]

1649–1714

EDW[ARD] ALEXANDER FRY, Index of chancery proceedings (Reynardson's division preserved in the Public record office. British record society: Index library (vol.xxix, xxxii): 1903–1904. pp. xxiii.259+[v].238. [55,000.]

1689–1805

A DIGESTED index to the chancery reports: containing the points of equity determined in the High court of chancery from the year 1689, to the year 1801. 1802. pp.xii.539. [8000.]

— Second edition. A digested index to the modern reports in chancery . . . 1869, to . . . 1805. 1807. pp.xi.626. [10,000.]

1789–1809

ROBERT BELT, A general index to the first fourteen volumes of the cases reported in chancery, by Francis Vesey. 1810. pp.[ii].616. [5000.]

d. *Court of common pleas*, see also *Court of king's bench.*

INDEX of placito de banco. Public record office: Lists and indexes (no.xxxii): 1909. pp.[iii].472+[ii].473–837. [15,000.]

e. *Courts of equity*

A GENERAL abridgment of cases in equity. . . . By a gentleman of the Middle temple. 1732. pp. [xxviii].417.[xxvii].

attributed to Matthew Bacon, Robert Foley, sir Geoffrey Gilbert, and Henry Pooley.

— The second edition. 1734. pp.[xxviii].417. [xxvii]. [2500.]

a corrected reprint; reprinted in 1739 as a 'third edition', in 1756 as a 'fourth', in 1792 as a 'third', in 1793 as a 'fifth'; also reprinted in vol.xxi of the English reports, *Edinburgh 1902; an interleaved copy of the 1734 edition, with ms. notes by Sir John Strange, and a copy of the 1756 edition, with voluminous ms. notes by Francis Hargrave, are in the British museum.*

— [supplement]. A general abridgment [&c.]. Vol.II. 1756. pp.[xxiv].780.

— — The second edition. 1769. pp.[xxii].780. [xliv].

— — The third edition. 1793. pp.[xxii].512+[ii].513–780.[xcii].

reprinted in vol.xxii of the English reports, *Edinburgh 1902.*

JOSIAH BROWN, A new abridgment of cases in equity . . . from 1735, to the present time. . . . Vol.I. 1793. pp.xix.535. [1250.]

a only; no more published.

RICHARD WHALLEY BRIDGMAN, Thesaurus juridicus: containing the decisions of the several courts of equity. 1799–1800. pp.xx.612+xiv.588. [15,000.]

RICHARD WHALLEY BRIDGMAN, An analytical index of the reported cases in the several courts of equity, as well chancery as exchequer, and in the High court of parliament. 1805. pp.[ii].viii. [xviii].640+[xv].764. [10,000.]

— — Third edition. 1822. pp.27.736+20.748+viii.715. [15,000.]

NICHOLAS BAYLIES, A digested index to the modern reports of the courts of common law in

England and the United States. Montpelier, Vt. 1814.

covers the period 1689–1809 in England and 1799–1812 in the United States.

JOHN FLATHER, A digested index to the reports of cases determined in the High court of chancery, and other courts of equity, in England and Ireland, from 1808 to 1822 . . . with a digest of the reported cases upon equity practice, from the earliest printed reports to the present time. 1823. pp.xvi.646. [7500.]

EDWARD CHITTY, An index to all the reported cases, statutes, and general orders, in or relating to the principles, pleading, and practice of equity and bankruptcy in the several courts of equity in England and Ireland, the Privy council, and the House of lords, from the earliest period. 1831. pp.xxxii.726+[iv].727–1646. [40,000.]

—— Second edition. 1837–1838. pp.[lx].vi. 620 + [vi].621–1104 + [iv].1105–2008 + 7.2009–2782. [60,000.]

—— Third edition, brought down to the year 1853, by James Macaulay. 1853. pp.[ii].viii.950+[iii].951–1796 + [iii].1797–2946 + [iii].2947–3986. [75,000.]

—— Fourth edition. Chitty's index [&c.]. . . .

revised . . . by William Frank Jones and Henry Edward Hirst [vols.iii–ix: by H. E. Hirst]. 1883–1889. pp.xii.1042 + ix.1043–2080 + viii.2081–3070 + viii.3071–4210 + xlii.4211–5372 + x. 5373–6369 + viii.6371–7363 + vii.7365–8368 + [418]. [100,000.]

OLIVER L. BARBOUR and E. B. HARRINGTON, An analytical digest of the equity cases decided in the courts of the several states, and of the United States, from the earliest period: and of the decisions in equity, in the courts of chancery and exchequer in England and Ireland, and the Privy council and House of lords, from Hilary term, 1822. Springfield, Mass. 1837. pp.7–684+[ii].viii. 664+[ii].xi.614. [17,500.]

— — Since 1836. By O. L. Barbour. 1843. pp. xxiv.17–737. [7500.]

GEORGE FARREN, The common law and equity digest. 1841. pp.iii–xx.146+[x].62. [4000.]

the title of vol.ii reads The equity digest.

f. *Court of exchequer*, see also *Court of king's bench*

ADAM MARTIN, Index to various repertories, books of orders, and decrees, and other records, preserved in the Court of exchequer. 1819. pp. viii.244. [10,000.]

[H. RODNEY], Index of ancient petitions of the chancery and the exchequer. Public record office: Lists and indexes (no.1): 1892. pp.vi.127. [15,000.]

[HORACE HEADLAM], List of special commissions and returns in the exchequer. Public record office: Lists and indexes (no.xxxvii): 1912. pp.[ii].136. [10,000.]

LIST of exchequer k. r., memoranda rolls, and exchequer l. t. r., Chancellor's rolls, memoranda rolls, originalia rolls, and pipe rolls. Public record office: 1926. ff.[ii].117. [3000.]*

g. *Court of king's bench*

A DIGEST of adjudged cases in the Court of king's bench, from the revolution to the present period. . . . By a gentleman of Lincoln's inn. 1775. pp.[iv].839.xxxv. [7500.]
published in parts 1773?

[SIR] T[HOMAS] E[DLYNE] TOMLINS, A digested index to the seven volumes of term reports in the Court of king's bench: containing a concise statement of all the points of law determined in that court, from Michaelmas term 26 Geo III. 1785, to Trinity term 38 Geo III. 1798, inclusive. 1799. pp.xliv.324. [2000.]

— — 1785–1798. Second edition. 1799. pp. xliv.324. [3000.]

— — 1785–1805. Third edition. 1806. pp.12. ix–xl.548. [5000.]

— — 1785–1811 and in the Court of common pleas, 1788–1810. Fourth edition. 1812. pp.8. xxxii.667.xix. [6000.]

JOHN BAYLY MOORE, A digested index to the term reports . . . containing all the points of law argued and determined in the Court of king's bench, from Michaelmas term, 1785, to Easter term, 1814, and in the Court of common pleas, from Easter term, 1788, to Hilary term, 1815. 1816. pp.lxxii.731+[ii].265. [7500.]

— — Second edition [to 1818 and 1819]. 1821. pp.lxxxviii.946+[iii].325. [10,000.]

JOHN TIDD PRATT, A digested index to the term reports . . . containing all the points of law . . . determined, in the King's bench, from . . . 1785, to . . . 1825; in the Common pleas, from . . . 1788, to . . . 1825; and in the Exchequer, from . . . 1792, to . . . 1825. 1826. pp.lxiv.1045.[cvi]. [10,000.]

JOHN HILLYARD CAMERON, A digest of cases determined in the Court of queen's bench, from Michaelmas term, tenth George IV. to Hilary term, third Victoria. Toronto 1840. pp.[ii].121. [1000.]

h. *Court of referees*

REGINALD C[AUTLEY] SAUNDERS, The consolidated index of cases decided by the Court of referees and contained in the Locus standi reports, 1867 to 1890. 1891. pp.xcviii.192. [4000.]

i. *Court of requests*

[P. S. L. HUNT, H. RODNEY and J. B. W. CHAPMAN], List of proceedings in the Court of requests . . . Vol.I. Public record office: Lists and indexes (no. xxi): 1906. pp.v.499. [15,000.]

no more published.

j. *Court of star chamber*

[J. B. W. CHAPMAN], List of proceedings in the Court of star chamber. . . . Vol.I. A.D. 1485–1558. Public record office: Lists and indexes (no.xiii): 1901. pp.viii.335. [12,500.]

no more published.

k. *Superior courts*

JOHN MEWS, A digest of all the reported decisions of the superior courts, from 1884 to 1888 inclusive. Together with a selection from those of the irish courts. 1889. pp.[iii].coll.2138. pp.58. [7500.]

— — [another edition]. The digest of english case law, containing the reported decisions of the superior courts, and a selection from those of the irish courts. 1898. pp.[x].66.xvi.coll.1068 + pp.xi.coll.1940 + pp.xi.coll.2170 + pp.xi.coll.1950 + pp.xi.coll.1592 + pp.xi.coll.1898 + pp.xi.coll.1654 + pp.xi.coll.1654 + pp.xi.coll.1872 + pp.xi.coll.1654 + pp.xi.coll.1740 + pp.xi.coll.1212 + pp.xi.coll.1976 + pp.xi.coll.2040 + pp.xi.coll.1858+pp.[iv].66.xvi.759. [200,000.]

— — Second [*sic*] edition. Mews' digest of english case law, containing the reported decisions of the superior courts and a selection from those of the scottish and irish courts to the end of 1924. . . . Under the general editorship of sir Alexander Wood Renton and Sydney Edward Williams [vols.ix–xxix: and Wyndham A. Bewes].

i. Abandonment–banker. 1925. pp.[ii].xxxiv. coll.1476. [7500.]

ii. Bankruptcy. 1925. pp.ix.coll.1716. [8500.]

iii. Barrister–common. 1925. pp.xx.coll. 1828. [9000.]

iv. Company. 1925. pp.ix.coll.1766. [9000.]

v. Compensation–cash. 1925. pp.xvi.coll. 1680. [8500.]

vi. County–custom. 1925. pp.xiii.coll.1600. [8000.]

vii. Customs and excise–ecclesiastical law. 1925. pp.xvi.coll.1968. [10,000.]

viii. Ejectment–execution. 1925. pp.xiv.coll. 1668. [8500.]

ix. Executor and administrator–heir-at-law. 1925. pp.xix.coll.1684. [8500.]

x. Highways and bridges–inspectorship. 1926. pp.xv.coll.1486. [7500.]

xi. Insurance–landlord and tenant. 1925. pp. xv.coll.1760. [9000.]

xii. Land registry–machinery. 1926. pp.xv. coll.1550. [8000.]

xiii. Machinery–mutual will. 1925. pp.xvi. coll.1904. [10,000.]

xiv. Name–poll. 1926. pp.xx.coll.1556. [8000.]

xv. Poor law–prescription. 1925. pp.xiv. coll.1944. [10,000.]

xvi. Press–receipt. 1926. pp.xvi.coll.1472. [7500.]

xvii. Receiver–sheriff. 1925. pp.xx.coll.1478. [7500.]

xviii. Shipping and marine insurance. 1926. pp.ix.coll.2040. [10,000.]

xix. Shops–truck act. 1925. pp.xx.coll.1534. [7500.]

xx. Trust and trustee–verdict. 1926. pp.xii. coll.1504. [7500.]

xxi. Vested, contingent and future interests–will. 1925. pp.xvi.coll.1388. [6500.]

xxii. Will–younger children. 1926. pp.xiii. coll.2072. [10,000.]

xxiii. Index of cases judicially noticed. 1927. pp.[iv].coll.1125. [25,000.]
this volume only extends to 1926.

xxiv. Table of cases in vols.I–XXIII. 1928. pp.xxvi.coll.1090. [100,000.]

——— Supplement . . . 1925 to 1935. By G. T. Whitfield Hayes. 1936. pp.ccxxiv.coll.3106. [12,500.]

——— Supplement . . . 1936 to 1946. 1949. pp.cciii. coll.1121 + 1122–2564. pp.2565–2581. [8000.]

i–xxi. [*consolidated as shown next above*].

xxii. 1946. pp.xii.coll.364.pp.365–395. [600.]

xxiii. 1947. By V. R. Aronson. pp.xx.coll. 430.pp.431–471. [600.]

xxiv. 1948. pp.xxix.coll.472.pp.473–523. [750.]

xxv. 1949. pp.xxxvi.coll.474.pp.475–526. [750.]

xxvi. 1950. By Peter Allsop. pp.xliv.coll. 454.pp.455–516. [750.]

xxvii. 1951. pp.xvi.coll.442.pp.443–483. [750.]

xxviii. 1952. pp.xxvi.coll.338.pp.339–378. [600.]

in progress; the successive editions incorporate series of annual and periodically consolidated supplements, only the current issues of which are set out here; this work is a continuation of one entered under section vi.a.β above.

THE YEARLY abridgment of reports. Being a full analysis of all cases decided in the superior courts.

1895–1896. By Arthur Turnour Murray. pp.lxiii.coll.336.pp.337–374. [1000.]

1896–1897. pp.lxiii.coll.336.pp.337–381.

1897–1898. pp.xlv.coll.292.pp.293–338. [750.]

[*continued as:*]

The yearly digest of reported cases . . . decided in the supreme and other courts.

1899. Edited by Edward Beal. pp.lx.coll.402. [1000.]

1900. pp.lxviii.coll.448. [1000.]
1901. pp.lxxii.coll.512. [1250.]
1902. pp.lxxvi.coll.564. [1250.]
1903. Edited by G. R. Hill. pp.lxxviii.coll. 440. [1000.]
1904. pp.lxxviii.coll.410. [1000.]
1905. pp.lxx.coll.418. [1000.]
1906. pp.xxxii.coll.406.pp.35. [1000.]
1907. pp.xxxi.coll.404.pp.34. [1000.]

— — Sidney W. Clarke, Butterworth's ten year digest of reported cases 1898 to 1807. A digest of reported cases decided in the supreme and other courts 1908. pp.[vi].coll.1356+pp.[iv].coll.1258 + pp.[iv].coll.1246 + pp.[iv].363. [10,000.]

— — — Annual supplement. Butterworth's yearly digest of reported cases.

1908. Edited by G. R. Hill. pp.xxxvii.coll. 708.pp.41. [1500.]
1909. Edited by Harry Clover. pp.xxxix. coll.678.pp.40. [1500.]
1910. pp.xxxvii.coll.670.pp.46. [1500.]
1911. pp.xxxix.coll.676.pp.41. [1500.]
1912. pp.xliii.coll.756.pp.45. [1500.]
— 1908–1912. Butterworth's five years' digest. By Gilbert Stone. pp.cccviii.coll. 902+pp.[ii].coll.1472. [7500.]

1913. pp.xli.coll.744.pp.51. [1500.]
1914. pp.xl.coll.738.pp.60. [1500.]
1915. Edited by Harold Meyer. pp.xlii.coll. 886.pp.67. [1500.]
1916. pp.xxxviii.coll.720.pp.49. [1500.]
1917. Edited by H. Meyer and C. L. Hales. pp.xxxiv.coll.664.pp.39. [1000.]
1918. Edited by H. Meyer and C. H. Chadwick. pp.xxxiv.coll.622.pp.38. [1000.]
1919. Edited by C. H. Chadwick. pp.xl.coll. 538.pp.39. [1000.]
1920. pp.xliv.coll.612.pp.46. [1000.]
1921. Edited by C. H. Chadwick and W. S. Goddard. pp.xxxviii. coll.502. pp.41. [1000.]
1922. Edited by W. S. Goddard. pp.xxxvi. coll.338.pp.32. [750.]
1923. pp.xxiii.coll.328.pp.34. [750.]
1924. pp.xxi.coll.338.pp.32. [750.]
1925. pp.xxi.coll.346.pp.32. [750.]
1926. pp.xx.coll.336.pp.34. [750.]
1927. pp.xix.coll.352.pp.25. [750.]
1928. pp.xx.coll.314.pp.28. [750.]
1929. pp.xix.coll.332.pp.26. [750.]
1930. pp.xviii.coll.334.pp.30. [750.]
1931. pp.xix.coll.366.pp.31. [750.]
1932. pp.xviii.coll.338.pp.28. [750.]

1933. pp.xviii.coll.350.pp.24. [750.]
1934. pp.xviii.coll.346.pp.22. [750.]
1935. pp.xvii.coll.324.pp.22. [750.]
1936. Edited by W. S. Goddard and Philip F. Skottowe. pp.xxi.coll.536.pp.31. [1000.]
1937. Edited by P. F. Skottowe. pp.xx.398. pp.18. [750.]
1938. pp.xix.coll.392.pp.15. [750.]
1939. pp.xx.coll.418.pp.15. [750.]
1940. pp.xix.coll.338.pp.11. [750.]
1941. pp.xi.coll.274.pp.6. [500.]
1942. pp.xi.coll.280.pp.5. [500.]

[*continued as:*]

The all England law reports digest of reported cases.

1943. pp.xi.coll.308.pp.5. [500.]
1944.
1945. pp.xi.coll.404.pp.17. [700.]
1946. pp.xii.coll.406.pp.13. [700.]
1947. pp.xv.coll.414.pp.21. [700.]
1948. pp.xvi.coll.466.pp.26. [700.]

no more published.

vii. *The justice of the peace*

E. W., Statuta pacis: or a perfect table of all the statutes (now in force) which any way concerns the office of a Justice of peace. 1644. pp.[xx].286. [750.]

KENNETH M. MACMORRAN, The Justice of the peace digest of cases reported during the years 1883 to 1908 inclusive. 1909. pp.lxxix.coll.1509. [6000.]

— — The Justice of the peace and local government review digest of cases reported during the years 1909 to 1930, inclusive. By R. C. Maxwell. 1931. pp.xxiv.coll.1035.pp.29. [3000.]

viii. *Miscellaneous*

LEGAL aid and advice for poor people. House of commons: Library: Bibliography (no.43): [1948]. pp.20. [89.]*

W. A. FEURTADO, Index to the laws of England specially relating to the colonies and british possessions abroad. Jamaica 1890. pp.[iii].52. [750.]

LESLIE F. MAXWELL, A bibliography of the law of british colonies, protectorates and mandated territories. Sweet & Maxwell's legal bibliography (vol.vii): 1949. pp.iv.110. [1000.]

UNION list of commonwealth law literature in libraries in Oxford, Cambridge and London. University of London: Institute of advanced legal studies: Publication (no.2): 1952. pp.[v].120. [1000.]*

Grenada.

P. M. C. SHERIFF, Comparative index of the laws of the colonies of Grenada & St. Vincent up to the 31st day of December 1905. Barbados [printed] [1906]. pp.[ii].26. [1000.]

Guatemala.

ALEJANDRO MARURE and ANDRÉS FUENTOS FRANCO, Catálogo razonado de la leyes de Guatemala . . . desde la independencia. Guatemala 1841. pp.143. [1400.]

—— [another edition]. 1856. pp.[ii].ix.361. [2000.]

Guiana.

O. E. SHARPLES, A digest of cases decided in the Supreme court of British Guiana during the years 1901, 1902, 1903, 1904, and the earlier half of the 1905, including cases decided in the appellate jurisdiction of the court. [*s.l.* 1906]: pp.[ii].ii. 251.x. [500.]

—— 1905–1909. 1910. pp.vi.234.x. [600.]

B. E. J. C. BELMONTE, An alphabetical digest and index appended of . . . decisions of the several courts of justice in British Guiana, from 1856 to 31st December, 1906, and of the statute laws of the colony . . . comprising the resolutions of the States general, A.D. 1774, and all subsequent statutes. 1907. pp.xiii.419. [3000.]

— — Supplementary . . . digest . . . 1907, to 21st August, 1908. 1908. pp.xiii.90. [400.]

LAWRENCE C. WROTH and GERTRUDE L. ANNAN, Acts of french royal administration concerning Canada, Guiana, the West Indies and Louisiana, prior to 1791. Public library: New York 1930. pp.151. [2083.]

Guinea.

FRANCISCO MARTOS AVILA, Índice legislativo de Guinea. Instituto de estudios políticos: Madrid 1944. pp.xxii.249. [3500.]

Hainault.

J[EAN] B[APTISTE] BIVORT, Ancien droit de Belgique. Analyse chronologique des chartes, coutumes, édits, ordonnances et règlements qui, depuis l'an 1200, ont régi les diverses localités qui composaient le comté de Hainaut au moment de l'invasion française . . . 1er juillet 1794. Bruxelles 1846. pp.99. [500.]

Hannover.

E. W. G. SCHLÜTER, Repertorium juris hannoverani, oder nachweisungen der wichtigsten erläuterungen der bewährtesten hannoverschen practiker zu dem im königreiche Hannover geltenden rechte, welche in deren werken und zeitschriften zerstreuet sind. Stade 1854. pp.xxvii.448. [5000.]

Hungary.

STEPHAN ASZALAY, Index seu compendium operis tripartiti, et generalis decreti, constitutionumquè inclyti regni Hungariæ. Tyrnaviæ 1694. pp.[xxviii].441.[xl]. [5000.]

ALEXANDER KUBINYI, Enchiridion lexici juris incliti regni Hungariae. . . . Revisus . . . studio & opera Joannis Csaplovics. Posonii 1810. pp.[iv]. 783. [5000.]

— — Editio tertia. 1832. pp.556. [5000.]

JOSEPH BENCSIK, Repertorium juris publici, privati, et criminalis hungarici. Posonii 1821. pp.[x].474. [20,000.]

BARON IGNATIUS EÖTVÖS, Index synopticus actorum comitalium in novem regni Hungaricae et partium ei adnexarum Comitiis signanter ab anno $178\frac{0}{1}$. usque $182\frac{5}{7}$. inclusive occurrentium. Budae 1829. pp.[viii].174. [3000.]

GEORG BINDER, Index der ungarischen gesetze . . . 1836–1904. Wien 1906. pp.xvi.276+[ii].147. [3000.]

MIKLÓS UJLAKI, Hetven év magánjogi irodalma. A magyar magánjog bibliográfiája 1861–1930. Budapest 1930. pp.xix.572. [7500.]

ALEXANDER L. KRISZTICS, Bibliography of the hungarian administration. Hungarian sociological institute: Publication (no.6): Budapest 1927. pp. 338.coll.339–347. [3050.]

KÁROLY BIHARI, Bihari index juris hungarici, Magyar jogmutató. Budapest 1936–

Iceland.

HALLDÓR HERMANNSSON, The ancient laws of Norway and Iceland. A bibliography. Cornell university library: Islandica (vol.iv): Ithaca 1911. pp.[ix].83. [750.]

Illinois.

JAMES F. CONOVER, A digested index of all the supreme decisions in law and equity of the supreme courts of the states of Ohio, Indiana, and Illinois. Philadelphia 1834. pp.xvi.512. [5000.]

EUGENE L. and WILLIAM L. GROSS, An index to all laws of the state of Illinois, both public and private, which are not printed at large in Gross' Statutes of 1869, except private acts of 1869. 1818 to 1869. Springfield, Ill. 1869. pp.xii.140. [15,000.]

interleaved.

CHARLES H. WOOD and JOSEPH D. LONG, A digest of the Illinois reports, from the earliest period to the year 1863[–1866]; embracing all the decisions of the Supreme court of the state. . . . Second . . . edition. Chicago 1867. pp.689 + 691–990. [12,500.]

— — [third edition]. 1872. pp.xii.585+[ii].587–1214. [15,000.]

GEO. R. WENDLING, An alphabetical index showing by parallel references the several cases in the Illinois reports, subsequently reversed, modified, explained, approved or maintained by the Supreme court of Illinois. Chicago 1874. pp.5–268. [3000.]

JOHN T. LONG, An index-digest of the decisions of the Supreme and Appellate courts of the state of Illinois. Chicago 1885. pp.811. [40,000.]

Indiana.

JAMES F. CONOVER, A digested index of all the reported decisions in law and equity of the Supreme courts of the states of Ohio, Indiana, and Illinois. Philadelphia 1834. pp.xvi.512. [5000.]

WARWICK H. RIPLEY, Analytical digest and index. Digest of Indiana decisions from . . . 1817 . . . to . . . 1881. Indianapolis 1883. pp.vi.997+999–1878. [39,083.]

JOHN G. RAUCH and NELLIE C. ARMSTRONG, A bibliography of the law of Indiana, 1788–1927, beginning with the Northwest territory. Indiana library and historical board: Indiana historical collections (vol.xvi): Indianapolis 1928. pp.xxxix. 77. [200.]

Indochina.

H. PETITJEAN, Répertoire chronologique et alphabétique des lois, décrets, ordonnances, etc. promulgués ou appliqués en Indochine depuis l'occupation de la Cochinchine (1861) jusqu'au

31 décembre 1917. Saïgon 1918. pp.[iii].xi.913. [2500.]

the list actually goes back to 1776.

Iowa.

SKELETON-digest of cases determined by the Supreme court of the state of Iowa. 1930 &c.

in progress.

Ireland.

i. *General*

LESLIE F. MAXWELL, A bibliography of irish law from the earliest times to December, 1935. Sweet & Maxwell's legal bibliography (vol.iv): 1936. pp.iv.88. [1000.]

— — Second edition. Compiled by L. F. Maxwell and W. H. Maxwell. 1957. pp.vii.128. [1500.]

ii. *Statute law*

GEORGE WALLER, A general index to the several statutes from the 33d. of George the second relating to the revenue of Ireland. [Dublin 1778]. pp.cxxiv. [500.]

WILLIAM BALL, An index to the acts passed in Ireland in the thirty-ninth and fortieth years of the reign of . . . George the third; together with an appendix, containing a short index to such acts of the Parliament of the United Kingdom, passed in the 41st, 42^{d} and 43^{d} years of the same reign, as appear to bind Ireland. Dublin 1804. pp.[213]. [4000.]

this is in effect a supplement to the index which forms vol.viii (1799) of The statutes at large, . . . in Ireland, *edited by Ball and others.*

[SIR THOMAS EDLYNE TOMLINS], Index to acts relating to Ireland, passed in the parliament of the United Kingdom . . . from January, 41 Geo III. A.D.1801, to December, 55 Geo III. A.D. 1814. 1815. pp.[v].108. [3000.]

— — 1801–1829. 1830. pp.[v].336. [8500.]

the title varies.

RICHARD NUN, An index to the statutes, passed in the parliament of Ireland, from the third year of Edward II. A.D. 1310, to the union, A.D. 1800. 1828.

ANDREW NEWTON OULTON, Chronological table

of the statutes, in force in, or affecting Ireland, from . . . 1310 to 1839. Dublin [1837–]1839. pp. [v].148. [5000.]

ANDREW NEWTON OULTON, Index to the statutes, at present in force in, or affecting Ireland, from the year 1310 to 1838. . . . Second edition. Dublin 1839. pp.[v].809. [20,000.]

—— First supplement. 1836. pp.[iii].82. [1500.]

—— Second annual supplement. 1837. pp.iv. 42. [600.]

—— Third annual supplement. 1838. pp.iv.64. [1000.]

—— Fourth annual supplement. 1839. pp.[iii]. 37. [600.]

—— Fifth annual supplement. 1841. pp.[iii].79. [1500.]

—— Sixth annual supplement. 1841. pp.[ii].31. [600.]

—— Seventh annual supplement. 1842. pp.[ii]. 77. [1500.]

—— Eighth annual supplement. 1843. pp.[iii]. 70. [1250.]

—— Ninth annual supplement. 1845. pp.[ii]. 95. [1750.]

—— Tenth annual supplement. 1846. pp.[ii]. 114. [2000.]

— — Eleventh annual supplement. 1847. pp.[ii].98. [1750.]

— — Twelfth annual supplement. 1848. pp.[ii].148. [2750.]

— — Thirteenth annual supplement. 1849. pp.[ii].80. [1500.]

the 5th–12th supplements were reissued with a collective titlepage reading Index to the statutes . . . 1839 to 1847.

INDEX to the legislation passed by the Oireachtas in the years 1922 to 1932, inclusive — and also certain tables in relation to such legislation. Saorstát Éireann: Dublin [1934]. pp.308. [500.]

— [another edition]. Index to the statutory rules, orders and regulations, 1922–1938. [1944]. pp.viii.287. [3000.]

— [another edition]. Index to the statutes, 1922–1948. With chronological tables showing their effect on pre-union irish statutes [&c.]. [1949]. pp.[ix].331. [3500.]

GEORGE GAVAN DUFFY and ART O'CONNOR, A register of administrative law in Saorstát Éireann, including the statutory rules and orders, from December 6, 1921, to December 31, 1933. Dublin [1935]. pp.v.113. [5000.]

INDEX to the emergency powers orders published in the statutory rules and orders series for the years 1939, 1940, and 1941, and also certain tables in relation to such orders. Dublin 1942. pp.52. [750.]

iii. *Case law*

JOHN FINLAY, A digest and index of all the irish reported cases in law and equity, from the earliest period to the present time, and also of the reported cases in ecclesiastical and criminal law. Dublin 1830. pp.xx.600. [5000.]

MATTHEW O'DONNELL and FRANCIS BRADY, An analytical digest of all the reported cases, statutes, and general orders, in . . . equity, in . . . Ireland at the House of lords. Dublin 1840. pp.vi.iii–xli.579. [10,000.]

CHARLES P. ARCHER, An analytical digest of all the reported cases in the several courts of common law in Ireland, from the earliest period to the present time. Dublin 1842. pp.[viii].502. [1500.]

THOMAS BRUNKER, A digest of all the reported cases decided in the superior and other courts of common law in Ireland, and in the Court of admiralty. Dublin 1865. coll.cxxxii.2344. [15,000.]

RICHARD WILSON GAMBLE and WILLIAM BARLOW, An index to all the reported cases in the several courts of equity in Ireland, from Trinity term 1838 to Hilary term 1867. Dublin 1868. pp.[iv]. 4.lii.664+[iv].665–1411. [12,500.]

WILLIAM COTTER STUBBS, The Irish law times digest of cases decided by the superior and other courts in Ireland, 1867–1893. Dublin 1895. pp. cxci.coll.792. [3000.]

— — 1894–1918. Editor: T. Henry Maxwell. 1921. pp.cccxciii.coll.2794. [8000.]

R. H. RYLAND, Digest of cases decided by the superior and other courts in Ireland. Dublin.

1919–1928. pp.civ.coll.724. [2000.]

1929–1938. pp.cxliv.coll.1056. [3000.]

HERBERT WOOD and ALBERT E[DWARD] LANGMAN, Calendar of the justiciary rolls or proceedings in the court of the justiciar of Ireland, I to VII years of Edward II. . . . Revised by Margaret C. Griffith. Dublin [1956]. pp.vii.406. [500.]

EDWARD F[RANCIS] RYAN, Notes of irish cases reported in the irish reports . . . 1949–1958. [Cork] 1960. pp.[iv].101. [1000.]

REGINALD A. HARRISON, The law reports of the Incorporated council of law reporting for Ireland

... and Northern Ireland, the Irish law times and the Irish jurist, 1949–1958. Digest of cases decided by the superior and other courts in Ireland and Northern Island. Dublin [1961]. pp.cviii.coll.816. [1750.]

Northern Ireland

M. A. COSTELLO, De annatis Hiberniae. A calendar of the first fruits' fees levied on papal appointments to benefices in Ireland, A.D. 1400 to 1535. . . . Volume I: Ulster. St. Patrick's college: [Catholic] Record society: Maynooth 1912. pp. xxxi.324. [500.]

no more published.

LIST of parliamentary and Stationery office publications of the government of Northern Ireland. 1923. pp.[ii].16. [200.]

reissued at frequent intervals, the last edition being:

Italy.

FRANCESCO BONAINI, Statuti della val d'Ambra del MCCVII. . . . Si aggiungono alcuni apunti per servire ad una bibliografia degli statuti italiani. Pisa 1851. pp.201. [550.]

FRANCESCO BERLAN [*and others*], Statuti italiani.

Saggio bibliografico. Venezia 1858. pp.xl.151. [1000.]

300 copies printed.

F[ILIPPO] BETTINI, Giurisprudenza italiana di XII anni. Repertorio generale alfabetico della giurisprudenza degli stati Sardi dal 1848 al 1859 inclusive in ogni materia. Torino 1861 [1862]. pp.1250. [25,000.]

— — Giurisprudenza italiana di dieci anni 1860 a 1869. Repertorio . . . della giurisprudenza italiana [&c.]. . . . Compilata a cura dell'avvocato Domenico Giuriati e di altri giureconsulti. . . . Seconda serie. 1872[–1873]. pp.[iv].1125. [22,500.]

— — Repertorio-sommario della giurisprudenza italiana. . . . Indicazione metodica delle sentenze . . . e delle leggi riportate negli anni 1870–1898. 1900. pp.[x].242. [50,000.]

[A. VALSECCHI], Bibliografia analitica degli statuti italiani esistenti nella privata biblioteca del d[r] Antonio Valsecchi. . . . Vol.I. Padova 1862. pp.xv.34.5.4.36.3.4.112.15.16.[vii]. [100.]

no more published.

ERNEST DUBOIS, Bibliographie juridique italienne. [1872–1873]. pp.51. [44.]

LUIGI MANZONI, Bibliografia statutaria e storica italiana. Bologna.

i. Bibliografia degli statuti, ordini e leggi dei municipii italiani. 1876–1879. pp.xxvii. 571+xvii.539. [10,000.]

vol.ii is entered unter Topography, below.

INDICE analitico della raccolta ufficiale delle leggi e dei decreti del regno dal 1861 al 1876. Roma 1876. pp.xv.616. [12,500.]

G. D'ETTORE, F. E. GIORDANO and C. GAMBUZZI, Indice generale della legislazione del regno d'Italia. Napoli 1880. pp.viii.628+[iii].629–1216. [25,000.]

BOLLETTINO di bibliografia giuridica italiana contemporanea. Compilato . . . dell'avv. Saladino Saladini-Pilastri. Istituto bibliografico internazionale: Bibliographia universalis: Firenze 1899. pp.8. ff.[vii]. [100.]

only one number was issued.

LEONE FONTANA, Bibliografia degli statuti dei comuni dell'Italia superiore. Torino 1907. pp. xv.510+[ii].504+525. [7000.]

ARRIGO SOLMI, La storia del diritto italiano. Fondazione Leonardo: Guide bibliografiche [vol. x]: Roma 1922. pp.[ii].99. [700.]

—— Histoire du droit italien. Paris 1926. pp.100. [700.]

IL PENSIERO giuridico italiano. Istituto nazionale per le relazioni culturali con l'estero: Bibliografia del ventennio: Roma 1941. pp.368+200+226+177+205. [10,000.]

ELENCO delle leggi e dei decreti emanati dal 1851 al 31 dicembre 1941–XX, con indicazione delle corrispondenti pubblicazioni ufficiali messe in vendita dalla Libreria dello stato. Roma 1942. pp.224. [3300.]

BIBLIOGRAFIA internazionale sui nuovi codici d'Italia (codici civile, della navigazione, di procedura civile). Istituto italiano di studi legislativi: Roma 1942–1943. pp.viii.120+x.133. [3207.]

MATTIA MININNI [CARACCIOLO], Bibliografia giuridica coloniale (Italia). Roma 1943. pp.[vi]. 125.x. [1250.]

CATALOGO della raccolta di statuti, consuetudini, leggi, decreti, ordini e privilegi dei comuni, delle associazioni e degli enti locali italiani, dal medioevo alla fine del secolo XVIII. Senato: Biblioteca: Roma.

i. A–B. [By Corrado Chelazzi]. 1943. pp. xxxv.290. [1000.]

ii. C–E. 1950. pp.xxviii.358. [1000.]
iii. F–K. 1955. pp.xxi.391. [1000.]
iv. L–M. 1958. pp.xv.481. [1200.]
v. N–Q. 1960. pp.xv.511. [1300.]
vi. R. 1963. pp.xv.317. [1000.]
in progress.

VINCENZO NAPOLETANO, Dizionario bibliografico delle rivisti giuridichi italiane su leggi vigenti. Milano.
1865–1954. pp.iii–xxiii.2028. [50,000.]
1955–1956. pp.iii–xi.456. [10,000.]
1957. pp.viii.452. [10,000.]
1958. pp.iii–xviii.815. [8000.]
1959. pp.iii–xix.839. [8000.]
1960. pp.xx.967. [8000.]

Jersey.

TABLE des décisions de la cour royale [de Jersey]. Jersey.
[i]. 1885–1888. 1896. pp.[iv].180. [500.]
[ii]. 1889–1893. 1895. pp.[iii].133. [400.]
iii. 1894–1900. 1906. pp.[iii].191. [600.]
iv. 1901–1907. 1908. pp.[ii].xxviii.210. [750.]
v. 1908–1916. 1930. pp.[ii].xxi.130. [500.]
vi. 1917–1930. 1931. pp.[iii].xvi.59. [400.]

Kentucky.

J. BARBOUR, Kentucky digest, embracing all the reported cases decided by the Court of appeals from its organization to the year 1878. Louisville, Ky. 1878. pp.xxiii.906+xiii.907–1845. [30,000.]

DOUGLAS C[RAWFORD] MCMURTRIE, A bibliography of Kentucky statute law 1792–1830. . . . Addition of titles in the Kentucky historical society, the university of Kentucky and the Filson club only, 1831–1952, by G. Glenn Clift. University of Kentucky: Margaret I. King library: Occasional contribution (no.49): [Lexington] 1953. pp. [ii].41. [201.]*

KENTUCKY session laws, legislative journals, collected documents. Checklist. University of Kentucky: Library: Occasional contribution (no.67): Lexington 1954. pp.[iii].24. [750.]*

Lagos.

SMALMAN SMITH, Analytical index to the ordinances regulating the civil and criminal procedure of the Gold Coast colony and of the colony of Lagos. 1888. pp.119. [3000.]

Leeward islands.

AN INDEX to the federal acts of the General

legislature of the colony of the Leeward islands from 1872 to 1889. [Antigua 1890]. pp.32. [350.]

DUDLEY HENRY SEMPER and ALAN CUTHBERT BURNS, Index of the laws of the federated colony of the Leeward Islands and of the several presidencies comprising the same. 1911. pp.xvi.160. [750.]

Liége, bishopric, city, and principality of.

LISTE chronologique des édits et ordonnances de la principauté de Liége, de 974 à 1505. Commission royale pour la publication des anciennes lois et ordonnances de la Belgique: Bruxelles 1873. pp.xxxix.96. [500.]

— 1507–1684. 1860. pp.xv.254. [1250.]

— 1684–1794. 1851. pp.[iii].xxxii.470. [2500.]

Livonia.

KARL GOTTLOB SONNTAG, Chronologisches verzeichniss der livländischen gouvernements-regierungs-patente von 1710 bis 1822. Riga 1823. pp.54.

Lombardy.

ANTONIO NEGRI, L'indicatore delle leggi ed ordinazioni dall'anno 1796 al tutto il 1834, nei rapporti giudiziarii pel regno lombardo-veneto. Milano 1835–1836. pp.378.82+266. [3000.]

Louisiana.

WILLIAM CHRISTY, A digest of Martin's Reports of the decisions of the supreme court of the state of Louisiana, from its establishment in the year 1813 . . . including those of the Superior court of the late territory of Orléans. New Orléans 1826. pp.viii.400. [2500.]

J. P. BENJAMIN and T. SLIDELL, Digest of the reported decisions of the Superior court of the late territory of Orleans, and of the Supreme court of the state of Louisiana. New Orleans 1834. pp.[ii].479. [6000.]

JOHN EDWARDS LEONARD, A digest of the decisions of the Supreme court of the United States, in Louisiana cases. New Orleans 1875. pp.[ii]. xxvi.379. [4000.]

ROBT. H. MARR, An annotated index of the acts of the legislature of Louisiana, from 1870 to 1888, inclusive, with references to the decisions of the Supreme court. New Orleans 1890. pp.403. [2500.]

JOSEPH A[RSENNE] BREAUX, A digest of decisions of the Supreme court of Louisiana, from the 40th annual through the 52nd annual. Also of the decisions referring to Louisiana law decided by the United States Circuit court of appeals and . . . Supreme court. New Orleans 1901. pp.[vi]. 1163. [9360.]

LAWRENCE C. WROTH and GERTRUDE L. ANNAN, Acts of french royal administration concerning Canada, Guiana, the West Indies and Louisiana prior to 1791. Public library: New York 1930. pp.151. [2083.]

Maine, U.S.A.

[SIMON GREENLEAF], A digest of Greenleaf's Reports of cases argued and determined in the Supreme judicial court of the state of Maine, from the year 1820, to the year 1832, inclusive. Portland 1835. pp.360. [2000.]

PHILIP EASTMAN, Digest of the decisions of the Supreme judicial court, of the state of Maine. Hallowell 1849. pp.xcvi.682. [6000.]

—— Supplemental digest. . . . By William Wirt Virgin. Portland 1870. pp.lxiii.560. [5000.]

Malabar.

MĀDHAVAN NAIR [NĀYAR], The Malabar law digest (1862–1941). Calicut 1941. pp.[v].xix.336. [1000.]

Malaya.

C. H. WITHERS PAYNE, The malayan digest, being a complete digest of every case in the colony of the Straits Settlements and the Federated Malay States reported from 1808. Singapore 1936. pp.[ix].305. [1504.]

BASHĪR A[ḤMAD] MALLĀL and NĀZIR A[ḤMAD] MALLĀL, Mallal's digest of malayan case law. Being a comprehensive digest of all decisions of the superior courts of Malaya from 1808–1939. Singapore 1940. pp.xxiv.coll.592. [1500.]

Malmédy.

LISTE chronologique des édits et ordonnances de la principauté de Stavelot et de Malmédy, de 650 à 1793. Bruxelles 1852. pp.[ii].viii.134. [750.]

Man, Isle of.

WILLIAM MACKENZIE, Index to all the statute or Tynwald laws of the Isle of Man. Douglas 1861.

pp.viii.3–87. [2000.]

— — Revised index to Isle of Man statutes . . . by Ramsey B. Moore. 1927. pp.266. [7500.] *interleaved.*

Manitoba.

ALAN C. EWART, The Manitoba digest, 1875–1899. Winnipeg 1900. pp.lxv.coll.688.pp.lxxiv. [2000.]

GEORGE PATTERSON and WILLIAM A. TAYLOR, Manitoba digest, 1875–1911, of cases reported in . . . Manitoba reports, together with a selection of Manitoba cases from the reports of the Supreme and Exchequer courts of Canada. Winnipeg 1913. pp.xcix.coll.1262.pp.30. [2500.]

MARJORIE MORLEY, A bibliography of Manitoba selected from holdings in the legislative library of Manitoba. [Winnipeg 1948]. ff.[i].16. [250.]*

Maryland.

INDEX to the laws and resolutions of the state of Maryland, from 1800 to 1813, inclusive. Annapolis 1815. pp.[228]. [5000.]

— — 1826–1831. 1832. pp.[348]. [6000.]

INDEX to the laws of Maryland, from the year 1838 to the year 1845, inclusive. Annapolis 1846. pp.754.

WILLIAM HENRY NORRIS, GEORGE WILLIAM BROWN and FREDERICK WM. BRUNE, Digest of the Maryland reports. Baltimore 1847. pp.lix.427+[ii].428–922. [12,000.]

— — [continuation]. By J. Shaaff Stockett, Richard T. Merrick and Oliver Miller. 1857. pp.lix.632. [10,000.]

— — [—]. By J. I. Cohen and James Fenner Lee. 1886. pp.[iv].xl.529. [6000.]

— — [—]. By Wm. H. S. Burguyn. 1878. pp. c.680. [7500.]

[WILLIAM BAXTER], Catalog of manuscripts and printed matter in the possession of the court of appeals of Maryland. Baltimore [printed] 1926. pp.29. [large number.]

Massachusetts.

BENJAMIN WHITMAN, An index to the laws of Massachusetts: from the adoption of the constitution to the year MDCCXCVI. Worcester 1797. pp. 152. [1500.]

LEWIS BIGELOW, A digest of the cases argued

and determined in the Supreme judicial court of the commonwealth of Massachusetts, from Sept. 1804, to Nov. 1815. Cambridge [Mass.] 1818. pp.viii.684. [5000.]

— — [second edition]. A digest of the reported cases [&c.]. Boston 1825. pp.lxxxiii.856. [7500.]

— — — Supplement. A digest of Pickering's Reports, . . . volumes II–VII. 1830. pp.xxxix.339. [2500.]

THERON METCALF, Digest of the cases decided in the Supreme judicial court of the commonwealth of Massachusetts, from March, 1816, to October, 1823. Boston 1825. pp.513. [3500.]

GEO[RGE] FRED[ERICK] WILLIAMS, Massachusetts citations. A table of cases overruled, denied, doubted, criticised, approved, and cited by the Supreme judicial court. Boston 1878. pp.vii.707. [27,500.]

EDMUND H. BENNETT, RUSSELL GRAY and HENRY W. SWIFT, Massachusetts digest. A digest of the reported decisions of the Supreme judicial court of the commonwealth of Massachusetts from 1804 to 1879. Boston 1881. pp.xxxiv.coll.2130+ pp.[ii].coll.2131–4230 + pp.[ii].coll.4231–6360. [35,000.]

[HENRY B. PEIRCE *and others*], Report to the Legislature of Massachusetts made by the Commissioners . . . upon the condition of the records, files, papers and documents in the Secretary's department. Boston 1885. pp.42. [100,000.]

GEORGE H. MOORE, Bibliographical notes on witchcraft in Massachusetts. Worcester [Mass.]. 1888. pp.32. [12.]

WILLIAM H[ENRY] WHITMORE, A bibliographical sketch of the laws of the Massachusetts colony from 1630 to 1686. Boston 1890. pp.xliii.150. [20.]

Mauritius.

W. GREENE, Index to the laws of Mauritius. . . . Fifth edition. Mauritius 1879. pp.[ii].iii.96. [1500.]

L. A. THIBAUD, General index to the laws of Mauritius in force. Mauritius 1886. pp.[ii].iii.139. [2000.]

— — Second edition. 1892. pp.[ii].iv.108. [2500.]

B. H. COLIN, Index to the regulations, bylaws and proclamations made under various ordinances and which are now in force. Port Louis 1917. pp.[iii].65. [1250.]

GÉRARD LALOUETTE, A digest of the decisions of the supreme court of Mauritius (1926–1943). Colony of Mauritius: Port Louis 1947. pp.[iii]. xvi.249. [1250.]

GÉRARD LALOUETTE, The Mauritius digest. Being a digest to the reported decisions of the supreme court of Mauritius to the end of 1950. Port-Louis [printed] [1957]. pp.[v].lxxxix.399+[iii].504+ [ii].463+[ii].402. [6000.]

Mecklenburg.

[WILHELM BÄRENSPRUNG], Repertorivm oder alphabetisches verzeichniss der vornehmsten sachen welche in den mecklenburgischen grundgesetzen . . . enthalten sind. Schwerin 1781. pp. x.428. [3000.]

BIBLIOTHEK der mecklenburgischen ritter- und landschaft. . . . Rechts- und staatswissenschaften. Rostock 1859. pp.[iii].v.291. [4000.]

Mexico.

ÍNDICES de todas las leyes, decretos, órdenes y providencias espedidas por las secretarías del despacho, en virtud de las facultades estraordinarias concedidas al gobierno en decreto de 25 de agosto de 1829. [México 1830]. pp.28. [500.]

REPERTORIO de la legislación ó índice alfabético y cronológico de las materias mas notables contenidas en la colección de leyes, decretos, y órdenes que se han espedido en la república desde el año de 1821 hasta el de 1837. Méjico 1840. pp.572. [7500.]

RAMÓN VICARIO, Índice alfabético de las materias contenidas en el código civil. México 1871. pp.20. [500.]

MANUEL CRUZADO, Memoria para la bibliografía jurídica mexicana. México 1894. pp.139. [250.]

CATÁLOGO alfabético de una parte de las obras impresas de la biblioteca de la Escuela nacional de jurisprudencia. México 1904. pp.337. [5000.]

MANUEL CRUZADO, Bibliografía jurídica mexicana. México 1905. pp.[v].385. [830.]

ÍNDICES cronológicos y alfabéticos de las leyes, convenciones . . . en todo el territorio de la federación, y de las leyes . . . del Distrito y de los territorios federales. México 1927 &c.

ÍNDICE legislativo mexicano. Todas las disposiciones del poder ejecutivo federal . . . septiembre

[-noviembre] 1939. Instituto panamericano de bibliografía y documentación: México 1939. pp. 48+56+60. [1250.]

no more published.

JOHN T[HOMAS] VANCE and HELEN L. CLAGETT, A guide to the law and legal literature of Mexico. Library of Congress: Latin american series (no.6): Washington 1945. pp.vi.269. [1250.]

ENSAYO bibliográfico de derecho constitucional mexicano y de garantias y amparo. Universidad nacional autonoma de México: Instituto de derecho comparado: México 1947. pp.xvii.173. [1851.]

HELEN L. CLAGETT, A guide to the law and legal literature of the mexican states. Library of Congress: Latin american series (no.13): Washington 1947. pp.v.180. [1000.]

Michigan.

[THOMAS MAC INTYRE COOLEY], A digest of the reported cases contained in the Michigan reports. Ann Arbor 1866. pp.xxviii.430.73. [3337.]

— — [second edition]. Digest of the Michigan reports. . . . By Edgar A. Cooley. 1872. pp.viii.495. [4000.]

——— Supplement . . . by Henry A[llen] Chaney. Detroit 1876. pp.iii–xii.471–916. [3000.]

Middlesex.

[W. I. STRACEY CLITHEROW], Calendar to a volume entitled the 'Brentford journal', being a record of proceedings at petty sessions held at Brentford, 1651–1714. [1911]. ff.[i].vi.221. [500.]*

Milan.

[LUCA PERONI], Indice delle leggi, degli editti, avvisi ed ordini ec., pubblicati nello stato di Milano dai diversi governi intermedi dal 1765 al 1821. Milano 1823. pp.vii.317+217. [7000.]

—— Continuazione . . . dall'anno 1822 al 1845 . . . colla presente aggiunta delle interne circolari di massima ed altri atti amministrativi dal 1816 al 1846, il tutto a cura dell'attuale aggiunto . . . Carlo Peroni. 1850. pp.73. [1300.]

Minnesota.

HOMER C. ELLER, Digest of decisions of the Supreme court of Minnesota as contained in . . . the Minnesota reports. St. Paul 1880. pp.xxxiv. 541+iii.543–1085. [9000.]

Mississippi, state of.

W. C. SMEDES, A digest of the cases decided and reported in the High court of errors and appeals and the Superior court of chancery of the state of Mississippi from 1818 to 1847. Boston 1847. pp.xxxvi.441. [4000.]

Missouri.

EVANS CASSELBERRY, A digest of the decisions of the Supreme court of Missouri, on all subjects, from 1820 to 1845. St. Louis 1845. pp.[ii].482.iii.

EVERETT W. PATTISON, A digest of the Missouri reports . . . 1821 . . . [to] 1872. St. Louis 1873–1875. pp.9–402+11–166.lxxi.273–381. [12,500.]

—— 1872 to . . . 1878. 1880. pp.5–446.cxx. [7500.]

Moravia.

FRANZ STARR, Vollständiges sach- und nachschlage-register zu sämmtlichen landesgesetzblättern der im Reichsrathe vertretenen königreiche und länder von deren beginn 1849 bis zum jahre 1873. . . . Dritter theil. Böhmen, Mähren und Schlesien. Wien 1874. pp.[ii].408. [5000.]

Morocco.

P. LOUIS RIVIÈRE, Table génerale, analytique et raisonnée des traités, codes, lois et règlements du Maroc . . . accompagnés des lois et décrets français concernant le Maroc . . . 1912–1923. 1923. pp. xii.129. [2500.]

HENRI BRUNO and PAUL MOUSSARD, Répertoire alphabétique de la jurisprudence de la Cour d'appel de Rabat. Institut des hautes études marocaines: Collection des centres d'études juridiques (vol.xxiv): [Rabat] 1947. pp.3–508+3–468. [5000.]

— — Tome III . . . 1945. . . . 1952. Par André Knoertzer, Hubert Carteret and Gilbert Pons . . . (vol.xxxxvii): 1955. pp.3–312. [1500.]

Natal.

PERCY E. COAKES, Digest of decisions and dicta of the Supreme court, Natal, 1873–1887. Durban 1889. pp.[ii].xiii.170.vi. [1000.]

Netherlands.

BERNARDUS MOURIK, Naamrol der rechtsgeleerde en historische schryvers, welke over alle rechtzaaken en voorvallen in de rechten in Holland, by de practizyns gebruikelyk, in t' nederduits geschreeven hebben. Amsterdam [*c*.1740]. pp.[xvi].472. [8500.]

CHARLES AUGUSTE D'HENRY, Indicateur général des lois, arrêtés et autres actes du gouvernement insérés au Journal officiel et dans la Gazette générale des Pays-Bas depuis leur création. Gand [1818]. pp.144. [1250.]

REGTSGELEERDE literatuur in Nederland. Amsterdam 1825–1837.

[*continued as:*]

Overzigt der regtsgeleerde en staathuishoudkundige letterkunde in Nederland. 1838.

[*continued as:*]

Overzicht der letterkunde van regtsgeleerdheid en staatswetenschappen in Nederland. 1839–1849.

[*continued as:*]

Letterkundig overzicht van geschriften tot rechtsgeleerdheid en staatswetenschappen betrekkelijk in Nederlanden. 1850–1873.

JOURNAL officiel du royaume des Pays-Bas. Tables chronologique et alphabétique des années 1814–1830. Bruxelles [1831]. pp.xvi.454. [1500.]

LISTE chronologique des édits et ordonnances des Pays-Bas [1780–1794: Pays-Bas autrichiens]. Commission royale pour la publication des anciennes lois et ordonnances de la Belgique: Bruxelles.

Règne de Charles-Quint (1506–1555). 1885 [–1890]. pp.xvii.520. [3500.]

Règne d'Albert et Isabelle (1598–1621). 1908. pp.xv.103. [750.]

Règnes de Philippe IV (1621–1665) et de Charles II (1665–1700). 1910. pp.xii.288. [1750.]

1700–1750. 1851. pp.[iii].xxxiv.492. [2500.]

1751–1780. 1853. pp.xv.455. [2500.]

1781–1794. 1858. pp.xxxix.413. [2000.]

[R. C. BAKHUIZEN VAN DEN BRINK], Overzigt van het Nederlandsche rijks-archief. . . . Eerste stuk. . . . Overzigt van het archief der voormalige Regtscollegien in Holland. 's Gravenhage 1854. pp.[ii].6.231.xliii. [large number.]

[MARTINUS NIJHOFF], Bibliotheca juridica. Catalogus van alle boeken sedert 1837 in het koningrijk der Nederlanden verschenen over staatswetenschappen, wetgeving en rechtsgeleerdheid. 's Gravenhage 1874. pp.[vi].209. [2750.]

REPERTORIUM van de nederlandsche jurisprudentie en rechtsliteratuur. 's-Hertogenbosch [1891–1918: Heusden; 1919–1937: Amsterdam; 1938 &c.: Assen].

[i]. 1878. pp.[iii].308. [2928.]
[ii]. 1879. pp.[iii].263. [2621.]
[iii]. 1880. pp.[iii].284. [2752.]
[iv]. 1881. pp.[iii].265. [2625.]
[v]. 1882. pp.[iii].252. [2569.]
[vi]. 1883. pp.[v].213. [2129.]
[vii]. 1884. pp.[vi].187. [2003.]
[viii]. 1885. pp.[iv].182. [1893.]
ix. 1886. pp.[iv].190. [2040.]
x. 1887. pp.[iv].192. [2047.]
xi. 1888. pp.[iv].207. [2253.]
xii. 1889. pp.[iv].205–407. [1907.]
xiii. 1890. pp.[iv].405–586. [2134.]
xiv. 1891. pp.[iii].238. [2377.]
xv. 1892. pp.4.228. [2330.]
xvi. 1893. pp.[vii].228. [2163.]
xvii. 1894. pp.[v].229–475. [2080.]
xviii. 1895. pp.[v].477–510[*sic*, 710]. [2095.]
xix. 1896. pp.[v].711–928. [1862.]
xx. 1897. pp.[v].929–1124. [1846.]
xxi. 1898. pp.[vii].252. [1545.]
xxii. 1899. pp.[vii].147. [1386.]
xxiii. 1900. pp.[v].285. [2055.]
xxiv. 1901. pp.[v].273. [1554.]
xxv. 1902. pp.[v].192. [1517.]
xxvi. 1903. pp.[v].205.35. [1740.]
xxvii. 1904. pp.[v].199.34. [1780.]

xxviii. 1905. pp.[v].195.32. [1656.]
xxix. 1906. pp.[v].212.35. [1879.]
xxx. 1907. pp.[v].193. [1646.]
xxxi. 1908. pp.[v].194.35. [1667.]
xxxii. 1909. pp.[v].209.36. [1821.]
xxxiii. 1910. pp.[v].239.39. [2086.]
xxxiv. 1911. pp.[v].225.36. [2027.]
xxxv. 1912. pp.[v].248. [1991.]

— Repertorium. . . . 1878–1912. Tweede opnieuw bewerkte druk. Heusden 1917 [–1918]. pp.480. [5000.]

aanbesteding-authentieke akten (in part) only; no more published.

xxxvi. 1913. pp.[v].280.42. [2333.]
xxxvii. 1914. pp.[v].255.40. [2242.]
xxxviii. 1915. pp.[v].260.39. [2311.]
xxxix. 1916. pp.[v].244.40. [2220.]
xl. 1917. pp.[v].257. [2318.]
xli. 1918. pp.[v].302.43. [2737.]
xlii. 1919. pp.[v].341.48. [2945.]
xliii. 1920. pp.[v].286.43. [2793.]
xliv. 1921. pp.[v].359. [2957.]
xlv. 1923. [*sic*, 1922]. pp.[v].336. [3028.]
xlvi. 1923. pp.[v].462. [3610.]
xlvii. 1924. pp.456. [3457.]

— Alphabetisch register . . . over de jaren 1900–1924. 1926. pp.[iii].346.

— Register volgens de wetsartikelen over de jaren 1900–1924. 1926. pp.190.

— — Alphabetisch register behoorende bij het wetsartikelen-register . . . door A. W. Verheyden. [*n.d.*]. pp.14.

xlviii. 1925. pp.[v].604. [3827.]
xlix. 1926. pp.[v].608. [4135.]
l. 1927. pp.648. [4629.]
li. 1928. pp.582. [4217.]
lii. 1929. pp.646. [4784.]
liii. 1930. pp.613. [4828.]
liv. 1931. pp.696. [5009.]
lv. 1932. pp.456+457–870. [5579.]
lvi. 1933. pp.399+401–806. [5553.]
lvii. 1934. pp.416+390. [5410.]
lviii. 1935. pp.390+391–784. [5213.]
lix. 1936. pp.376+377–785. [5116.]
lx. 1937. pp.436+437–824. [5260.]
lxi. 1938. pp.404+405–767. [5105.]
lxii. 1939. pp.368+369–747. [4810.]
lxiii. 1940. pp.407+409–812. [4913.]
lxiv. 1941. pp.383+385–741. [4402.]
lxv. 1942. pp.351+353–671. [4002.]
lxvi. 1943. pp.336+337–627. [3826.]
lxvii. 1944. pp.248+ . [.]

reissued with quinquennial (afterwards triennial)

titlepages and indexes (afterwards indexes only); no more published.

S[YBRANDUS] J[OHANNES] FOCKEMA ANDREAE, Overzicht van oud-nederlandsche rechtsbronnen. Haarlem 1881. pp.67. [750.]

— — Tweede druk, herzien . . . door A. S. de Blécourt en A. M. baron van Tuyll van Serooskerken. Haarlem 1923. pp.185.

supplements appear in the Tijdschrift voor rechtsgeschiedenis *(Haarlem 1927), vii.61–108, 454–458; (1933), xii.157–206.*

L[EO] J. VAN OPPEN and J. C. SASSE, Nederlandsche rechtsliteratuur. 's-Gravenhage 1884–1886. pp.ix.384 + 454 + vii.302 + vii.402 + vii.621. [13,000.]

[VICOMTE] CH[ARLES] TERLINDEN, Liste chronologique provisoire des édits et ordonnances des Pays-Bas. Règne de Philippe II (1555–1598). Bruxelles 1912. pp.viii.319. [2500.]

F. L. HARTONG, Register der protocollen van notarissen in Nederland. Samengesteld in opdracht van de Broederschap der notarissen in Nederland van ± 1550 tot heden. Rotterdam 1916. pp.578. [very large number.]

a supplement was published in 1925.

C. GRAHAM BOTHA, An eighteenth century law library. Cape Town 1935. pp.[ii].14. [75.]
refers to the Court of justice at the Cape.

J. A. AUDIER and H. J. JERPHANION, Van Stockum's naam- en zaakregister van wetten, algemeene maatregelen van bestuur en koninklijke besluiten, verschenen in het Staatsblad van het koninkrijk der Nederlanden, gedurende de jaren 1813 tot 1939. Den Haag 1939. pp.[vii].808. [15,000.]
— — Supplement. 1940. pp.[viii].237. [5000.]

KLAPPER op de wetgeving te vinden in het Staatsblad van het koninkrijk der Nederlanden, het Verordeningenblad voor het bezette nederlandse gebied, de Nederlandse staatscourant en het Publicatieblad van het militair gezag van 15 mei 1940 tot ... 1949. Zwolle 1950. pp.263. [1500.]

RENÉ DEKKERS, Bibliotheca belgica juridica. Een bio-bibliographisch overzicht der rechtsgeleerdheid in de Nederlanden van de vroegste tijden ab tot 1800. Koninklijke vlaamse academie voor wetenschappen, letteren en schone kunsten van Belgie: Verhandelingen (Letteren, vol.xiii, no.14): Brussel 1951. pp.xix.236. [3500.]

CATALOGUS van het nederlands fonds. Ministerie van justitie: Bibliotheek: Brussel 1954. pp.iii–xv. 93. [600.]

New Brunswick.

JAMES GRAY STEVENS, A digest of the reported and unreported cases determined in the Supreme court of judicature of the province of New Brunswick, from the year 1825 to Easter term 1873 inclusive. Saint John 1874. pp.xviii.484. [4000.]

— — Second edition . . . to Easter term (inclusive) 1879. Toronto 1880. pp.[iii].1353. [5000.]

pages 24 a–d occur between 24 and 25.

GEORGE W. BURBIDGE, Index to the statutes of New Brunswick, 1854–1878.

— [another edition]. Handbook to the consolidated statutes of New Brunswick, . . . to which is added a general index of the statutes . . . since 1854 . . . By G. Bidlake. Fredericton 1916. pp.32.96.196. [4000.]

— — An index to the statutes . . . 1917–1921. 1922. pp.15.35.

HORACE A. PORTER, Digest of New Brunswick case law. Toronto 1918. pp.[iii].xxx.coll.806. [3000.]

New Hampshire.

JOHN JAMES GILCHRIST, A digest of the reports of cases argued and determined in the Superior court of judicature of New-Hampshire. . . . Vols.I–XII. Concord 1846. pp.xcii.584.

INDEX to the laws of New Hampshire recorded in the office of the Secretary of state, 1679–1883. Manchester, N.H. 1886. pp.viii.594. [15,000.]

ALBERT H[ARRISON] HOYT, Notes, historical and bibliographical, on the laws of New Hampshire. Worcester, Mass. 1896. pp.19. [12.]
100 copies printed.

New Orleans.

J. P. BENJAMIN and T. SLIDELL, Digest of the reported decisions of the Superior court of the late territory of Orleans, and of the Supreme court of the state of Louisiana. New Orleans 1834. pp. [ii].479. [6000.]

New York, province and state of.

JOHN L. WENDELL, A digest of cases decided and reported in the Supreme court of judicature, and in the Court for the correction of errors, of the state of New York, from May 1828 to May 1835. Albany 1836. pp.xxxii.684. [4000.]

THOMAS W. CLERKE, A practical elementary digest of the reported cases in the Supreme court of judicature, and the Court for the correction of errors of the state of New York; together with the reported cases of the Superior court for the city and county of New York, from the earliest times. [Second edition]. New York 1845. pp.clix. 544 + [ii].545–1216 + xvii.648 + [ii].649–1333. [35,000.]

GEORGE W. CLINTON, A digest of the decisions at law and in equity, of the several courts of the state of New York. Albany 1852. pp.3–15.880+ [iv].881–1504+[iv].1505–1927.228. [35,000.]

— — Supplement. 1855. pp.xv.316. [5000.]

WILLIAM H. BOGART, Index to the documents of the legislature of New York . . . 1842 to . . . 1854. State of New York: [Documents of the] Senate (1855, no.33): Albany 1855. pp.278. [5000.]

WILLIAM H. BOGART, Index to the laws of the state of New-York, 1842 to 1855. State of New-York: [Documents of the] Senate (1856, no.110): Albany 1856. pp.296. [6000.]

T. S. GILLETT, General index of the laws of the state of New York. Albany 1859. pp.[iii].745. [35,000.]

— — 1858–1865. By Henry H. Havens. 1866. pp.335. [15,000.]

BENJAMIN VAUGHAN ABBOTT and AUSTIN ABBOTT, A digest of New York statutes from the earliest period to the year 1860. New York 1865–1866. pp.xci.681+796+791+799+768. [40,000.]

— — New edition, complete to the year 1873. 1873–1875. pp.clxxxvii.634+811+800+781+799+744. [60,000.]

— — 1873–1882. By Austin Abbott. 1883. pp. vii.1147+[ii].1209. [25,000.]

JOEL TIFFANY, Condensed digest of the Court of appeals [and the Commission of appeals] of the state of New York, as reported in Comstock's . . . Selden's . . . Kernan's . . . Smith's reports . . . volumes I to XXVII inclusive of the New York reports. Albany 1866. pp.lxix.584. [8000.]

— — Vol.II[–III] . . . as reported in Tiffany's . . . Hand's . . . Keyes' . . . Sickel's reports . . . volumes XXVIII to LXII inclusive of the New York reports. By Oliver L. Barbour. 1877. pp.xviii.815+xii. 994. [12,500.]

WILLIAM WAIT, A digest of New York reports, from the organization of the state to the year 1869, containing the decisions of all the courts of the state, except such as are digested in Clinton's Digest, Second edition. . . . Volume I. Albany 1869. pp.xix.839. [15,000.]

WILLIAM WAIT, A table of cases affirmed, reversed or cited in any of the volumes of the reports of the state of New York . . . [1794–]1872. Albany 1872. pp.vi.732. [20,000.]

—— Supplement . . . 1872 to 1880. . . . By R. E. Andrews. 1880. pp.[iii].562. [20,000.]

FREDERICK C. BRIGHTLY, A digest of the decisions of the courts of the state of New York, from the earliest period to September 1875. New York 1875. pp.iii–viii.coll.ix–xcviii.2258+pp.[ii].coll. 2261–4474. [40,000.]

HENRY G. DANFORTH and ROBERT B. WICKES, Digest of the New York Court of appeal reports, embracing the decisions contained in Abbott's Court of appeals decisions, Keyes' reports, and in the New York reports, volumes one to ninety-four inclusive. New York &c. 1884. pp.[ii].1088. [22,500.]

WILLIAM H[ENRY] SILVERNAIL, Index to the session laws of the state of New York . . . from sessions of 1775 down to session of 1897. New York &c. 1897. pp.iii–vii.899. [18,000.] .

— — Supplementary index . . . down to session of 1901. 1901. pp.iv.316. [6000.]

E[MILE] HENRY LACOMBE and A[RTHUR] H[AYNSWORTH] MASTEN, Table of cases involving questions of law peculiar to the city and county of New York. Fourth edition . . . by James M. Valles . . . Lamar Hardy. New York 1916. pp.374. [1000.]

ERNEST HENRY BREVER, The New York state court of claims. New York state library: Bibliography bulletin (no.88): Albany 1959. pp.55.

New Zealand.

MAURICE W. RICHMOND, The New Zealand digest: reported cases determined by the Supreme court and Court of appeal of New Zealand, and cases on mining law, from 1869–1892 inclusive. Council of law reporting: Wellington [1893]. pp.cxii.coll.916. [10,000.]

— — Supplement . . . 1893–1897 . . . to which is added an index of cases judicially noticed... during the years 1861–1897. [1898]. pp.xlviii. coll.370. pp.[181]. [3000.]

E. Y. REDWARD, Index to the laws of New Zealand, general, local, and provincial. Being fourteenth edition of 'Curnin's index'. Wellington 1905. pp.viii.273. [2500.]

— — Twenty-second edition. 1921. pp.viii.392. [5000.]

A BIBLIOGRAPHY of the laws of Australia, New Zealand, Fiji and the western Pacific from the earliest times. With lists of reports of cases, digests and collections of statutes and rules. Sweet & Maxwell's legal bibliography (vol.i): 1938. pp. vii.144. [1500.]

Nicaragua.

ÍNDICE general de las leyes patrias. Managua 1919 &c.

in progress.

Normandy.

CH[ARLES] PATEY, Factums normands conservés à la Bibliothèque nationale. Caen 1888. pp.13. [237.]

North-West Provinces, Pakistan.

INDEX to the leading decisions of the Sudder

dewanny adawlut, North western provinces. Roorkee 1859. pp.[ii].ciii. [750.]
interleaved.

Norway.

JACOB HENRIC SCHOU, Chronologisk register over de kongelige forordninger og aabne breve, som fra aar 1670 til 1775 [–1813] aars udgang ere udkomme, tilligemed et nøiagtigt udtog af de endnu gieldende, for saavidt samme i almindelighed angaae undersaatterne i Danmark og Norge. Kiøbenhavn 1777–1814.
details of this work are set out under Denmark: Law, above.

OLE FALK EBBELL, Alphabetisk register til de fyv første bind eller 21 første aargange (1814–1834) af samlinger af love, anordninger, kundgjørelser, aabne breve, resolutioner m.m. Christiania 1837. pp.[vii].160. [3000.]
—— 1835 til 1845.... Udgivet af Otto Kaltenborn. 1848. pp.[vi].223. [4500.]

A[NDREAS] AAGESEN, Fortegnelse over retssamlinger, retsliteratur m.m. i Danmark, Norge, Sverig og til dels Finland. Kjøbenhavn 1876. pp.[vii].167. [3000.]

HALLDÓR HERMANNSSON, The ancient laws of Norway and Iceland. A bibliography. Cornell university library: Islandica (vol.iv): Ithaca 1911. pp.[ix].83. [750.]

Nova Scotia.

FRED[ERICK] T. CONGDON, A digest of the Nova Scotia common law, equity, vice-admiralty and election reports. Toronto 1890. pp.xvi.coll.1640. pp.1641–1663. [4000.]

— — 1888–1907. By J. M. Geldert. Toronto 1910. pp.xl.coll.894. [3000.]

BENNETT H. ARMSTRONG, A digest of the Nova Scotia reports . . . and of all Nova Scotia cases decided in the Supreme court of Canada and the Imperial privy council between the years 1888 and 1903. Toronto 1903. pp.[vi].coll.716. pp.721–749. [1500.]

INDEX to the public statutes of Nova Scotia in force at the end of the first session of the thirty-fifth General assembly. Halifax 1912. pp.[37]. [1000.]

INDEX to the local and private acts of Nova Scotia passed by the Legislature during the years 1901 to 1912, inclusive. Halifax 1912. pp.158. [2250.]

Nyasaland.

[SIR] CHARLES F[REDERIC] BELCHER, A list of orders of his majesty in council, and local ordinances with the subsidiary legislation thereunder in force on 31st July, 1925 (excluding war and emergency legislation). Zomba 1925. pp.27. [500.]

W. A. E. ROSSITER, Index to the laws in force. Nyasaland protectorate. Zomba 1937. pp.55. [750.]

— — [another edition]. 1946. pp.68. [1000.]

Ohio.

JAMES F. CONOVER, A digested Index of all the reported decisions in law and equity of the supreme courts of the states of Ohio, Indiana, and Illinois. Philadelphia 1834. pp.xvi.512. [5000.]

P. B. WILCOX, A digest of the first sixteen volumes of the Ohio reports. Columbus 1848. pp.xxiii.iii–viii.607.xx. [3000.]

M[ASKELL] E. CURWEN, A revising index to the statute law of the state of Ohio, showing the present state of the law by indicating the changes that have been made since the publication of Swan's Statutes. Dayton 1849. pp.91. [1000.]

W. Y. GHOLSON and J. W. OKEY, Digest of the Ohio reports. Cincinnati 1867. pp.xx.677.181. [7500.]

J. BRYANT WALKER and CLEMENT BATES, Ohio digest, containing all reported Ohio cases to the year 1875. Cincinnati 1875. pp.xiii.878+vii.881–1709. [22,500.]

A. H. MCVEY, A digest of the reported decisions of the courts of Ohio. . . . Third edition Cleveland 1876. pp.[xvii].561+[ii].639. [10,000.]

WILLIAM J[AMES] TOSSELL, Ohio cross-reference tables and annotations . . . 1885–1923. Indianapolis [1923]. pp.3–1159.

Oklahoma.

R[ICHARD] J[AY] SHIVE, Oklahoma criminal digest. Third edition . . . edited . . . by C[harles] W[infield] Van Eaton. Oklahoma City 1935. pp. xxiii.813. [2400.]

—— Supplement. 1914. pp.[ii].282. [1000.]

Ontario.

CHRISTOPHER ROBINSON and F. J. JOSEPH, A digest of the reported cases determined in the courts of common law and equity in the now province of

Ontario, from . . . 1823. Toronto 1880. pp.xvi. coll.2528 + pp.[ii].coll.2529–4736. pp.4737–4839. [30,000.]

HARRIS H. BLIGH, The Ontario law index, embracing all legislation of the province of Ontario, down to and including the year 1895. Toronto 1895. pp.[iii].268. [5000.]

— — Supplement . . . 1896 to 1900. 1900. pp.104. [2000.]

J. F. SMITH, E. B. BROWN and R. S. CASSELS, The Ontario digest, 1891–1895. Toronto 1896. pp. xcvii.1056. [3000.]

J. F. SMITH [*and others*], The digest of Ontario case law . . . from . . . 1823, to . . . 1900. Toronto 1902–1904. pp.[iv].coll.2320+pp.[iv].coll.2321–4748+pp.[iv].coll.4749–7148+pp.[vi].coll.7149–7788.pp.7789–8608.vi. [40,000.]

EDWIN BELL, The Ontario digest (1901–5). Toronto 1906. pp.lxxxiv.coll.984. [3000.]

BRUFF GARRETT, Index to Ontario statute amendments (1914–1920). Toronto 1921. ff.[v].63. [2500.]

— — [supplement]. Bruff Garrett's index of amendments . . . for the years 1928– . . . 1931.

Henry L[ennox] Cartwright . . . editor. [1931]. pp.[iv].vi.110. [3500.]

Oudh.

GOKARAN NATH MISRA [GOKARṆA-NĀTHA MIṢRA], The Oudh digest, being a digest of all the reported decisions relating to Oudh (from 1859 to 1905). Lucknow 1906. pp.[vii].lxv.xxiii.coll.1776. [10,000.]

— — 1906–1915–. 1917. pp.[iii].2.civ.[viii]. coll.2652. [20,000.]

MUḢAMMAD NŪR AL-ḢASAN, A digest and easy referencer of Oudh case law . . . (1874–1913). Lucknow 1914. pp.[vii].553.lxvii. [2000.]

MOHAN-LĀL KHARBANDA, Oudh digest, civil, criminal & revenue, 1859–1940. Allahabad 1941 &c.

Pacific ocean and region.

A BIBLIOGRAPHY of the laws of Australia, New Zealand, Fiji and the western Pacific from the earliest times. Sweet & Maxwell's legal bibliography (vol.vi): 1938. pp.vii.144. [1500.]

Panjab.

E. REYNOLDS, A digest of the civil, criminal and

revenue cases, published in the Punjab record during the years 1866–1875. Lahore 1876. pp.[v]. vii.247. [1500.]

A DIGEST of the cases reported in the Punjab record. Lahore.

1890. By Madan Gopal. pp.[ii].v.coll.68. [200.]
1891. By J. A. Sinclair. pp.[ii].v.coll.88. [200.]
1892. pp.[ii].v.coll.110. [200.]
1893. By H. A. B. Rattigan. pp.[ii].v.coll.140. [200.]
1894. pp.[ii].vi.coll.260. [250.]
1895. pp.[ii].iv.coll.168. [200.]
1896. pp.[ii].iv.coll.90. [150.]
1897. pp.[ii].iii.coll.128. [150.]
1898. pp.[ii].iv.coll.114. [150.]
1899. pp.[ii].iii.coll.76. [150.]
1900. By Alweyne Turner. pp.[ii].iv.coll.80. [200.]
1901. pp.
1902. pp.
1903. pp.[ii].iv.coll.96. [150.]
1904. pp.[ii].iv.coll.110. [150.]
1905. pp.[ii].iv.coll.104. [200.]
1906. pp.
1907. pp.[ii].iv.coll.92. [150.]

1908. pp.[ii].iv.coll.106. [200.]
1909. By C. H. Oertel. pp.[ii].iv.coll.70. [150.]
1910. pp.
1911. pp.[ii].iv.coll.72. [150.]
1912. pp.[ii].v.coll.90. [250.]
1913. pp.
1914. pp.[ii].coll.84. [200.]
1915. pp.[ii].coll.90. [200.]
1916. pp.
1917. pp.[ii].coll.98. [250.]
1918. pp.[ii].coll.92. [200.]
1919. pp.[ii].coll.122. [250.]

DĪWĀN-CHAND OBHRĀI, The Punjab referencer, being a digest and analytical summary . . . of cases reported . . . (civil, criminal and revenue). Madras 1914. pp.[ii].11.167.lv. [500.]

A. B. BROADWAY and A. L. DANSON, Consolidated digest of the civil and revenue cases reported in the Punjab record, 1866 to 1911. Lahore 1914. pp. lxiii.coll.2880. [7500.]

DĪWĀN-CHAND OBHRĀI, The Punjab ready referencer, 1866–1915, or the consolidated subject-index of the cases reported. . . . B–civil portion. Madras 1918. pp.[ii].2.1192 + [ii].1193–2254. [50,000.]

— — C–revenue portion. 1918. pp.[ii].60. [1250.]

section A is entered under Crime: India, above.

SITA-RAM KOHLI, Catalogue of Khalsa darbar records. Lahore 1919–1927. pp.[v].158+[v].315. [20,000.]

A. N. KHANNA and VEDA VYĀSA, A complete digest of the Punjab case-law. (1866–1930[1931]). Lahore 1931– . pp.[iii].coll.1056.388+pp.[ii]. coll.460.xliv.461–1488+

— — Continuation. Octavinial Punjab digest (civil, criminal & revenue), 1931–1938. . . . By A. N. Khanna. Lahore 1939. pp.[ii].coll.800+pp. [iii].coll.801–1680+pp.[ii].coll.400.118. [10,000.]

ĀNANDA-MOHANA SŪRI and HARIDĀSA SŪRI, An exhaustive & up-to-date Punjab digest, civil, criminal & revenue, 1931 to 1938. Lahore [1939–1940]. pp.[vi].xii.iii.coll.748 + pp.[ii].coll.749–1718+pp.[iii].v.coll.1717–3230. [10,000.]

Paraguay.

HELEN L[ORD] CLAGETT, A guide to the law and legal literature of Paraguay. Library of Congress: Latin american series (no.14): Washington 1947. pp.vi.59. [250.]

Patna.

ADITYA NARAYAN LAL [ĀDITYA-NĀRAYAṆA LĀLA], The Patna digest, criminal & revenue, with decisions of the Privy council, 1926–1935. Gaya 1936. pp.[vii].xxxvi.coll.694. [1500.]

Pennsylvania.

THOMAS I. WHARTON, A digest of cases adjudged in the Circuit court of the United States for the third circuit, and in the courts of Pennsylvania. Philadelphia 1822. pp.xxi.690. [7500.]

— — Fourth edition. 1843. pp.xxx.829+[iii]. 902. [25,000.]

FREDERICK C. BRIGHTLY, A digest of the decisions of the courts of the state of Pennsylvania, from 1754 to 1877. Philadelphia 1877. pp.viii.coll. ix–lxviii.1313+pp.[ii].coll.1321–2906. [25,000.]

— — 1877–1882. 1883. pp.[ii].coll.ix–xxviii. 2909–4048. [7500.]

GEORGE WHARTON PEPPER and WILLIAM DRAPER LEWIS, Pepper and Lewis' new digest. A digest of the laws of Pennsylvania from 1700 to 1894. Philadelphia 1896. pp.xliii.coll.2838+pp.[ii].coll. 2849–5844. [20,000.]

— — 1895 to 1897. 1898. pp.cix.coll.814. [2500.]

FREDERICK E[WING] RAY, Digest of official opinions with statutes and cases cited, November 1, 1933 to December 31, 1942. Department of justice: [Harrisburg] 1943. pp.[v].223. [5000.]

Peru.

MARIANO FELIPE PAZ SOLDAN, Índice analítico de los códigos civil y de enjuiciamientos, del Reglamento de tribunales y de las leyes secundarias que tienen relación con ellos. Callao 1853. pp. [iv].120.

— — Apéndice. Índice analítico de los reglamentos de tribunales, juzgados y jueces de paz. Lima 1854. pp.[18].

JUAN FRANCISCO OLIVO, Índice detallado de las leyes y resoluciones legislativas de carácter general . . . desde . . . 1900 hasta el 1° de julio de 1916. Cámara de diputados: Lima 1916. pp.v.255. [2500.]

— — Índice de leyes [&c.]. 2 edición. 1919–1920. pp. + . [5000.]

HELEN L[ORD] CLAGETT, A guide to the law and legal literature of Peru. Library of Congress: Latin american series (no.20): Washington 1947. pp.vii.188. [1000.]

Pomerania.

APPARATUS diplomaticus-historicus. Oder verzeichniss allerhand zur pommerschen und rugianischen historie dienlichen landes-gesetzen, constitutionen, rescripten, privilegien, gerichtlichen judicaten . . . theils gedruckten . . . mehren theils aber nie gedruckten. . . . Zweite . . . auflage. Greiffswald 1735. pp.108.40.34. [3500.]

AUGUSTIN [VON] BALTHASAR, Historische nachricht von denen landes-gesetzen im hertzogthum Pommern, sonderlich königlich-schwedischen antheils, und selbigem incorporirten fürstenthum Rügen. [Greiffswald] 1740. pp.[xxxiv].178. [2000.]

JOHANN CARL CONRAD OELRICHS, Entwurf einer pommerschen juristischen bibliothek. Berlin 1763. pp.[iv].viii.84. [200.]

C. G. R. GESTERDING, Litteratur des pommerschen lehnrechts. Greifswald 1773. pp.[viii].144. [100.]

Portugal.

MANOEL MENDEZ DE CASTRO, Repertorio das ordenações do reyno de Portugal novamente recopiladas. Lisboa 1604. ff.viii.136. [6500.]

— — Accrescentado . . . pelo licenciado Martim Alveres de Castro . . . e nesta ultima impressão . . . pelo licenciado Mathias de Fonseca. Coimbra 1743. pp.400. [11,250.]

[ANTONIO BARNABÉ DE ELESCANO BARRETO E ARAGÃO], Demetrio moderno, ou o bibliografo juridico portuguez. Lisboa [1780–]1781. pp.[xi]. 216. [250.]

JOSÉ ANASTASIO DE FIGUEIREDO, Synopsis chronologica de subsidios ainda os mais raros para a historia e estudo critico da legislação portugueza. Academia real das sciencias: Lisboa 1790. pp.xi. 412.[iv]+[iii].371.[vii]. [3000.]

JOÃO PEDRO RIBEIRO, Indice chronologico remissivo da legislação portugueza posterior à publicação do Codico filippino. . . . Segunda impressão. Lisboa 1805–1830. pp.[xi].381.[iv]+[iii].368.[iv] + [iv].299 + [iv].347.[v] + [xi].488 + [ii].viii.301. [20,000.]

MANOEL FERNANDES THOMAZ, Repertorio geral, ou indice alphabetico des leis extravagantes do reino de Portugal. Coimbra 1815–1825. pp.[iv]. xv.560+[iv].569.iv. [30,000.]

MANOEL BORGES CARNEIRO, Additamento geral das leis, resoluções, avisos, &c. desde 1603 ate' o presente. Lisboa 1817. pp.291. [1500.]

—— Segunda additamento [&c.]. [1818]. pp. 239. [1000.]

ANTONIO MANOEL DO REGO ABRANCHES, Indice chronologico e remissivo da novissima legislação portugueza. Lisboa 1836. pp.[iii].275. [2000.]

JOAQUIM RAPHAEL DO VALLE, Classificação geral da legislação portugueza, desde a publicação do Codigo philippino até à data. Lisboa 1841. pp.449. [4000.]

JOSÉ JUSTINO D'ANDRADE E SILVA, Repertorio geral ou indice alphabetico e remissivo de toda a legislação portugueza publicada o anno de 1815 até o de 1849, em continuação de Fernandes Thomaz. Lisboa 1850. pp.[iv].300+[ii].246. [5000.]

TITO DE NORONHA, A imprensa portugueza no seculo XVI, seus representantes e suas producções. Ordenações do reino. Porto 1873. pp.[vii].108. [7.]

250 copies printed.

[PEDRO WENCESLAU DE] BRITO ARANHA, A

imprensa em Portugal nos seculos XV e XVI. Às ordenações d'el-rei d. Manuel. Sociedade de geographia de Lisboa: Quarto centenario do descobrimento da India: Lisboa 1898. pp.29. [5.]

[ARNALDO FARÍA DE ATAÍDE E MELO], Index das notas de varios tabelliães de Lisboa, entre os annos de 1580 e 1747. Biblioteca nacional: Subsídios para a investigação histórica em Portugal: Lisboa 1930–1944. pp.145+371+574. [3000.]

Prussia.

W. B. FISCHER, Repertorium des neuesten preussischen rechts, oder wesentlicher inhalt der bis zum ende des jahrs 1823 erschienenen preussischen gesetze und ministerial-verfügungen. . . . Zweite . . . auflage. Oels 1824. pp.[iv].664. [3000.]

— — I. ergänzungs-bogen. 1825. pp.[ii].90. [400.]

HAUPT-REGISTER zur gesetz-sammlung für die königlichen preussischen staaten. Berlin.

1806–1863. 1864. pp.[iii].1144. [50,000.]

1806–1883. 1885. pp.[ii].974 + [ii].975–1880. [75,000.]

1884–1903. 1904. pp.[ii].655. [25,000.]

OTTO MÜHLBRECHT, Die literatur der preussischen staats- und rechtswissenschaft. Uebersicht der in den jahren 1849 bis ende 1867 in Deutschland im druck erschienenen . . . schriften, welche sich auf den Preussischen staat beziehen. Berlin 1868. pp.120. [2327.]

EMIL STEFFENHAGEN, Deutsche rechtsquellen in Preussen vom XIII bis zum XVI jahrhundert. Leipzig 1875. pp.viii.248. [150.]

Quebec.

J. F. DUBREUIL, The reference book, being a detailed index of the statutes affecting the province of Quebec . . . and of all acts passed since confederation by the . . . legislature of the province. Montreal 1879. pp.322. [10,000.]

HARRIS H. BLIGH, The Quebec law index, embracing all the legislation of the province of Quebec from 1867, down to and including the year 1898. Montreal 1898. pp.[vi].283. [6000.]

PIERRE GEORGES ROY, Index des jugements et délibérations du conseil souverain de 1663 à 1716. Archives de la province de Québec: Québec 1940. pp.[ii].287. [5000.]

TABLE analytique des mémoires et autres documents consultés par la commission. Provinces de

Québec: Commission royale d'enquête sur les problèmes constitutionnels: [Quebec] 1956. pp. [ii].211. [2000.]*

Rennes.

J. L. LEHIR and CH. NOUVEL, Table générale et raisonnée du recueil des arrêts de la cour royale de Rennes de 1800 à 1835 inclusivement. Rennes [1836]. pp.400. [4750.]

Rhin, Haut-.

JACQUES THURNER, Table générale et alphabétique des actes de la préfecture du département du Haut-Rhin depuis le 5 messidor an IX jusqu'au 1er septembre 1858. Colmar 1858. pp.[iv].288. [3000.]

Rhine provinces.

PH. I. SERINI, Chronologische zusammenstellung der während der provisorischen französischen verwaltung in der deutschen Rheinlanden publicirten älteren französischen gesetze. Mannheim 1848. pp.[v].298. [4000.]

Rhode Island.

JOHN RUSSELL BARTLETT, Index to the printed

acts and resolves of, and of the petitions and reports to the General assembly of the state of Rhode Island and Providence plantations, from the year 1850 to 1862. Providence 1863. pp. xxxiv.104. [3000.]

— — 1863 to 1873. By Joshua M. Addeman. 1875. pp.lxviii.131. [4000.]

J. HARRY BONGARTZ, Check list of Rhode Island laws. Providence 1893. pp.8. [600.]

GRACE E. MACDONALD, Check-list of legislative documents in the Rhode Island state archives. State bureau of information: Annual bulletin (no.1): Providence 1928. pp.24. [1000.]

Rhodesia, Southern.

CHRONOLOGICAL table of statutes. Southern Rhodesia. [Salisbury 1940]. pp.[ii].38. [500.]*

Rhodesia and Nyasaland.

INDEX to the subsidiary legislation of the Federation of Rhodesia and Nyasaland: Federal information department: Salisbury.

1957. pp.v.43. [500.]
1958. pp.v.44. [500.]

1960. pp.v.47. [500.]
1962. pp.v.62. [750.]

Romania.

REPERTORIUL general al legilor, regulamentelor şi altor dispoziţiuni de ordin legislativ. Consiliul legislativ: Bucureşti.
1940. pp.cccxxvi. [6000.]
1941. pp.516. [8000.]
1942. pp.459. [8000.]

Rome.

THEODOR VON DYDYŃSKI, Beiträge zur handschriftlichen überlieferung der justinianischen rechtsquellen. . . . I. Institutionen. Heft I. Berlin 1891. pp.112. [298.]
no more published.

JOHANN OLDENDORP, Titulorum juris civilis index. . . . Imperatorum ac jurisconsultorum catalogus. Item regulae juris ad locos communes redactae. Lugduni 1551. pp.142. [1600.]

JACQUES LABITTE, Index legvm omnivm qvæ in pandectis continentvr: in qvo singulæ ad singulos iurisconsultorum libros ex quibus desumptæ sunt, vt earum monet inscriptio, referuntur. Parisiis 1557. ff.[x].100.40. [10,000.]

— — Editio neapolitana adcuratior. Neapoli 1759. pp.[xii].xxiv.344. [10,000.]

INDEX rervm et verborvm, qvæ in pandectis tractantvr, copiosissimvs. Antverpiae 1567. pp. [511]. [15,000.]

— — [another edition]. Index omnivm legvm et paragraphorvm qvæ in pandectis codice et instit. continentur, per literas digestus. Lvgdvni 1571. pp.[511]. [15,000.]

[ANTOINE LE COMTE], Pandectarum seu digestorum tituli ordini alphabetico dispositi. Parisiis [*c.*1570]. single leaf. [710.]

[CLAUDE BROSSETTE], Les titres du droit civil, et du droit canonique, raportez sous les noms françois des matières, suivant l'ordre alphabétique. Lyon 1705. pp.[xviii].361. [4500.]

CARL FERDINAND HOMMEL, Sceleton juris civilis, sive juris prudentia universa paucis tabulis delineata. Editio 4ª. Lipsiae 1767. pp.24. [175.]

CARL FERDINAND HOMMEL, Corpvs ivris civilis. Lipsiae 1768. pp.xvi.804. [40,000.]

— — Hommel redivivus, oder nachweisung der bei den vorzüglichsten älteren und neueren civilisten vorkommenden erklärungen einzelner stellen des Corpus juris civilis. Herausgegeben von Theodor Schimmelpfeng. Cassel 1858–1859. pp.xxviii.597+722+455. [75,000.]

CHRISTIAN GOTTLIEB HAUBOLD, Institvtiones ivris romani litterariae. Tomvs I, partem biographicam et bibliographicae capita priora, maxime qvae ad ivs anteivstinianevm spectant, continens. Lipsiae 1809. pp.xxviii.370. [2000.]
no more published.

CHRISTIAN GOTTLIEB HAUBOLD, Doctrinae pandectarvm lineamenta, cvm locis classicis ivris in primis ivstinianei et selecta litteratvra maxime forensi. Lipsiae 1820. pp.xxii.525. [2500.]

CHRISTIAN GOTTLIEB HAUBOLD, Institvtionvm ivris Romani privati historico-dogmaticarvm lineamenta, observationibvs maxime litterariis distinta.... Avxit Carolvs Edvardvs Otto. Lipsiae 1826. pp.xxx.526+107. [5000.]

INDEX omnivm titvlorvm qvi in libris ivris civilis et canonici invenivntur. Halis Saxonvm 1844. pp.47. [1500.]

EDUARD BÖCKING, Grundriss zu pandektenvorlesungen (mit ausschluss des erbrechts), nebst quellen- und litteratur-angaben und einer quellenchrestomathie. . . . Dritte auflage. Bonn 1845. pp.[ii].24.[126]. [5000.]

the earlier editions were not published.

INDEX alphabeticus omnium titulorum qui continentur in corpore digestorum, codicis, novellarum-constitutionum nec non institutionum. Pisis 1852. pp.57. [1500.]

[A. F. R.] TEICHMANN, Bibliographische uebersicht des römischen, deutschen, französischen und englischen rechts. Basel 1876. pp.118. [5000.]

MAX CONRAT, Geschichte der quellen und litteratur des römischen rechts im früheren mittelalter. . . . Erster band. Leipzig [1889–]1891. pp.xi. 549. [2000.]

no more published.

H. ERMAN, Das römische recht, 1884 bis 1894. Juristischer litteraturbericht (part 2): Leipzig 1895. pp.33. [200.]

CESARE BERTOLINI, Bibliografia: 1895–1899: diritto romano, libri; 1900–1906: diritto greco e diritto romano, libri, periodici. Roma 1912. pp. iv.306 [6000.]

P[IETRO] DE FRANCISCI, Il diritto romano. Guide bibliografiche [no.13]: Roma 1923. pp.143. [1724.]

PAUL COLLINET, Bibliographie des travaux de droit romain en langue française. Société de bibliographie classique: Collection de bibliographie classique: 1930. pp.[vi].41. [1324.]

PAUL COLLINET, Répertoire des bibliographies, vocabulaires, index, concordances et palingénésies du droit romain. 1933. pp.13. [100.]

THE PAUL KRUEGER collection of books on roman and general law in the Library of Congress. [Washington] 1934. ff.[i].244. [4691.]

BIONDO BIONDI, Diritto romano. Università cattolica del sacro cuore: Guide bibliografiche (III.1): Milano 1944. pp.xx.391. [3500.]

RAYMOND MONIER, Bibliographie des travaux récents de droit romain en français, en allemand, en anglais, en italien et en roumain. 1944. pp.48. [618.]

—— [another edition]. Par R. Monier et Maxime Lemosse. Université de Paris: Institut de droit romain: Publications (vol.iii): 1949. pp.60. [810.]

L[UCIEN] CAES and R[OGER] HENRION, Collectio bibliographica operum ad ius romanum pertinentium. Bruxelles.

i. Opera edita in periodicis miscellaneis encyclopaediisque. 1949–1950. pp.447+256. [10,000.]
ii. Theses. vol.i. Theses Galliae. 1950. pp.3–447. [6000.]

E[DOARDO] VOLTERRA, Saggio bibliografico di diritto agrario romano. Osservatorio italiano di diritto agrario: Testi legislativi e documenti: Firenze 1951. pp.141. [1450.]

Russia.

V. PFAF, Систематическій каталогъ книгъ на русскомъ языкѣ Императорской Публичной Библіотеки по части правовѣдѣнія, политическихъ и статистическихъ наукъ. С.-Петербургъ 1863. pp.445. [law: 3331.]

there is another titlepage, on which the author's name does not appear, but instead that of prince [Nikolai Borisovich] Yusupov as editor.

ОПИСАНІЕ документовъ и бумагъ, хранящихся въ Московскомъ архивѣ министерства юстиціи. Санктпетербургъ [vols.iii–xiv: Москва] 1869–1905. pp.[iii].xxxix.431.ii.10 + [vii].viii.199.vi.70.iv.211.ii.11 + [xii].353.ii.220 + [ix].193.viii.534 + xv.509.160 + xv.276.199.216 +

xiii.214.428 + xiii.179.iv.459.xi + ix.363.163 + vii. 527.39 + xv.511.57 + [ix].551.76 + [vii].546.83 + [vii].339.84. [10,000.]

P[LATON IVANOVICH] BARANOV, Опись именнымъ высочайшимъ указамъ и повелѣніямъ . . . 1704–1725[–1762]. Архивъ правительствующаго сената: Санктпетербургъ 1872–1878. pp.[ii].xxxi.169 + [ii].xiv.1002 + [ii].xxxi.517 + 304. [12,233.]

СИСТЕМАТИЧЕСКІЙ каталогъ книгъ Библиотеки присяжныхъ повѣренныхъ. С.-Петербургъ 1875. pp.22. [250.]

КАТАЛОГЪ книгамъ библіотеки Государственнаго совѣта. С.-Петербургъ 1877. pp.[ii]. 47.vi. [1500.]

— [another edition]. 1878. pp.[ii].72.viii. [2000.]

V[ALTASAR] BOGIŠIĆ, Aperçu des travaux sur le droit coutumier en Russie. 1879. pp.22. [50.]

E. SHAIKEVICH and A[NDREI FILIPPOVICH] POVORINSKY, Алфавитный указатель юридическихъ вопросовъ разрѣшенныхъ гражданскимъ кассаціоннымъ департаментомъ Правительствующаго Сената, въ 1879 и 1880 годахъ. 2-ое изданіе. Санкт-Петербургъ 1881. pp.[iv].200. [800.]

A[NDREI FILIPPOVICH] POVORINSKY, Систематическій указатель русской литературы по гражданскому праву. Санктпетербургъ 1886. pp.xvi.393.

— — Изданіе второе. 1904. pp.xxi.896. [16,625.]

F. DENISENKO, Указатель свода законовъ, продолженій и позднѣйшихъ узаконеній. Москва 1890. pp.48. [250.]

N[IKOLAI] P[AVLOVICH] ZAGOSKIN, Наука исторіи русскаго права. Ея вспомогательныя знанія, источники и литература. Казань 1891. pp.xxviii.530. [4687.]

N[IKOLAI] P[ETROVICH] LIKHACHEV, Каталогъ летучихъ изданій и ихъ перепечатокъ. Манифесты, указы и другія правительственныя распоряженія въ отдѣльныхъ изданіяхъ и перепечаткахъ, разные отдѣльные листы и брошюры. С.-Петербургъ 1895. pp.xiii.v[*sic*, iv].467. [2500.]

КАТАЛОГЪ библіотеки Московскаго архива Министерства юстиціи. Москва 1895. pp.[ii]. 140. [2000.]

A[NDREI FILIPPOVICH] POVORINSKY, Систематическій указатель русской литературы по судоустройству и судопроизводству, гражданскому и уголовному. С.-Петербургъ 1896–1905. pp.xxv.835+[iii].xiv.495. [18,777.]

библіотека Александровской Военно-юридической академіи. Систематическій каталогъ. Часть первая. Русскія книги юридическаго содержанія. С.-Петербургъ 1899. pp.[vi].283. [2750.]

FEDOR IVANOVICH LEONTOVICH, Исторія русскаго права. Вып. 1. Литература исторіи русскаго права. Варшава 1902. pp.iv.597. lxviii. [5000.]

S. P. NIKONOV, Гражданское право. Указатель литературы. Харьковъ 1904. pp.[ii]. 127.[ix]. [2500.]

LIST of recent books on political and social conditions in Russia. Library of Congress: Washington 1905. ff.3. [18.]*

A[NDREI] V. ODINTSOV, Указатель книгъ и статей о государственномъ контролѣ. Петроградъ 1918. pp.[ii].29. [403.]

BRIEF list of references on the soviet government of Russia. Library of Congress: [Washington] 1925. ff.11. [105.]*

E. KELMANN and H. FREUND, *edd.* Die juristische literatur der Sowjet-Union. Bio-bibliographische beiträge zur geschichte der rechts- und staatswissenschaften (supplement 2): Berlin 1926. pp.108. [750.]

V[LADIMIR] V. SOKOLOV, Систематическйи указатель юридической литературы. Издание второе. Москва 1926. pp.324. [4022.]

SOVIET law. American foreign law association: Bibliographies of foreign law series (no.6): [New York] 1933. pp.67. [350.]

RUSSIA. A check list preliminary to a basic bibliography of materials in the russian language. Part 4. Law and institutions prior to 1918. Library of Congress: Reference department: Washington 1944. ff.62. [1002.]*

JOHN N[EWBOLD] HAZARD and WILLIAM B[ERNHARD] STERN, Bibliography of the principal materials on soviet law. American foreign law association: Proceedings (no.27): [New York 1945]. pp.46. [500.]

BORIS MEISSNER, Russland-bibliographie. Universität Hamburg: Forschungsstelle für völkerrecht und ausländisches öffentliches recht: Hektographierte veröffentlichungen (ser. C2, vol.i): Hamburg 1950.*

i. Die grundordnung des staates. Folge 1. UdSSR und RSFSR. Allgemeines. pp. [iv].128. [1200.]

ii. Gliedrepubliken und autonome nationale gebietskörperschaften der UdSSR und RSFSR. pp.[iv].107. [1000.]

no more published.

V[LADILENA] V[ASILEVNA] MISHARINA [*and others*], Новинки популярной общественно-политической литературы (1955–1956 гг.). Рекомендательный указатель литературы. Государственная . . . публичнаябибл иотека СССР имени В. И. Ленина: Москва 1957. pp.52. [150.]

[K. YA. DRAGOMIRETSKAYA *and others*], Советское государственное право. Библиография 1917–1957. Академия наук СССР: Институт права им. А. Я. Вышинского: Москва 1958. pp.776. [7500.]

[P. S. ROMASHKIN *and others*], Литература по советскому праву. Библиографический указатель. Академия наук СССР: Институт государства и права: Москва 1960. pp.280. [5000.]

Saar.

[ ] GILL, Alphabetisches register über die im Amtsblatt der Regierungs-kommission des Saargebietes in den jahrgängen 1 bis 8 (1920 bis einschliessl. 1927) erschienenen verordnungen, bekenntmachungen, erlasse u. verfügungen. Saarlouis 1928. pp.176. [4000.]

Saint Gall.

UEBERSICHT der gedruckten ältern und neueren lokal-statuten, öffnungen und gemeinds-reglemente des kantons St. Gallen. St. Gallen &c. 1847. pp.[iv].100. [218.]

St Lucia.

P. M. C. SHERIFF, Index of the laws of St. Lucia (exclusive of the civil code and code of civil procedure) in force on the 31st December, 1907. [St. Lucia 1908]. pp.[v].34. [1000.]

St Vincent.

P. M. C. SHERIFF, Comparative index of the laws of the colonies of Grenada & St. Vincent up to the 31st day of December 1905. Barbados [printed] [1906]. pp.[ii].26. [1000.]

Salzburg.

FRANZ STARR, Vollständiges sach- und nachschlage-register zu sämmtlichen landesgesetzblättern der im Reichsrathe vertretenen königreiche und länder von deren beginn 1849 bis zum jahre 1873. . . . Erster theil. Niederösterreich, Oberösterreich und Salzburg. Wien 1873. pp.vi. 358. [5000.]

Santiago del Estero.

ÍNDICE de todas las leyes orgánicas y especiales de carácter permanente desde el año 1856 hasta el año 1942. Dirección general de estadística: Santiago del Estero 1942. pp.32. [600.]

Sardinia.

BORON ANGELO, Repertorio della legislazione costituzionale sarda ossia doppio indice degli atti del governo . . . dall'anno 1848 a tutto il 1859. Torino 1860. pp.xliv.148. [1500.]

Savoy.

G. FLANDIN, Répertoire par ordre alphabétique et chronologique des édits, lettres-patentes, billets royaux, manifestes, ordonnances, règlemens, instructions, circulaires et autres actes du gouvernement, émanés depuis le mois de mai 1804, jusqu'à la fin de 1834. Moutiers 1836. pp.viii.404. [2000.]

Saxe-Meiningen.

E. SCHAUBACH, Uebersicht über die im herzogthum S.-Meiningen in ansehung der evangelischen landeskirche erschienenen gesetze und verordnungen. Meiningen 1857. pp.iv.113. [350.]

Saxony.

BENJAMIN GOTTFRIED WEINART, Litteratur des staatsrechts und der statistik von Sachsen. Meissen 1802. pp.xii.282+viii.181. [2500.]

WILHELM THEODOR RICHTER, Alphabetisches repertorium zur gesetzgebung des königreichs Sachsen . . . vom jahre 1818 an bis mit 1838. Leipzig 1839. pp.viii.488+[ii].396. [10,000.]

—— Supplement . . . 1839 bis 1841. 1841. pp.[vi].345. [5000.]

Scandinavia.

A[NDREAS] AAGESEN, Fortegnelse over retssamlinger, retsliteratur m.m. i Danmark, Norge,

Sverig og til dels Finland. Kjøbenhavn 1876. pp.[vii].167. [2750.]

SCANDINAVIA. American foreign law association: Bibliographies of foreign law series (no.2): [New York] 1926. pp.19–31. [75.]

ÅKE SANDLER and ERNST [RAGNAR] EKMAN, Government, politics, and law in the Scandinavian countries. A selected, critical bibliography. University of Minnesota: Program in scandinavian area studies: [Minneapolis] 1954. pp.24. [200.]

a preliminary duplicated edition appeared in 1952.

STIG IUUL [*and others*], Scandinavian legal bibliography. [Institut för jämföranda rättsvetenskap:] Acta (vol.iv): Stockholm &c. 1961. pp.196. [3500.]

Schleswig-Holstein.

[EDUARD AMBROSIUS], Chronologisches verzeichniss über verschiedene königliche und fürstliche verordnungen und verfügungen für die herzogthümer Schleswig und Holstein. Flensburg [vols.iii–viii: Schleswig].

i. 1579–1730. 1796. pp.xvi.108. [300.]
ii. 1731–1738. 1797. pp.111. [200.]

iii. 1739–1750. 1799. pp.134. [200.]
iv. 1750–1760. 1799. pp.102. [250.]
v. 1760–1770. 1801. pp.196. [200.]
vi. 1770–1780. 1803. pp.232. [500.]
vii. 1780–1790. 1804. pp.246. [1000.]
viii. 1790–1799. 1804. pp.198. [600.]

Scotland.

[SIR JAMES STEWART], An index or abridgement of the acts of parliament, made by . . . kings and queen of Scotland. Edinburgh 1685. pp.292. [2500.]

— — [second edition]. The index or abridgement . . . from 1424 to . . . 1707. 1707. pp.[xi].297. [2500.]

INVENTARY of works done for the state by his majesties printer in Scotland, Dec. 1642–Oct. 1647. Edinburgh 1815. pp.17. [150.]

INDEX to the decisions of the Court of session, contained in all the original collections, and in mr. Morison's Dictionary of decisions. Edinburgh 1823. pp.xiii.536. [27,500.]

ARCHIBALD SWINTON, Digest of decisions in the Registration appeal court at Glasgow, in the years 1835, 1836, 1837, and 1838; with notes of decisions in other districts; and a supplement, containing the cases decided in 1839. Edinburgh 1840. pp.[ii].ii. 270. [500.]

PATRICK SHAW, Digest of cases decided in the supreme courts of Scotland, 1800–1842. Edinburgh 1843. pp.18.911+[ii].913–1800. [15,000.]

— — 1800–1868, and, on appeal, by the House of lords, from 1726 to 1868. By A. B[eatson] Bell and W[illiam] Lamond. [1868–1869]. pp.xxiv.768 +[iii].769–1536+[iii].1537–2336. [40,000.]

JAMES BADENACH NICOLSON, Digest of the decisions of the Registration appeal court under the Reform act, 1868. Edinburgh 1869. pp.46. [80.]

HENRY JOHNSTON, C. C. MACONOCHIE and HUGH J. E. FRASER, An analytical digest of cases decided in the supreme courts of Scotland and on appeal by the House of lords from . . . 1877, to . . . 1885. Edinburgh 1886. pp.viii.coll.938.pp.[ii].lii. [3500.]

HANDY book of reference to decisions in the Court of session, Court of justiciary, and House of lords, from July 1885 to August 1893. Edinburgh 1894. pp.206. [2250.]

A DIGEST of cases decided in the sheriff courts of Scotland. Glasgow &c.

1885–1894. By George Guthrie. 1895. pp. [v].346. [1750.]

1885–1904. 1906. pp.[v].626. [3000.]

1905–1914. 1915. pp.[iii].283. [1500.]

1915–1924. By R. H. Sherwood Calver. 1926. pp.[iv].251. [1250.]

1925–1934. By C. de B. Murray. 1936. pp.[v]. 187. [800.]

1935–1944. By Donald Mackay. 1948. pp. [iv].172. [1000.]

in progress.

DIGEST of all the cases decided in the supreme courts of Scotland and reported in the various series of reports. Edinburgh.

1895–1898. By J[ames] C[ondie] S[andeman] Sandeman. pp.[iii].coll.476. [2000.]

1895–1900. pp.[iii].coll.692. [3000.]

[*continued as:*]

The scots digest. Digest of all the cases [&c.].

1900–1903. pp.[iii].coll.336. [1500.]

1905–1915 [*on cover:* 1904–1914]. By R. H. Maconochie and James Bell Ballinghall. pp.[iii].coll.1256.pp.1257–1403. [4000.]

1914–1923. By William Dunbar. pp.[iv]. coll.674.pp.676–715. [2750.]

1923–1930. pp.[iv].coll.504. pp.505–538. [1500.]

1930–1937. pp.[iv].coll.424. pp.425–545. [1250.]

1937–1944. pp.[iv].coll.294. pp.295–316. [750.]

1945–1946. pp.[iv].coll.56.pp.57–64.

1946–1947. pp.[iv].coll.70.pp.71–78.

in progress; only the final cumulative issues are set out.

JOHN A. WELSH, Index of cases commented upon in judgments in the Court of session and in scottish appeals to the House of lords from October 1893 to July 1904. Edinburgh 1906. pp.[vii].199. [2500.]

R. CANDLISH HENDERSON, The scots digest of scots appeals in the House of lords from 1707 and of the cases decided in the supreme courts of Scotland, 1800 to 1873. Edinburgh 1908–1912. pp. viii.coll.1312 + pp.[iv].coll.1396 + pp.[iv].coll. 1296 + pp.[iv].coll.450.pp.433–789.coll.791–800. [27,500.]

AN ANALYTICAL digest of cases decided in the supreme courts of Scotland and, on appeal, in the House of lords. Faculty of advocates: Edinburgh &c.

1868–1922. 1924–1926. pp.viii.coll.1530 + [v].coll.1734 + pp.[v].coll.1632 + pp.xiii. pp.[v].coll.1486 + pp.[v].coll.1584 + pp. coll.1482. [30,000.]

1922–1930. By Kenneth D. Cullen. 1932. pp.xii.coll.1490. [3000.]

1930–1940. By J[ames] Lindsay Duncan. 1947. pp.iii–xii.coll.1684. [3500.]

1941–1950.

1951.

in progress; only the final cumulative issues and the current supplements are set out.

DIGEST of justiciary cases, 1868–1925. Faculty of advocates: Edinburgh &c. 1927. pp.viii.coll. 906.pp.[ii].96. [3500.]

the numbered pages at the end of the volume are blank.

LESLIE F. MAXWELL, A bibliography of scottish law from the earliest times . . . together with a list of roman law books in the english language. Sweet & Maxwell's legal bibliography (vol.v): 1937. pp.vii.148. [1500.]

— — Second edition. Compiled by L. F. Maxwell and W. H. Maxwell. 1957. pp.vii.188. [2250.]

N[ORMAN] M[ACDONALD] W[ALKER] WALKER, Digest of Sheriff court cases selected from the

Scots law times, 1893–1943. Edinburgh 1944. pp. [iii].coll.154.pp.155–167. [500.]

Seine-Inférieure.

[H. CREVIER], Table générale, par ordre alphabétique, du recueil des actes des corps administratifs, et particulièrement de la préfecture de la Seine-Inférieure. Dieppe 1842–1843. pp.199+236 +[iv].304. [7500.]

although the title remains unaltered in vol.iii, only the four preliminary pages contain the completion of the work; the rest of the volume sets out the texts of election laws.

Serbia.

PREGLED razvoja međunarodno-pravnih odnosa jugoslovenskih zemalja od 1800 do danas. I sveska. Pregled međunarodnik ugovora i drugih akata od međunarodno-pravnog značaja za Srbijn od 1800 do 1918 godine. Institut za međunarodnu politiku i privredu: Sekcija za međunarodno pravo: Beograd 1953. pp.244. [1148.]

Seychelles.

ROBERT STEPHEN DE VERE, Index of the laws of

Seychelles. Victoria (Mahé) 1930. pp.[vii].83. [2500.]

Sicily.

DIEGO ORLANDO, Biblioteca di antica giurisprudenza siciliana. Palermo 1851. pp.204. [162.]

Sierra Leone.

F. F. PINKETT, Numerical and alphabetical index of the ordinances of Sierra Leone. 1887. pp.[iii].40. [400.]

—— [another edition]. Chronological and alphabetical index [&c.]. Revised. [1900]. pp.[ii]. 129. [3000.]

Silesia.

FRANZ STARR, Vollständiges sach- und nachschlage-register zu sämmtlichen landesgesetzblättern der im Reichsrathe vertretenen königreiche und länder von deren beginn 1849 bis zum jahre 1873. . . . Dritter theil. Böhmen, Mähren und Schlesien. Wien 1874. pp.[iii].408. [5000.]

Singapore.

LIST of regulations, etc. presented pursuant to

ordinances. Legislative assembly: Singapore 1959 &c.

in progress.

Somaliland.

INDEX to the laws enacted during 1941 to 1946. Somaliland protectorate: [Aden 1947]. pp.[ii].44. [750.]

— Index to the laws enacted during 1947 [&c.].
1947. pp.[ii].12. [200.]
1948. pp.[ii].10. [150.]

Spain.

[CELSUS HUGO DESCOUSU], Las leyes de todos los reynos de Castilla: abreuidas reduzidas en forma de reportorio decisiuo por la orden del a.b.c. por Hugo de Celso. Valladolid 1538. ff.[viii].ccclxiiii. [6000.]

[—] — nueuamente por el doctor Aguilera . . . y por el doctor Victoria . . . corregido y añadido de muchas leyes que faltanã. 1547. ff.[vii].ccclxxii. [6000.]

[—] — Reportorio vniversal de todas las leyes destos reynos de Castilla. . . . Agora nueuamente van añadidas . . . y corregido . . . por . . . Andres

Martinez. Medina del Campo 1553. ff.[viii]. cccxxxix. [7500.]

DIEGO DE ATIENÇA, Reportorio de la nueva recopilacion de las leyes del reyno. Alcala de Henares 1571. pp.[xi].coll.288. [3000.]

— — [another edition]. 1598. pp.[xii].coll.304. [4500.]

GERARDUS ERNESTUS [FRANCK] DE FRANCKENAU, Sacra Themidis Hispanae arcana, jurium legumque ortus, progressus, varietates et observantiam [&c.]. . . . Editio secunda novis accessionibus locupletata a Francisco Cerdano et [Cerdá y] Rico. Matriti 1780. pp.xvi.108.350. [200.]

FELIX DEL VALLE LINACERO, Leyes penales vigentes actualmente en España, recopiladas de nuestros codigos, ordenanzas y colecciones de decretos. Madrid 1840. pp.clii.56. [250.]

ÍNDICE de las ordenes mas precisas é interesantes espedidas por el gobierno de España desde el año de 1811 al de 1841 inclusives. Madrid 1842. pp.88. [1000.]

[F. W. HALFPENNY], Specimen of a catalogue of the books on foreign law lately presented by

Charles Porton Cooper, esq., to the Society of Lincoln's inn. 1847. pp.vi.80. [80.]

the Specimen *consists of the section on spanish law.*

COLECCIÓN de fueros y cartas-pueblas de España, por la Real academia de la historia. Catálogo. Madrid 1852. pp.[vii].309. [2000.]

the title is misleading; the work is a catalogue of laws and the like arranged in the order of the towns &c. at which they were promulgated.

MANUEL GORMAZ, Índice alfabético del codigo civil. Santiago 1857. pp.157. [2250.]

FRANCISCO SÁNCHEZ DE CASTRO, Apuntes de literatura y bibliografía juridica de España. Madrid 1883. pp.163. [1500.]

JOSÉ VILLA-AMIL Y CASTRO, Reseña de algunos códices jurídicos de la biblioteca del Escorial. Madrid 1883. pp.94. [40.]

MANUEL TORRES CAMPOS, Bibliografía española contemporánea del derecho y de la política, 1800–1880. Madrid 1883. pp.208. [4000.]

— — 1881 a 1896. 1897 [*on cover:* 1898]. pp.168. [2500.]

RAFAEL DE UREÑA Y SMENJAUD, Las ediciones de los fueros y observancias del reino de Aragón anteriores à la compilación de 1547. Madrid 1900. pp.40. [10.]

[PEDRO A. DE AZEVEDO], Inventario dos livros das portarias do reino. Real archivo da Tôrre do tombo: Lisboa 1909–1912. pp.xvi.522+[iii].434. [10,000.]

THOMAS W[AVERLY] PALMER, Guide to the law and legal literature of Spain. Prepared under the direction of Edwin M[ontefiore] Borchard. Library of Congress: Washington 1915. pp.174. [750.]

BIBLIOGRAFÍA jurídica hispánica. . . . Por José de Peray March. Tomo I. Barcelona [1921]. pp.184. [750.]

this volume covers the publications of 1912; no more published.

[E. VARÓN VALLEJO and A. GONZÁLEZ PALENCIA], Consejo de Castilla. Sala de Alcaldes de casa y corte. Catálogo por materias. Archivo histórico nacional: Madrid 1925. pp.xx.851. [22,500.]

FAUSTINO GIL AYUSO, Noticia bibliográfica de textos y disposiciones legales de los reinos de Castilla impresos en los siglos XVI y XVII. Biblioteca nacional: Madrid 1935. pp.xi.465. [1750.]

JOHN THOMAS VANCE, The background of hispanic-american law: legal sources and juridical literature of Spain. Catholic university of America: Washington 1937. pp.x.281. [1000.]

— — [another edition]. New York 1943. pp. viii.296. [1000.]

JESÚS MUÑOZ Y NÚÑEZ DE PRADO, Índices cronológico y alfabético de la legislación de interés general desde el 24 de julio de 1936 hasta el 24 de julio de 1939. Pamplona 1939. pp.79. [1400.]

ÍNDICE progresivo de legislación. Pamplona.
1930–1940. [By Estanislao de] Aranzadi. pp. 1015. [60,000.]
1930–1949. pp.1612. [140,000.]
followed by a monthly Apendice.

CARLOS A LUQUE COLOMBRES, Libros de derecho en bibliotecas particulares cordobesas, 1573–1810. Universidad nacional de Córdoba: Instituto de estudios americanistas: Cuaderno de historia (vol. ix): 1945. pp.xvii.80. [125.]

ARCHIVO general de protocolos de Barcelona. Sección histórica. Índice cronológico, alfabético. I. Siglos XIII, XIV, XV y XVI. Colegio notarial: Barcelona 1948–1950. pp.225+256. [large number.]

F. FERNÁNDEZ DE VILLAVICENCIO [*and others*], Bibliografía jurídica española. Consejo superior de investigaciones científicas: Instituto de derecho comparado: Colección: Bibliografías (no.1): Barcelona 1954. pp.127. [800.]

AURELIO GUAITA, Bibliografía española de derecho administrativo. Instituto do derecho comparado: Colección (ser. F, no.4): Barcelona 1955. pp.113. [1402.]

GREGORIO PASCUAL NIETO, Bibliografía de derecho civil, mercantil y procesal civil. Aguilar 1956. pp.v–xv.451+[vii].453–1002. [20,000.]

BIBLIOGRAFÍA jurídica española. Madrid.

1956. Por José Manuel Perez-Prendes and Ángel Sanchez de La Torre. 1958. pp.3–100. [1400.]

1957. 1959. pp.3–106. [1450.]

JAVIER MALAGÓN-BARCELO, La literatura jurídica española del siglo de oro en la Nueva España. Biblioteca nacional de México: Instituto bibliográfico mexicano (vol.3): México 1959 [*colophon*: 1960]. pp.3–175. [244.]

Stavelot.

LISTE chronologique des édits et ordonnances

de la principauté de Stavelot et de Malmédy, de 650 à 1793. Bruxelles 1852. pp.[ii].viii.134. [750.]

Straits Settlements.

SIR WILLIAM GEORGE MAXWELL, A chronological table of . . . the imperial acts . . . the indian acts . . . and . . . the ordinances of the Straits Settlements. . . . Ninth edition. Revised by A. B. Voules. Singapore 1916. pp.[ii].ii.279.[xiv]. [2250.]

— — Thirteenth edition. The chronological table of Straits Settlements laws. . . . Revised by J. V. Mills. 1925. pp.[ii].iv.492. [3500.]

from this date new editions have appeared annually, with more frequent corrections slips.

INDEX of Straits Settlements laws on 1st July, 1933. Compiled in Deputy public prosecutor's office, Penang. Singapore 1934. pp.[ii].100. [2500.]

C. H. WITHERS PAYNE, The malayan digest, being a complete digest of every case in the colony of the Straits Settlements and the Federated Malay States reported from 1808. Singapore 1936. pp. [ix].305. [1504.]

D. K. WALTERS, Index to the municipal ordinances of the Straits Settlements. Singapore 1939. pp.iii–xxiii.198. [6000.]

A CHRONOLOGICAL and alphabetical list of emergency legislation in force on 18th December, 1940. Singapore 1941. pp.[vii].50. [500.]

Styria.

FRANZ STARR, Vollständiges sach- und nachschlage-register zu sämmtlichen landesgesetzblättern der im Reichsrathe vertretenen königreiche und länder von deren beginn 1849 bis zum jahre 1873. . . . Zweiter theil. Steiermark, Kärnthen und Krain. Wien 1873. pp.[iii].288. [4000.]

Swabia.

GEORG KARL VON MAYR, General-index über alle landes-verordnungen, welche durch die königlich baierische regierungs-blätter von Baiern in München, von der Oberpfalz in Amberg, von Franken in Bamberg, und von Schwaben in Ulm, von den jahren 1802, 1803, 1804, und 1805 promulgirt und bekannt gemacht worden sind. München 1806. pp.[viii].428. [2000.]

— — 1806 — 1809–1810. 1809. pp.[viii].793. [2500.]

Sweden.

REGISTER öfwer den på kongl. maj:ts nådiga befallning utgifna samling af foerfattningar och stadgar. Stockholm 1808. pp.[ii].142. [2500.]

C. U. LEYONMARCK, Register öfwer den utaf framledne herre cancellie-rådet och riddaren Anders Anton v. Stjerneman gjorde samling af riksdags-beslut, bewillningar, arfföreningar, regements-former, resolutioner på ståndens allmänna beswär, m.m., ifrån år 1521 til år 1731. inclusive. Stockholm 1820. pp.[ii].759. [10,000.]

A[NDREAS] AAGESEN, Fortegnelse over retssamlinger, retsliteratur m.m. i. Danmark, Norge, Sverig og til dels Finland. Kjøbenhavn 1876. pp.[vii].167. [3000.]

[BARON] JOHANNES [REINHOLD GUSTAF] RUDBECK, Beskrivande och illustrerad förteckning över de upplagar av Sveriges landskapslagar, landslagar och stadslagar som av trycket blivit utgivna intill dess Sveriges rikes lag blev gillad och antagen på riksdagen år 1734. Bibliografi. Stockholm 1915. pp.[iii].viii.85. [42.]
350 copies printed.

NILS REGNER, Svensk juridisk litteratur, 1865–1956. Institut för rättsvetenskaplig forskning (vol.xvi): Stockholm 1957. pp.xxxii.610. [12,000.]

[HILLEVI VRETBLAD], Katalog över Juridiska biblioteket i Stockholm. Stockholm 1958. pp. xviii.995. [30,000.]

Switzerland.

A[LOYS] V[ON] ORELLI, Grundriss zu den vorlesungen über schweizerische rechtsgeschichte (mit literatur- und quellenangabe). Zweite auflage. Zürich 1884. pp.[ii].24. [200.]

CHARLES GILLIÉREN, Répertoire des lois fédérales. Lausanne 1885. pp.iv.80. [1250.]

SCHWEIZERISCHES recht. Schweizerischer buchhändlerverein: Schweizerische bücherkataloge: Frauenfeld [printed] 1939. pp.[xii].201. [2250.]

Tanganyika.

H[ARRY] R[OBERT] F[REDERICK] BUTTERFIELD, Index to the laws of the Tanganyika territory in force. Dar es Salaam 1935. pp.[iii].xii.94. [3000.]

— — [another edition]. By G. M. Pillai. 1941. pp.[iii].xxv.88. [3000.]

LIST of publication published by the government of Tanganyika. Dar es Salaam.
1944. pp.[8]. [100.]

AUDREY A. WALKER, Official publications of British east Africa. Part II. Tanganyika. Library of Congress: General reference and bibliography division: Washington 1962. pp.x.134. [715.]*

Tarn.

L. BONHOURE, Table abrégée du Bulletin des actes administratifs de la préfecture du Tarn depuis . . . 1er janvier 1816 jusqu'au 31 décembre 1857 inclusivement. Castres 1858. pp.32. [500.]

Tasmania.

HUGH MUNRO HULL, An index to the statute law in force in Tasmania. [Hobart 1874]. pp.xi. [500.]
— — [another edition]. Tasmania. The statute

index; containing I. — An alphabetical index to the statutes of Tasmania in force. . . . II. — A chronological account of all the acts passed by the Legislature since 1826. III. — A table of english statutes which have been extended to Tasmania. Hobart Town 1877. pp.iv.43. [500.]

JOHN KIDSTON REID, Index to the statutes of Tasmania and acts of the Federal council of Australasia in force on June 1, 1897. Hobart 1897. pp.36. [1000.]

— — Fifth edition. 1921. pp.59. [2750.]

Tennessee.

HENRY CLAY KING, The Tennessee digest of the judicial decisions of the state of Tennessee from the year 1796 to May, 1880. . . . Second edition. Chicago 1880. pp.651+653–1420+1421–2185. [20,000.]

CHECK lists of laws and codes of the state of Tennessee, 1792–1939. Tennessee historical record survey: Special publications series (no.5): Nashville 1940. pp.[ii].ff.21. [150.]*

PRELIMINARY check-list of Tennessee legislative documents. Tennessee state library & archives: Nashville 1954. pp.[32]. [550.]

Texas.

C. N. BUCKLER, A civil digest of the Texas reports. Kansas City, Mo. [printed] 1894. pp. 786+3–739+632. [40,000.]

Transvaal.

C. J. M. WILDE, Index op de rapporten over de jaren 1877–1888 en 1893–1897 van het Hof te Pretoria. Leiden 1904. pp.xi.ff.89.pp.91–99. [574.]

Trinidad.

A TABLE of all the orders in council and ordinances which were either wholly or partially in force on the 31st of December, A.D. 1871. [*s.l.* 1872]. pp.[ii].34. [500.]

INDEX to all the orders in council and ordinances which were either wholly or partially in force on the 31st day of December, A.D. 1871. [*s.l.* 1872]. pp.[ii].51. [500.]

CHRONOLOGICAL table of the royal orders in council and ordinances promulgated in this colony between the 25th April, A.D. 1831, and the 30th June, A.D. 1877. Port-of-Spain 1877. pp.xvii.142. [1250.]

Trinidad and Tobago.

INDEX to proclamations, orders in council, regulations, &c. for the year 1945. [Port of Spain]. 1949. pp.x. [250.]

Tyrol.

REPERTORIUM über die in den zwölf ersten bänden der provinzial-gesetzsammlung für Tyrol und Vorarlberg enthaltenen verordnungen. Innsbruck 1828. pp.587. [5000.]

— Bänden XIII. bis einschliesslich XXV. 1842. pp.563. [5000.]

FRANZ STARR, Vollständiges sach- und nachschlage-register zu sämmtlichen landesgesetzblättern der im Reichsrathe vertretenen königreiche und länder von deren beginn 1849 bis zum jahre 1873. . . . Vierter theil. Tirol-Vorarlberg, Küstenland und Dalmatien. Wien 1874. pp.[iii]. 428. [6000.]

Uganda.

CHRONOLOGICAL table and index of the laws of the Uganda protectorate. [Entebbe] 1905. pp. [iv].38. [2000.]

— — [another edition]. [1909]. pp.[xi].61. [3000.]

T. C. DANDS, Index to the laws of the Uganda protectorate in force. . . . With a table of references to amending legislation. Entebbe 1937. pp.[vi]. xxvi. [1000.]

— — [another edition]. Compiled by Leo Gama. 1943. pp.88. [2000.]

United States.

i. *Bibliographies*

LAWRENCE KEITT, An annotated bibliography of bibliographies of statutory materials of the United

States. Harvard series of legal bibliographies (vol.ii): Cambridge [Mass.] 1934. pp.xvii.191. [479.]

ARTHUR SYDNEY BEARDSLEY, Legal bibliography and the use of law books. University textbook series: Chicago 1937. pp.xv.514. [1000.]

JOHN S[AEGER] BRADWAY, A tentative bibliography of material on legal aid work. [Durham, N.C.] 1940. pp.xi.247. [3700.]*

WILLIAM L[AWRENCE] FRIEND, Anglo-american legal bibliographies. An annotated guide. Library of Congress: Washington 1944. pp.xii.166. [298.]

ii. *History*

[CHARLES SWIFT RICHÉ HILDEBURN], The Charlemagne Tower collection of american colonial laws. Historical society of Pennsylvania: Philadelphia [printed] 1890. pp.299. [1029.]

privately printed; includes a few historical Americana.

RICHARD BRANDON MORRIS, Early american court records: a publication program. New York university: School of law: Anglo-american legal history series (1st ser., no.4): New York 1941. pp.[ii].37 [large number.]

iii. *General*

JOHN C. DEVEREUX, Court of claims. Reports and digest of opinions delivered since the organization of the court. New York 1856. pp.261.53. [735.]

HORACE RUBLEE, Catalogue of the State library of Wisconsin. Madison 1859. pp.122. [3000.]
— — [another edition]. 1872. pp.319. [4000.]

GUY A. BROWN, Catalogue of the Nebraska state library. Des Moines, Iowa, 1871. pp.51. [500.]

[HIRAM A. HUSE], Catalogue of the Vermont state library. Montpelier 1872. pp.xv.200. [2500.]

O. H. MILLER, Catalogue of the Pennsylvania state library. . . . Part I. — Law books and state papers. Harrisburg 1873. pp.xvi.332. [4000.]

DIGEST of the official opinions of the Attorneys-general of the United States. Washington.
1789–1881. By A. J. Bentley. 1885. pp.xix. 491. [6000.]
1881–1906. By James A. Finch. 1908. pp.iv. 623. [6000.]
1906–1921. By George Kearney and Emily A. Spilman. 1926. pp.iv.393. [4000.]

T. H. MCKEE, Reports of the Committee on claims, House of representatives, from the fourteenth congress, 1815, to the forty-ninth congress, 1887, inclusive. Washington 1887. pp.79. [1500.]

T. H. MCKEE, Reports of the Committee on the judiciary, United States Senate, from the fifteenth congress, 1816, to the forty-ninth congress, 1887, inclusive. Washington 1887. pp.35. [1500.]

T. H. MCKEE, Reports of the Committee on the judiciary, House of representatives, from the fourteenth congress, 1815, to the forty-ninth congress, 1887, inclusive. Washington 1887. pp.29. [1750.]

T. H. MCKEE, Reports of the Committee on expenditures in Department of justice, House of representatives, from the organization of the committee, January 16, 1874, to the close of the forty-ninth congress, 1887. Washington 1887. pp.7. [100.]

T. H. MCKEE, Reports of the Committee on revision of laws, House of representatives, from the organization of [the] committee, July 25, 1868, to the close of the forty-ninth congress, 1887. Washington 1887. pp.6. [50.]

CATALOGUE of the library of the Law department of the Mutual life insurance company. New York 1895. pp.[ix].120. [2000.]

ORVILLE A[UGUSTUS] PARK, An index to the publications of the various bar associations. Atlanta 1899. pp.86. [2000.]

CHARLOTTE A. DURE, Law book catalogue of the Minnesota state library. St. Paul 1903. pp.621. [20,000.]

JOHN C[HARLES] TOWNES, Law books and how to use them. Austin, Tex. [1909]. pp.xi.191. [500.]

ROBERT J. MAWHINNEY, Digest of the opinions and briefs of the Solicitor of the Treasury, January 1, 1880, to December 31, 1910. Washington 1911. pp.510. [3000.]

— — 1911–1912. 1913. pp.105. [1500.]

A. J. SMALL, Bibliographical and historical check list of proceedings of bar and allied associations.

American association of law libraries: Des Moines 1923. pp.99. [1350.]

THE FEDERAL judiciary: a list of recent writings. Library of Congress: [Washington] 1928. ff.8. [89.]*

AMERICAN law. A finding list of books on this subject in public and private collections in Paris. American library: Paris 1929. pp.3–141. [1750.]

RALPH O. BRICKER, Research manual of legal bibliography and one of law books. Los Angeles [1936]. ff.[ii].v.64. [200.]

DENNIS A[LOYSIUS] DOOLEY, *ed.* Index to state bar association reports and proceedings, including also American bar association, Association of the bar of the city of New York, Canadian bar association, New York county lawyers' association. American association of law libraries: New York 1942. pp.xii.640. [20,000.]

CONDENSED catalog of the Supreme court library of the state of North Carolina. [Raleigh] 1942. pp.47. [1400.]

AN OUTLINE for methods in search for legal authorities. Thirteenth edition. [St. Paul 1942]. pp.16. [100.]

REBECCA LAURENS LOVE NOTZ, Legal bibliography and legal research. Second edition. Washington 1947. pp.[v].234. [1000.]

— Supplement. 1949. pp.[iii].237–296. [400.]

— Part III. Research problems 1949–1950. 1949. pp.[ii].297–380.*

limited to United States law; part III is not bibliographical.

LEONARD OPPENHEIM, Materials on legal bibliography. New Orleans [1948]. ff.[ii].79. [1000.]*

NELSON J. MOLTER, A selected list of law books available in the Maryland state library. Revised edition. Annapolis 1954. pp.viii.108. [2500.]

ANNUAL inventory and check list for field law libraries. Department of the army: Washington 1954. ff.vi.pp.106. [336.]*

CUMULATIVE index to published hearings and reports of the Subcommittee to investigate the administration of the Internal security act and other internal security laws of the Committee on the judiciary, 1955–195 . Washington 1957. pp. ii.844.

HENRY T. ULASEK and MARION JOHNSON, Preliminary inventory of the records of the United States district court for the southern district of New York. National archives: Preliminary inventories (no.116): Washington 1959. pp.v.68. [very large number.]*

MARION M. JOHNSON, MARY JO GROTENRATH, Preliminary inventory of the records of the United States district eourt for the eastern district of Pennsylvania. National archives: Preliminary inventories (no.124): Washington 1960. pp.v.44. [large number.]*

iv. *Statute law*

SAMUEL BURCH, General index to the laws of the United States of America, from March 4th, 1789, to March 3d, 1827. Washington City 1828. pp.3–331. [10,000.]

A SYNOPTICAL index to the laws and treaties of the United States of America, from March 4, 1789, to March 3, 1851. Boston 1856. pp.[iv].747. [25,000.]

PRICE list of laws of the United States. Superintendent of documents: [Price list] (no.10): Washington 1907. pp.[4]. [40.]
frequently re-edited under various titles.

CHARLES J[ACOB] BABBITT, Hand-list of legislative sessions and session laws, statutory revisions, compilations, codes, etc., and constitutional conventions, of the United States and its possessions and of the several states. State library of Massachusetts: [Boston 1912]. pp.634. [7500.]

INDEX analysis of [*afterwards:* Index to] the federal statutes (general and permanent law): Washington.

1789–1873. . . . By Middleton G. Beaman, A. K. McNamara. 1911. pp.v.1146. [40,000.]
1874–1931. . . . By Walter H. McClenon and Wilfred C. Gilbert. 1933. pp.[v].1432. [60,000.]

OFFICIAL cumulative index to state legislation. A complete record and a numerical and subject index of all Bills introduced in all state legislatures. National association of state libraries and American association of law libraries: New York 1915. pp.[658]. [60,000.]

— — [supplement]. 1916. pp.[iv].56.[181]. [15,000.]

BRIEF list of books on the legislative system of the United States. Library of Congress: Washington 1919. ff.2. [21.]*

JAMES B[ENNETT] CHILDS, Popular names of federal statutes. . . . Revised. Washington 1926. pp.[ii].19. [1000.]

STATE law index. An index and digest to [An index to] the legislation of the states of the United States. [Library of Congress: Legislative reference service:] Washington.

i. 1925–1926. By Margaret W. Stewart. 1929. pp.viii.583. [14,000.]

ii. 1927–1928. pp.viii.1034. [20,000.]
iii. 1929–1930. pp.viii.1092. [20,000.]
iv. 1931–1932. pp.viii.1095. [20,000.]
v. 1933–1934. pp.x.1126. [20,000.]
vi. 1935–1936. pp.viii.646. [15,000.]
vii. 1937–1938. pp.vii.700. [16,000.]
viii. 1939–1940. pp.viii.706. [16,000.]
ix. 1941–1942. pp.viii.765. [17,000.]
x. 1943–1944. pp.vii.789. [17,500.]
xi. 1945–1946. pp.vii.729. [20,000.]
xii. 1947–1948. pp.ix.895. [25,000.]*

no more published.

GRACE E. MACDONALD, Preliminary check-list of session laws prior to 1850 [1850–1933]. New York 1935–1934. ff.[iii].61+[ii].39. [10,000.]

— — Check-list of session laws. 1936. pp.[iii]. 266. [11,000.]

GRACE E. MACDONALD, Preliminary check-list of statutes, including revisions, compilations, digests, codes and indexes. New York 1936. ff.[ii].112. [4000.]

WILLARD O. WATERS, Check list of american laws, charters and constitutions of the 17th and 18th centuries in the Huntington library. Huntington library lists (no.1): San Marino, Cal. 1936. pp.vii.140. [933.]

DIGEST of public general bills, with index. Library of Congress: Legislative reference service: Washington.

Seventy-fourth congress. Second session. By W. C. Gilbert. 1936. pp.[ii].242. [2500.]

Seventy-fifth congress. 1937–1938. pp.[ii].410+[ii].254. [6000.]

Seventy-sixth congress. 1939–1940. pp.[ii].471+xlii.211. [5000.]

Seventy-seventh congress. 1942. pp.xxxiv.335+xxviii.99. [5000.]

Seventy-eighth congress. 1944–1945. pp.xxxviii.308+xliii.206. [5000.]

Seventy-ninth congress. 1945–1946. pp.xxv.371+xxxviii.182. [7000.]

Eightieth congress. 1947–1948. pp.xxxiv.433+xxvii.152. [7000.]

Eighty-first congress. 1949–1950. pp.xl.556+xlviii.268. [10,000.]

Eighty-second congress. 1951–1952. pp.l.598+xl.283. [10,000.]

Eighty-third congress. 1953–1954. pp.xlv.634+xli.319. [12,000.]

Eighty-fourth congress. 1955–1956.*

Eighty-fifth congress. 1957–1958.*

Eighty-sixth congress. 1959–1960.*

Eighty-seventh congress. 1961–1962.*

in progress; this is the final cumulative issue of each session.

SOURCES of information on legislation. . . . A bibliographical list of published material reporting legislative bills and enactments. Library of Congress: State law index: Special report (no.1 [&c.]): Washington.

1937–1938. Compiled by Jacob Lyons under the direction of Margaret W. Stewart . . . (no.1): 1938. pp.[ii].38. [389.]
— Supplement. 1940. pp.56. [328.]*
1939 . . . (no.3): 1940. pp.[ii].36. [327.]
no more published.

INDEX to circulars and orders. Department of justice: [Washington 1942]. pp.47. [1800.]

CLIFFORD L. LORD, List and index of presidential executive orders, unnumbered series. Historical records survey, New Jersey: Work projects administration: Newark 1943. pp.xiv.388. [2250.]*

v. *Case law*

a. *Digests*

α. *General*

A DIGESTED index to the reported decisions of

the several courts of law [and equity] in the United States. New York [vols.iii–v: Philadelphia].

i. [Supreme court, Vermont, Connecticut, New York, New Jersey, Pennsylvania]. By John Anthon. 1813. pp.xi.490. [4000.]

ii. [Supreme court, Massachusetts, &c.]. By Thomas Day. 1816. pp.[iii].651. [3000.]

iii. [Maryland, Virginia, North Carolina, South Carolina, Kentucky, Tennessee]. By Thomas I. Wharton. 1824. pp.602. [5000.]

iv. [Vermont, Maine, New Hampshire, Massachusetts, Connecticut, New York, New Jersey]. 1825. pp.691. [6000.]

v. [Supreme court, Vermont, Maine, New Hampshire, New Jersey, Maryland, Virginia, &c.]. By Thomas S. Smith and Francis J. Troubat. 1830. pp.xi.9–554. [5000.]

RICHARD S. COXE, A digest of the decisions in the Supreme court, circuit courts, and district courts of the United States. Philadelphia 1829. pp.viii.752. [10,000.]

RICHARD PETERS, A full and arranged digest of cases, decided in the supreme, circuit and district courts of the United States, from the organization of the Government of the United States. Philadelphia 1838–1839. pp.xxv.7–722+ix.704+x.709. [20,000.]

—— [second edition]. A full and arranged digest of the decisions in common law, equity, and admiralty, of the courts of the United States, from . . . 1789 to 1847. 1848. pp.819+779. [22,500.]

THERON METCALF and JONATHAN C. PERKINS [vols.ii–iii: GEORGE TICKNOR CURTIS], Digest of the decisions of the courts of common law and admiralty in the United States. Boston 1840–1846. pp.[iv].700+[iii].826+iv.724. [45,000.]

—— A supplement . . . by John Phelps Putnam. 1847. pp.lv.844+[ii].996. [20,000.]

——— A table of the cases contained in the . . . Digest, and in the . . . Supplement. By George P. Sanger. 1849. pp.[iii].787.

—— United States digest. . . . Annual digest.

i. 1847. By J. P. Putnam. pp.cxlvi.6–498. [10,000.]
ii. 1848. pp.xxiv.502. [8000.]
iii. 1849. pp.xxvi.581. [9000.]
iv. 1850. pp.xxiv.585. [9000.]
v. 1851. pp.xxiv.621. [9000.]
vi. 1852. pp.xxiv.810. [12,500.]
vii. 1853. pp.xxiii.826. [12,500.]

viii. 1854. pp.xxiii.760. [12,500.]
ix. 1855. pp.xxiii.744. [12,500.]
x. 1856. By George Silsbee Hale. pp.xxxvii. 780. [12,500.]
xi. 1857. pp.xxxviii.719. [12,500.]
xii. 1858. pp.xxxviii.906. [15,000.]
xiii. 1859. By G. S. Hale and H. Farnam Smith. pp.xlii.840. [15,000.]
xiv. 1860. By H. F. Smith. pp.xl.1151. [20,000.]
xv. 1861. pp.xxxix.651. [12,500.]
xvi. 1862. pp.xxxix.669. [12,500.]
xvii. 1863. pp.xxxviii.699. [12,500.]
xviii. 1864. pp.xxxvii.767. [12,500.]
xix. 1865. By Henry W. Frost. pp.xxxviii. 613. [10,000.]
xx. 1866. pp.xl.669. [12,500.]
xxi. 1867. pp.xl.771. [12,500.]
xxii. 1868. By B. F. Burnham. pp.xxxix.774. [12,500.]
xxiii. 1869. By H. W. Frost and B. F. Burnham. pp.xl.788. [12,500.]

— New series.
i. 1870. pp.li.843. [7500.]
ii. 1871. pp.lv.835. [7500.]
iii. 1872. pp.lv.833. [7500.]
iv. 1873. pp.xxxi.800. [7500.]

v. 1874. pp.xxvii.863. [7500.]
vi. 1875. pp.xxiii.872. [7500.]
vii. 1876. pp.xlii.968. [10,000.]
viii. 1877. pp.li.895. [10,000.]
ix. 1878. pp.lx.818. [10,000.]
x. 1879. By John E. Hudson and Geo. Fred. Williams. pp.iv.838. [15,000.]
xi. 1880. By G. F. Williams. pp.iv.962. [17,500.]
xii. 1881. pp.vi.937. [17,500.]
xiii. 1882. pp.iv.1020. [17,500.]
xiv. 1883. pp.vi.940. [17,500.]
xv. 1884. By G. F. Williams and Isaac F. Paul. pp.iv.859. [17,500.]
xvi. 1885. pp.iv.750. [15,000.]
xvii. 1886. pp.iv.735. [15,000.]
xviii. 1887. By I. F. Paul. pp.iv.737. [15,000.]
xix. 1888. pp.iv.759. [14,000.]

FREDERICK C. BRIGHTLY, A digest of the decisions of the federal courts, from the organization of the government to the present time. Philadelphia 1868. pp.viii.976. [10,000.]

UNITED STATES digest; a digest of decisions of the various courts within the United States, from the earliest period to the year 1870. Boston.

i. Abandonment–assignment. By Benjamin

Vaughan Abbott. 1874. pp.xx.820. [16,000.]
ii. Assignments–bills. 1874. pp.[ii].880. [17,000.]
iii. Bonds–costs. 1874. pp.[ii].847. [17,000.]
iv. Counties–discovery. 1875. pp.[ii].840. [17,000.]
v. Disorderly houses–evidence. 1875. pp.[ii]. 939. [19,000.]
vi. Exceptions–high treason. 1875. pp.[ii].913. [18,000.]
vii. Highways–judge. 1875. pp.[ii].883. [18,000.]
viii. Judgment–master. 1875. pp.[ii].997. [20,000.]
ix. Master–passenger. 1875. pp.[ii].955. [19,000.]
x. Patents–presumptions. 1876. pp.[ii].855. [17,000.]
xi. Principal–sales. 1876. pp.[ii].957. [19,000.]
xii. Salvage–taxes. 1876. pp.[ii].921. [18,000.]
xiii. Telegraph–variance. 1876. pp.832. [17,000.]
xiv. Vendor–Wyoming. With index. 1876 pp.[iii].845. [15,000.]
— A table of the cases contained in the . . . Digest. 1878. pp.[iii].929. [175,000.]

BENJAMIN VAUGHAN ABBOTT, Abbott's national digest. A digest of the reports of the United States courts from the organization of the government to the year 1884. New York 1884–1885. pp.xxiv.816+[ii].808+[ii].829+[ii].913. [30,000.]

— — 1884–1888. 1889. pp.vi.760. [7500.]

THOMAS W. WATERMAN, The american chancery digest, being an analytical digest of all the reported decisions on equity of the United States courts and of the courts of the several states, to the present time. . . . Third edition. New York &c. 1851. pp.[ii].cxlvii.562 + viii.710 + viii.673. [20,000.]

HOWARD ELLIS, The Reporter digest: being a digest of the Reporter, volumes I.–XVII. (1876–1884), and the American law times reports, volumes I.–IV. (1874–1877). Boston &c. 1886. pp.[ii].1233. [15,000.]

A. C. FREEMAN [vol.iii: ALBERT J. BRUNNER], Digest of the american decisions . . . 1760–1837 [–1869]. San Francisco 1882–1888. pp.3–825+vi.1245+viii.1415. [40,000.]

A BRIEF digest to the first [&c.] volumes of American state reports. San Francisco.

i–vi. 1889. pp.[iii].134. [4000.]

vii–xii. 1890. pp.[ii].174. [5000.]
xiii–xviii. 1891. pp.176. [5000.]
xix–xxiv. 1892. pp.179. [5000.]
xxv–xxx. By C. B. Labatt. 1893. pp.182. [6750.]
xxi–xxxvi. By C. B. Labatt and Chas. T. Boone. 1894. pp.150. [5000.]
xxvii–xlii. By Edwin D. Smith. 1895. pp.161. [5000.]
xliii–xlviii. 1896. pp.184. [6000.]
xlix–liv. 1897. pp.196. [7000.]
lv–lx. 1898. pp.194. [7000.]
lxi–lxvi. 1899. pp.195. [7000.]
lxvii–lxxii. 1900. pp.192. [7000.]
lxxiii–lxxviii. By Peter V. Ross. 1901. pp.193. [7000.]
lxxix–lxxxiv. 1902. pp.186. [6000.]
lxxxv–xc. 1903. pp.173. [5000.]
xci–xcvi. 1904. pp.317. [7000.]
xcvii–cviii. [By Charles L. Thompson]. 1906. pp.431. [10,000.]
cix–cxiv. 1907. pp.314. [6000.]
cxv–cxx. 1908. pp.335. [6000.]
cxxi–cxxvi. 1909. pp.362. [6000.]
cxxvii–cxxxii. 1910. pp.392. [6000.]

a digest was also published for vols.xcvii–cii, but most of the copies were destroyed by fire.

β. *Courts of last resort*

ISAAC GRANT THOMPSON, Digest of decisions in the courts of last resort of the several states contained in the American reports . . . 1780–1879. Albany 1879. pp.xxi.3–890. [5000.]

— — 1877–1884. By Irving Browne. 1885. pp.lx.3–760. [5000.]

— — [1884–1888] and table of cases. San Francisco 1888. pp.v.231. [2000.]

WILLIAM MACK, A digest of the decisions of the courts of last resort of the several states, from the year 1887 to the year 1892, contained in the American state reports. San Francisco 1892. pp.1354. [12,500.]

W. L. RICHARDS, Digest of decisions of United States Supreme court . . . Circuit court of appeals, Indian territory court of appeals. Atoka 1898. pp.[ii].156.

EDMUND SAMSON GREEN, Digest of the decisions of the courts of last resort of the several states, from 1887 to 1904, contained in the American state reports. San Francisco 1904. pp.xviii.1446+x.1447–2932+xiv.2933–4451. [60,000.]

according to the covers the period dealt with is 1886–1902.

— — Volume four, 1904 to 1909. 1909. pp. xxxix.1598. [20,000.]

— — Volume five, 1909 to 1911. 1912. pp. xxvi.1187.xix.374. [15,000.]

STEWART RAPALJE, A digest of the decisions of the courts of last resort of the several states . . . to the year 1888, contained in the . . . American decisions and the American reports. San Francisco &c. 1910. pp.1293+[ii].1295–2574+[ii].2575–3987. [50,000.]

CATALOGUE of the library of the United States circuit court of appeals. [New Orleans] 1917. pp.[ii].52. [750.]

— [another edition]. 1933. pp.[ii].iii.157. [2000.]

b. *Lists and indexes*

W[ILLIA]M G. MYER, An index to the reports of the Supreme court of the United States. St. Louis, Mo. 1878. pp.3–537.2–8. [30,000.]

TABLE of cases reported in volumes 1–72, inclusive, of the American State Reports. San Francisco 1900. pp.3–243. [10,000.]

E. DE LOS MAGEE, Index-digest to the monographic notes in the American state reports, volumes 1 to 91. San Francisco 1903. pp.267. [15,000.]

WM. S. TORBERT, Table of cases alphabetically arranged as to the several states in the American decisions, 100 vols., American reports, 60 vols., American state reports, 100 vols. San Francisco 1905. pp.754. [40,000.]

A.L.R. CUMULATIVE index-digest. . . . Combined indexes to cases and annotations. Rochester, N.Y. &c.

1919–1928. 1929. pp.[ii].1482+1483–2832. [60,000.]

1929–1935. 1936. pp.2275. [40,000.]

in progress; these volumes are based on a succession of cumulative indexes for shorter periods.

I[SIDORE] J[ACOB] LOWE, Key to the year of decisions of cases in the United States Supreme court, the opinions of the attorneys, general and other legal reports. 79th Congress: 1st session: Senate: Document (no.73): Washington 1945. pp.iii.16. [1000.]

vi. *Supreme court*

HENRY WHEATON, A digest of the decisions of the Supreme court of the United States, from its establishment in 1789, to February term 1820, including the cases decided in the Continental court of appeals in prize cases, during the war of the revolution. New York 1821. pp.xxxii.527. [2500.]

— — 1821–1829. . . . By two gentlemen of the New York bar. 1829. pp.xxxii.312. [3000.]

B[ENJAMIN] R[OBBINS] CURTIS, Digest of the decisions of the Supreme court of the United States from the origin of the court to . . . 1854. Boston 1856. pp.cliii.601. [30,000.]

A COMPLETE indexed digest of the United States Supreme court reports from the organization of the court in 1789 to October term, 1894. Rochester 1897. pp.1118+1154+1176. [50,000.]

— Supplement . . . 1894–1897. 1898. pp.[vi]. 267.127[*sic*, 141]. [2500.]

LIST of references on the appointment of the justices of the Supreme court. Library of Congress: Washington 1905. ff.4. [18.]*

HERMANN HENRY BERNARD MEYER, List of works relating to the Supreme court of the United States. Library of Congress: Washington 1909. pp.124. [1000.]*

— — [supplement]. Select list [&c.]. 1912. ff.7. [68.]*

— — — 1912–1916. 1916. ff.6. [78.]*
— — — 1916–1922. 1922. ff.8. [110.]*

LIST of references on judicial legislation by decisions of the U.S. Supreme court declaring laws unconstitutional. Library of Congress: Washington 1922. ff.11. [131.]*

— Supplementary list . . . including power of Congress to review these decisions. 1924. pp.15. [189.]*

LIST of references on the popular election of supreme court judges, state and federal. Library of Congress: [Washington] 1924. ff.6. [49.]*

FLORENCE S[ELMA] HELLMAN, List of references on the Supreme court of the United States with particular reference to the doctrine of judicial review. Library of Congress: [Washington] 1935. pp.17. [184.]*

MILDRED R[UTH] SENIOR, The supreme court: its power of judicial review with respect to congressional legislation. Selected references. George Washington university: Division of library science: Publication (no.1): Washington 1937. pp.[v].75. [600.]

ANNE L[AURA] BADEN, List of speeches, etc., on the United States Supreme court issue as printed in the Congressional record, 75th congress, first session, v.81, current file. Compiled . . . under the direction of Florence S[elma] Hellman. Library of Congress: [Washington] 1937. pp.29. [422.]*

FLORENCE S[ELMA] HELLMAN, The Supreme court issue. A selected list of references. Library of Congress: [Washington] 1937. ff.33. [403.]*
— — [another edition]. 1938. pp.42. [490.]*

[MARGARET W. STEWART and AGNES M. BROWN], United States supreme court cases declaring state laws unconstitutional, 1912–1938. Library of Congress: State law index: Special report (no.2): Washington 1938. pp.v.20. [400.]

DOROTHY CAMPBELL TOMPKINS, The Supreme court of the United States. A bibliography. University of California: Bureau of public administration: Berkeley 1959. pp.viii.217. [1750.]*

MARION M. JOHNSON, Preliminary inventory of the records of the Supreme court of the United States. National archives: Preliminary inventories (no.139): Washington 1962. pp.v.20. [very large number.]*

vii. *State law*

COMPARATIVE summary and index of state legislation. State library: Bulletin: Legislation (no.1 &c.): Albany.

[i]. 1890. pp.82. [1303.]
[ii]. 1891. pp.87–223. [2844.]
[iii]. 1892. pp.229–291. [995.]
[iv]. 1893. pp.297–450. [2806.]
[v]. 1894. pp.457–547. [1325.]
[*continued as:*]

Legislation by states.
vi. 1895. pp.310. [4535.]
vii. 1896. pp.315–424. [1566.]
viii. 1897. pp.487–735. [3668.]
ix. 1898. pp.741–909. [1653.]
x. 1899. pp.395. [4884.]
xi. 1900. pp.441–612. [1606.]
[*continued as:*]

Comparative summary and index of legislation.
[xii]. 1901. pp.815–1229. [5658.]
[xiii]. 1902. Edited by Robert H. Whitten. pp.415–693. [2208.]
[xiv]. 1903. pp.269–771. [7500.]
[xv]. 1904. pp.[258]. [2500.]
[*continued as:*]

Index of legislation.
[xvi]. 1905. pp.[428]. [7500.]
[xvii]. 1906. pp.248. [2500.]
[xviii]. 1907. Edited by Frederick D. Bramhall. pp.599. [7500.]

[xix]. 1908. Edited by Clarence B. Lester. pp.264. [2500.]
no more published.

CATALOGUE of an exhibit of the early laws of several states in the union. New Jersey state bar association: Atlantic City 1931. pp.16. [100.]

viii. *Miscellaneous*

LIST of references on jurisdiction of the courts in cases involving executive action and discretion. Library of Congress: Washington 1915. ff.13. [129.]*

LIST of references on the selection of judges: appointment vs. election. Library of Congress: Washington 1916. ff.2–7. [67.]*

— [another edition]. List of references on the election versus the appointment of judges. 1927. ff.6. [62.]*

— — Supplementary. 1939. ff.11. [135.]*

A LIST of manuals of justices of the peace, notaries and legal forms. Library of Congress: Washington 1922. ff.7. [72.]*

GAISELLE KERNER and IRA N. KELLOGG, Preliminary inventory of the records of the Court of claims section of the Department of justice.

National archives: Preliminary inventories (no.47): Washington 1952. pp.v.29. [very large number.]*

GAISELLE KERNER, Preliminary inventory of the records of the United States court of claims. National archives: Preliminary inventories (no. 58): Washington 1953. pp.v.31. [large number.]*

GAISELLE KERNER, Preliminary inventory of the records of the office of the pardon attorney. National archives: Preliminary inventories (no. 87): Washington 1955. pp.v.13. [large number.]*

Uruguay.

CATÁLOGO alfabético [Catálogo] de leyes. Biblioteca del poder legislativo: Montevideo.

1928. pp.xvi. [500.]
1929–1930. pp.xx.
1930–1931.
1932. pp.155. [109.]

CATALOGO de leyes. Biblioteca del poder legislativo: Montevideo.

1932. pp.165. [115.]
in progress?

URUGUAY. American foreign law association: Bibliographies of foreign law series (no.9): New York 1933. pp.95. [250.]

HELEN L[ORD] CLAGETT, A guide to the law and legal literature of Uruguay. Library of Congress: Latin american series (no.26): Washington 1947. pp.vi.123. [750.]

[ANATOLIO PALAMARCHUK and VICTOR BACCINO PONS], Bibliografía jurídica del Uruguay. Universidad de Montevideo: Facultad de derecho y ciencias sociales: Biblioteca de publicaciones oficiales (sección 3, vol.lxxxv): Montevideo 1956. pp.xvii.499. [3338.]

Venezuela.

RESUMEN cronológico de las leyes y decretos del credito publico de Venezuela, desde el año 1826. Caracas 1873. pp.[iv].cxxxix.412. [7500.]

HELEN L[ORD] CLAGETT, A guide to the law and legal literature of Venezuela. Library of Congress: Latin american series (no.16): Washington 1947. pp.viii.128. [750.]

BOLETÍN de la biblioteca de los tribunales del Distrito federal. [Contribución a la bibliografía del derecho procesal civil venezolano . . . 1856–1952]. Caracas.

i. 1951. pp.256. [1300.]
ii. 1952. pp.287. [1400.]
iii. 1953. pp.316. [1500.]

iv. 1954. pp.314. [1500.]
v. 1955. pp.255. [1300.]
no more published.

Venice.

ANDREAS TRIVISANUS, Index omnivm materiarvm, qve in Venetiarum statutis continentur, alphabetico ordine digestus. Venetijs 1548. pp. [110]. [1500.]

Vermont.

DANIEL ROBERTS, A digest of all the reported decisions of the Supreme court of the state of Vermont. Burlington 1878. pp.xxv.866. [7500.]

Victoria.

GEORGE BRISCOE KERFERD and JOHN BURNETT BOX, A digest of the cases decided in the Supreme court of Victoria, from A.D. 1846 to A.D. 1871. Melbourne 1871. pp.[ii].lxxxi.coll.824. [2500.]

G. W. WATERHOUSE and F. W. EDMONDSON, A digest of reported cases in the Supreme court, Court of insolvency, and the Courts of mines and vice-admiralty of the colony of Victoria, from 1861 to 1885. Melbourne &c. 1886. pp.[vii].coll.

cxxx.pp.cxxxiii–cxxxv.coll.1600. [7500.]

P[ERCY] E[RNEST] JOSKE, Index to the victorian statutes (consolidation and sessional volumes) 1928–1933. Melbourne 1935. pp.lxxiii.816. [10,000.]

Virginia.

TEMPORARY index of bills approved by the governor, and joint resolutions. Richmond 1938 &c.

E[DWARD] GRIFFITH DODSON, Lists of numbers of bills passed by each house, showing those approved by the governor. . . . Lists of numbers of joint resolutions agreed to by both houses. Richmond [1944]. pp.15+15. [900.]

E[DWARD] GRIFFITH DODSON, Cumulative index of bills and joint resolutions introduced. Richmond [1945].

Vorarlberg.

REPERTORIUM über die in den zwölf ersten bänden der Provinzial-gesetzsammlung für Tyrol und Vorarlberg enthaltenen verordnungen. Innsbruck 1828. pp.587. [5000.]

— Bände XIII. bis einschliesslich XXV. 1842. pp.563. [5000.]

FRANZ STARR, Vollständiges sach- und nachschlage-register zu sämmtlichen landesgesetzblättern der im Reichsrathe vertretenen königreiche und länder von deren beginn 1849 bis zum jahre 1873. . . . Vierter theil. Tirol-Vorarlberg, Küstenland und Dalmatien. Wien 1874. pp.[iii]. 428. [6000.]

Wales.

[W. H. STEVENSON], Calendar of various chancery rolls. . . . Welsh rolls. 1912. pp.ix.552. [welsh: 1000.]

covers the period 1277–1294.

IFAN AB OWEN EDWARDS, A catalogue of Star chamber proceedings relating to Wales. University of Wales: Board of celtic studies: History and law series (no.i): Cardiff 1929. pp.ix.226. [2000.]

E. A. LEWIS, An inventory of the early chancery proceedings concerning Wales. University of Wales: Board of celtic studies: History and law series (no.iii): Cardiff 1937. pp.ix.296. [2000.]

EMYR GWYNNE JONES, Exchequer proceedings (equíty) concerning Wales, Henry VIII–Elizabeth. Abstracts of bills of inventory of further proceedings. University of Wales: Board of celtic studies: History and law series (no.iv): Cardiff 1939. pp.xiv.412. [750.]

Wisconsin.

JAMES SIMMONS, A digest of Wisconsin reports, from the earliest period to the year 1868; comprising all the published decisions of the Supreme court of Wisconsin. Albany [N.Y.] 1868. pp.7. 891. [9000.]

— — 1868–1874. 1874. pp.xlii.648. [6000.]

MERRITT STARR, Index-digest of the Wisconsin reports, embracing all the decisions of the Supreme court of Wisconsin. Chicago 1883. pp.822. [15,000.]

[LYMAN JUNIUS NASH], Table of laws amended, repealed or created by laws of 1911. Madison 1911. pp.14.

Württemberg.

R[OBERT VON] MOHL, C. SCHEURLEN and C. G. WÄCHTER, Die literatur des gesammten württembergischen rechtes aus dem letzten jahrzehend historisch-kritisch dargestellt. Stuttgart 1830. pp. [ii].356. [300.]

C. A. SÜSKIND and G. WERNER, Repertorium der evangelischen kirchengesetze in Württemberg. Stuttgart [1860–]1862–1867. pp.viii.653 + [ii]. 670+[ii].634. [15,000.]

Zanzibar.

LIST of Zanzibar decrees enacted up to . . . 1940. Zanzibar protectorate: Zanzibar 1941. pp.8. [250.]

INDEX to the laws of the Zanzibar protectorate. Compiled by F. J. Jasavala. Zanzibar protectorate: Zanzibar 1950. pp.[iii].42. [1250.]

Zürich.

J. J. TREICHLER, Verzeichniss der mit 1. Januar 1868 ganz oder theilweise in kraft bestehenden und in die offiziellen gesetzsammlungen aufgenommenen gesetze und verordnungen des kantons Zürich. Zürich 1868. pp.135. [414.]

Special Subjects

Bankruptcy.

EDWARD CHITTY and FRANCIS FORSTER, A digested index to the common law reports relating to conveyancing and bankruptcy, commencing with the reign of Elizabeth, in 1558, to the present time. 1841. pp.xxiv.1164. [15,000.]

A DIGEST of the cases decided relating to bankruptcy and the county courts, in the year 1862. [1863]. pp.xxxiv. [200.]

THE ENGLISH and empire digest . . . being a complete digest of every english case reported from early times to the present day, with additional cases from the courts of Scotland, Ireland, the empire of India, and the dominions beyond the seas. Volume IV [–V]. Bankruptcy. 1920. pp.xxxv. 598+cl.601–1194. [9638.]

BUSINESS failures: a select list of references. Library of Congress: Washington 1932. ff.16. [203.]*

A. PISSAVY, La jurisprudence des faillites et les liquidations judiciaires. Répertoire et analyse des plus récentes décisions de justice sur les plus importants litiges. 1934. pp.422. [989.]

GRACE HADLEY FULLER, Selected list of references on bankruptcy in the U.S. with special reference to bankruptcy legislation, 1929–1939. Compiled . . . under the direction of Florence S[elma] Hellman. Library of Congress: [Washington] 1940. pp.48. [461.]*

— Supplement. 1941. pp.23. [46.]*

Black, Jeremiah Sullivan.

JA[ME]S L. KENNEDY, Index to judicial opinions of Jeremiah Sullivan Black, chief justice of the Supreme court of Pennsylvania. Greensburg [1935]. pp.37. [282.]

Blackstone, sir William.

[D. DOUGLAS], A catalogue of sir William Blackstone's writings . . . manuscript, as well as printed. By a gentleman of Lincoln's-inn. [1782]. pp.[ii]. iv.[iv].148. [27.]

published as part of the author's Biographical history of sir William Blackstone.

CATALOGUE of the exhibits of the Hampton L. Carson collection of books, documents . . . illustrative of the growth of english-american law. Historical society of Pennsylvania: Philadelphia 1924. pp.54. [Blackstone: 69.]

CATHERINE SPICER ELLER, The William Blackstone collection in the Yale law library. A bibliographical catalogue. Yale law library: Publications (no.6): [New Haven] 1938. pp.xvii.114. [271.]

Capital punishment.

ORAZIO VIOLA, Bibliografia italiana della pena di morte. [Catania] 1904. pp.71. [600.]

SELECT list of references on capital punishment. Library of Congress: Washington 1910. ff.19. [103.]*

HERMANN H[ENRY] B[ERNARD] MAYER, *ed.* Select list of references on capital punishment. Library of Congress: Washington 1912. pp.[ii].45. [282.]

[—] — [another edition]. Capital punishment. A bibliographical list. 1931. pp.33. [313.]*

[—] — — Additional references. 1935. ff.24–27. [47.]*

CRIMINAL justice, to which is annexed an appendix on capital punishment. House of commons:

Library: Bibliography (no.38): [1947]. ff.[i].30. [153.]*

— Capital punishment (being a revision of the appendix . . .) . . . (no.51): [1948]. pp.13. [63.]*

Contempt of court.

LIST of references on contempt of court. Library of Congress: Washington 1916. ff.3. [30.]*

— [another edition]. 1924. ff.4. [54.]*

Contracts.

BRIEF list of references on the effect of war on contracts (with special reference to the european war). Library of Congress: Washington 1919. ff.5. [59.]*

LIST of references on cost-plus contracts. Library of Congress: Division of bibliography: [Washington] 1922. ff.4. [30.]*

THE ENGLISH and empire digest . . . being a complete digest of every english case reported from early times to the present day, with additional cases from the courts of Scotland, Ireland, the empire of India, and the dominions beyond the seas. Volume XII. Contract. 1923. pp.lxxxi.632. [5168.]

ELEANOR M. MITCHELL, The Public contracts

(Walsh-Haley) act: selected references. Compiled . . . under the direction of Laura A. Thompson. Department of labor: Library: Washington 1940. ff.16. [150.]*

Conveyancing.

EDWARD CHITTY and FRANCIS FORSTER, A digested index to the common law reports relating to conveyancing and bankruptcy, commencing with the reign of Elizabeth, in 1558, to the present time. 1841. pp.xxiv.1164. [15,000.]

FREDERICK THOMAS SERGEANT, Aids to students of conveyancing. 1847. pp.[iv].99. [400.]

Copyright.

R. R. BOWKER, Copyright, its law and literature. . . . With a bibliography of literary property by Thorvald Solberg. 1886. pp.55.60. [1750.]

SUBJECT list of works on the laws of industrial property . . . and copyright in the library of the Patent office. Patent office library series (no.3 = Bibliographical series, no.2): 1900. pp.82. [813.]

— [second edition]. Patent office library series: Subject lists (n.s. BF–BL): 1909. pp.84. [1000.]

THORVALD SOLBERG, Foreign copyright laws. A list of the foreign copyright laws now in force, with citations of printed texts and translations, etc. Library of Congress: Copyright office: Bulletin (no.7): Washington 1904. pp.86. [750.]

THORVALD SOLBERG, Copyright in Congress, 1789–1904. A bibliography, and chronological record of all proceedings in Congress in relation to copyright. Library of Congress: Copyright office: Bulletin (no.8): Washington 1905. pp.468. [1000.]

HENRIETTE MERTZ Copyright bibliography. Preliminary edition. Library of Congress: Washington 1950. pp.iv.213. [5000.]*

Corn laws.

LIST of references on the corn laws of Great Britain. Library of Congress: Washington 1916. ff.4. [38.]*

Court of international justice. [*see also* **International court of justice.**]

SELECT list of references on the Hague tribunal.

Library of Congress: Washington 1904. ff.3. [14.]*

LIST of references on a permanent court of international justice. Library of Congress: [Washington] 1921. ff.2. [20.]*

— [another edition]. List of references on the Permanent [&c.]. 1923. ff.21. [210.]*

— — References supplementing [Recent references].*

1926. ff.31. [295.]
1928. ff.26. [272.]
1929. ff.10. [108.]
1930. ff.17. [189.]
1931. ff.14. [157.]
1932. ff.15. [149.]
1933. ff.19. [154.]
1934. ff.9. [69.]
1935. ff.14. [127.]
1936. ff.9. [85.]
1937. ff.8. [76.]

LIST of references on international courts with special reference to the Permanent court of international justice. Library of Congress: [Washington] 1923. ff.27. [258.]*

J. DOUMA, Bibliographical list of official and unofficial publications concerning the Permanent court of international justice. The Hague 1926. pp.159. [1299.]

— — Supplement. 1927. pp.80. [548.]

— — Supplement . . . with cumulative indexes. 1928. pp.79. [412.]

— — Supplement . . . with combined index to the preceding lists.

1929. pp.82. [402.]
1930. pp.102. [473.]
1931. pp.87. [401.]
1932. pp.97. [471.]
1933. pp.79. [413.]
1934. pp.82. [417.]
1935. pp.80. [364.]
1936. pp.97. [530.]
1937. pp.83. [303.]
1938. pp.72. [255.]
1939. pp.71. [222.]

— — Supplement 1940–1945. pp.40. [366.]

INDEX général des publications de la Cour (séries A, B et C). Leyde.

i. Première–onzième sessions (1922–1926). 1927. pp.127.124. [2500.]
ii. Douzième–dix-huitième sessions (1927–

1930). 1932. pp.148.144. [3000.]

iii. Vingtième – trente-cinquième sessions (1931–1935). 1936. pp.129.130. [2500.]

a fourth part comprises an index to the statute and rules of the court.

EDVARD HAMBRO, The case law of the International court. A repertoire of the judgements, advisory opinions and orders. . . . With a bibliography prepared by J. Douma. Leyden 1952. pp. [xvii].699. [3000.]

— — II. 1952–1958. 1960. pp.[xviii].376. [2823.]

Deportation.

DEPORTATION of aliens. A bibliographical list. Library of Congress: [Washington] 1931. pp.11. [127.]*

Desertion.

FRED[ERICK] T. WILSON, Digest of laws, rulings and decisions governing the military crime of desertion. Washington 1882. pp.80. [164.]

Divorce.

SELECT list of references on divorce. Library of Congress: Washington 1910. ff.20. [145.]*

— [another edition]. 1915. ff.76. [939.]*

A LIST of references on uniform divorce laws. Library of Congress: [Washington] 1923. ff.8. [75.]*

— [another edition]. 1925. ff.9. [82.]*

Ecclesiastical law.

CASPAR THURMAN, Bibliotheca canonicorum, in qua de canonicis, et canonicatibus, . . . et quæ eo pertinent, . . . agitur. Halæ Magdeburgicæ 1700. pp.[viii].80. [1250.]

[CLAUDE BROSSETTE], Les titres du droit civil, et du droit canonique, raportez sous les noms françois des matières, suivant l'ordre alphabétique. Lyon 1705. pp.[xviii].361. [4500.]

[CAESAR HERIONUS], Index generalis omnium conclusionum et rerum notabilium quæ continentur in decisiones sacræ Rotæ romanæ coram . . . Bartholomæo Olivatio. Romæ 1784. pp.477. [12,500.]

EDWIN MADDY, Digest of cases argued and determined in the Arches and Prerogative courts of Canterbury, the Consistory court of London, and the High court of delegates; and contained in the reports of sir George Lee, Phillimore, Addams, and Haggard. 1835. pp.268. [1000.]

ALFRED WADDILOVE, A digest of cases decided in the Court of arches, the Prerogative court of Canterbury, the Consistory court of London, and an appeal therefrom to the Judicial committee of the Privy council. 1849. pp.cxxxi.382. [2500.]

[FRANÇOIS] ÉMILE CHAVIN DE MALAN, De l'étude et de la bibliographie du droit ecclésiastique. 1851. pp.[iii].71. [1000.]

RODERICH STINTZING, Geschichte der populären literatur des römisch-kanonischen rechts in Deutschland am ende des fünfzehnten und im anfang des sechzehnten jahrhunderts. Leipzig 1867. pp.lii.564. [2000.]

[JOHANN] FRIEDRICH SCHULTE, Die canonistischen handschriften der bibliotheken. 1. der K. k. universität, 2. des Böhmischen museums, 3. des fürsten Georg Lobkowitz, 4. des metropolitankapitels von St. Veit in Prag. Königliche böhmische gesellschaft der wissenschaften: Abhandlungen (6th ser., vol.ii, no.2): Prag 1868. pp.116. [293.]

FRIEDRICH MAASSEN, Geschichte der quellen und der literatur des canonischen rechts im abendlande bis zum ausgange des mittelalters. . . . Erster band.

Gratz &c. 1870. pp.lxx.982. [5000.]
no more published.

JOH[ANN] FRIEDRICH VON SCHULTE, Die geschichte der quellen und literatur des canonischen rechts von Gratian bis auf die gegenwart. Stuttgart 1875–1880. pp.viii.265+xviii.582+xxi.783+[iii]. 415. [7500.]

JOHANN FRIEDRICH VON SCHULTE, Die geschichte der quellen und literatur des evangelischen kirchenrechts in Deutschland und Oesterreich. Stuttgart 1880. pp.[v].305. [1500.]

ADOLPHE TARDIF, Histoire des sources du droit canonique. 1887. pp.[iii].iii.410. [1000.]

CH[ARLES] L[OUIS] FROSSARD, Étude historique et bibliographique sur la discipline ecclésiastique des églises reformées en France. 1887. pp.48. [45.]

BERNHARD HÜBLER, Kirchliche rechtsquellen. Grundriss mit ausgewählten belegstellen. Berlin 1888. pp.vi.74. [250.]

— — Vierte . . . auflage. Kirchenrechtsquellen. Urkundenbuch zu vorlesungen über kirchenrecht. 1902. pp.x.130. [500.]

ADOLPH FRANTZ, Die litteratur des kirchenrechts, 1884 bis 1894. Juristischer litteraturbericht (part 7): Leipzig 1896. pp.[ii].18. [100.]

M[IKHAIL EGOROVICH] KRASNOZHEN, Указатель литературы церковнаго права по 1910 г. Ученыя записки Императорскаго Юрьевскаго университета (vol.xviii, no.9): Юрьев 1910. pp.48. [900.]

GIUSEPPE ERMINI, Guide bibliografice per lo studio del diritto comune pontificio. Istituto di studi romani: Bologna 1934. pp.iii–xxi.123. [1174.]

STEPHAN [GEORG] KUTTNER, Repertorium der kanonistik (1140–1234). I. Prodromus corporis glossarum. Biblioteca apostolica vaticana: Studi e testi (vol.lxxi): Città del Vaticano 1937. pp.iii–xx.536. [750.]

GUISCARDO MOSCHETTI, Bibliographia iuris canonici, ex ephemeridibus ab a. 1918 ad a. 1934. Romae [1942]. pp.3–336. [7500.]

JOACHIM ROMANUS BAR and WOJCIECH ZMARZ, Polska bibliografia prawa kanonicznego od wynalezienia druku do 1940 roku. Tom II za lata 1800–1940. Towarzystwo naukowe Katolickiego uniwersytetu lubelskiego: Rozprawy wydziału kanoniczno-teologicznego (no.4): Lublin 1947. pp.355. [3500.]

CANON law abstracts. Canon law society of Great Britain: Galashiels.

1–4. 1958–1959. pp.144. [700.]
5–6. 1960. pp.68+64. [500.]
7–8. 1961. pp.76+59. [500.]
9–10. 1962. pp.84+76. [750.]
11– . 1963. pp.80+ .

in progress?

Evidence, law of.

THE ENGLISH and empire digest . . . being a complete digest of every english case reported from early times to the present day, with additional cases from the courts of Scotland, Ireland, the empire of India, and the Dominions beyond the seas. Volume XXII. Evidence. 1925. pp.ciii.636. [6969.]

HUBERT WINSTON SMITH, Scientific proof and relations of law and medicine. Urbana, Ill. 1946. pp.26. [65.]

Experts.

LIST of references on expert testimony. Library of Congress: Washington 1900. ff.2. [15.]*

Extradition.

LIST of books and magazine articles on international extraction examined and referred to in the proceedings to extradite James Lynchehaun pending before Charles W. Moores, United States Commissioner at Indianapolis. Public library: Indianapolis [1903]. pp.[9]. [250.]

LIST of references on international extradition. Library of Congress: Washington 1914. ff.12. [139.]*

— Additional references. 1931. ff.3. [26.]*

Friendly societies.

JOHN TIDD PRATT, Index to acts relating to friendly societies. 1860. pp.31. [500.]

Illegitimacy.

LIST of recent references on illegitimacy. Library of Congress: Washington 1923. ff.6. [74.]*

Inheritance (law).

LIST of references on the amount of wealth transferable by bequest and inheritance. Library of Congress: Washington 1917. ff.3. [24.]*

A. M. HANNAY, Inheritance of farm real estate, 1920–1945. A list of references. Department of agriculture: Library: Library list (no.22): Washington 1946. pp.34. [219.]*

International court of justice. [*see also* **Court of international justice.**]

BIBLIOGRAPHY of the International court of justice. Carnegie library of the Peace palace: The Hague.

i. 1946–1947. pp.[v].148–193. [497.]
ii. 1947–1948. pp.[iii].80–118. [354.]
iii. 1948–1949. pp.[iii].90–130. [385.]
iv. 1949–1950. pp.[iii].114–157. [330.]
v. 1950–1951. pp.[ii].133–183. [377.]
vi. 1951–1952. pp.[iii].120–175. [441.]
vii. 1952–1953. pp.[iii].110–161. [323.]
viii. 1953–1954. pp.[iii].144–199. [350.]

in progress.

J. J. G. SYATAUW, Decisions of the International court of justice. A digest. 1962. pp.237. [47.]

Jews, Judaism.

CARL FERDINAND HOMMEL, Bibliotheca jvris rabbinica et Saracenorvm arabica. Byrvthi 1762. pp.63.[xvii]. [250.]

SAMUEL EISENSTADT, עין משפט Repertorium bibliographicum litteraturae totius iurisprudentiae hebraicae. Hierosolymae 1931. pp.[iv].464. [xxxii]. [4492.]

VERZEICHNIS jüdischer verfasser juristischer schriften. Stuttgart 1936. pp.[iv].53.*

Jury system.

LIST of works relating to the jury in roman law. Library of Congress: Washington [?1907]. ff.4. [25.]*

SELECT list of references on the jury system. Library of Congress: Washington 1912. ff.8. [106.]*

LIST of recent references on the jury system. Library of Congress: [Washington] 1923. ff.5. [66.]*

— [another edition]. The jury system: a bibliographical list. 1931. pp.23. [341.]*

— — Supplement. 1935. pp.13. [174.]*

BRIEF list of references on women as jurors. Library of Congress: [Washington] 1923. ff.2. [17.]*

— Additional references. 1927. single leaf. [14.]*

Notary.

VLADIMIR PAPPAFAVA, Delle opere che illustrano il notariato. Zara 1880. pp.[ii].362. [1000.]

ALBERT AMIAUD, Recherches bibliographiques sur le notariat français. 1881. pp.xvi.233. [1500.]

330 copies printed.

ADAM NIEMIROWSKI, Bibliografia powszechna notarjatu. Biblioteka umiejętności prawnych: Warszawa 1884. pp.[iv].303. [3000.]

VLADIMIR PAPPAFAVA, Povjestne crtice i bibliografija o biljež̌ništvu. Zadar 1895. pp.192. [2500.]

also published with french and dutch titlepages.

[J. F. L. MONTIJN and P. J. DAM], Catalogus van de boeken betrekkelijk het notariat aanwezig in de universiteits-bibliotheek te Amsterdam. Broederschap van candidaat-notarissen in Nederland en zijne koloniën: Amsterdam 1910. pp.3–11.382. [4000.]

JOSE MARIA ADRIÃO, Ensaio de bibliografia critica do notariado português. Lisboa 1923. pp.247. [127.]

Pre-emption.

BAKHSHISH LAL, A digest of cases on pre-emption, as prevailing in Behar, Lower Bengal, Malabar,

Guzerat, United Provinces of Agra and Oudh, and the Punjab. Patna City 1905. pp.[viii].xvii. coll.574. [909.]

— — Supplementary digest . . . 1905 to May 1914. 1914. pp.[iii].xiii.134. [250.]

Probate, law of.

SELECT list of works relating to probate law. Library of Congress: Washington 1905. ff.7. [45.]

Probation.

SELECT list of references on methods of probation and juvenile courts. Library of Congress: Washington 1909. ff.18. [270.]*

— [another edition]. List of references on probation [&c.]. 1914. ff.23. [313.]*

— — [supplement]. List of recent references [&c.]. 1921. ff.10. [729.]*

LIST of references on the reformatory and probation system. Library of Congress: Washington 1918. ff.6. [60.]*

LIST of references relating to probation. Library of Congress: Washington 1933. ff.4. [57.]*

CAROLINE SHURTLEFF HUGHES, Annotated bibliography on probation. Attorney general's advisory committee on crime: [Washington 1937]. ff.[ii]. 17. [94.]*

DOROTHY [LOUISE] CAMPBELL TOMPKINS, Probation since World war II: a bibliography. University of California: Institute of governmental studies: Berkeley 1964. pp.viii.311. [2000.]*

Recidivism.

RECIDIVISM. Library of Congress: Washington 1933. single leaf. [10.]*

Registration.

ÉMILE DE BRANDNER, 1818–1855. Répertoire général des décisions judiciaires et administratives rendues en Belgique depuis 1818 jusqu'en 1855 en matière d'enregistrement, de timbre, de greffe. Bruxelles 1886. pp.820. [11,500.]

Tribunals.

TRIBUNALS of inquiry established under the Tribunals of inquiry (evidence) act 1921. House of commons: Library: Bibliography (no.58): [1949]. pp.6. [12.]*